D1756407

MEDICAL OFFICERS
ON THE INFAMOUS
BURMA RAILWAY

MEDICAL OFFICERS
ON THE INFAMOUS
BURMA RAILWAY

ACCOUNTS OF LIFE, DEATH & WAR CRIMES
BY THOSE WHO WERE THERE

COMPILED BY

John Grehan

Frontline Books

MEDICAL OFFICERS ON THE INFAMOUS BURMA RAILWAY

This edition published in 2022 by Frontline Books,
an imprint of Pen & Sword Books Ltd,
47 Church Street, Barnsley, S. Yorkshire, S70 2AS

ISBN: 978-1-39909-562-4

CIP data records for this title are available from the British Library

For more information on our books, please visit
www.frontline-books.com
email info@frontline-books.com
or write to us at the above address.

Printed and bound by CPI Group (UK) Ltd, Croydon, CR0 4YY
Typeset by Dave Cassan in 10.5/12.5 point Swiss and American Typewriter.

Contents

Introduction   vii

1   History of "F" Force   1
2   Extract of a Report by Major B.A. Hunt, AAMC   45
3   Report on PoW Camps 1 (Shimo Songkrai), 2, 3, and 5 visited 23 and   48
    24 June 1943
4   Report on No.2 Camp (Songkrai)   51
5   Report on No.3 Camp (Kami Songkrai)   63
6   Report on No.4 Camp (Konkoita)   69
7   General report on conditions at No.5 Camp (Changaraya)   72
8   Tanbaya Hospital   74
9   Medical Report, Tanbaya Hospital   81
10 Report of conditions of Prisoners of War in Thailand May to December   93
    1943
11 Report by Assistant-Surgeon Wolfe, IMD   103
12 Report on Tropical Ulcers at Tanbaya   107
13 The Wardmaster System   122
14 Extract from the report of Capt. Wilson R.A.M.C. nutrition expert with   131
    "F" Force
15 Sickness and Death Rates   135
16 Report on Tanbaya Hospital subsequent to departure of main body 24   143
    Nov 43
17 Extract from Health of "F" Force – May to November, 1943   145
18 Selection of Correspondence and Reports between "F" Force and I.J.A.   161
19 Postscript: War Crimes Trials, Tokyo and Singapore, September and   194
    October 1946

Index of Persons   206

Introduction

When Lieutenant General Percival surrendered the 'fortress' of Singapore on 15 February 1942, he believed that he had saved both the civilian population and his own British and Commonwealth troops from a terrible fate. What he did not know was that he was committing them to unimaginable horrors at the hands of the Japanese which, in many cases, led to their deaths in shocking and degrading conditions.

What was not appreciated at the time of the surrender was the Japanese warrior ethic of *bushido* which demanded that the Japanese soldier should never, under any circumstances, surrender to the enemy. To die for the Emperor and the country was 'glorious', but to surrender would bring only disgrace and it was far more honourable to commit suicide than become a prisoner of war. This explained why the Japanese treated the Allied troops who had surrendered with such utter disrespect, as was pointed out during the military trials of war criminals in the Netherlands East Indies which took place between 1946 and 1949: 'Those who had surrendered to the Japanese—regardless of how courageously or honorably they had fought—merited nothing but contempt; they had forfeited all honor and literally deserved nothing.'[1] All that followed must be viewed from that ingrained belief.

As prisoners of war, the Allied troops (though not officers) could be compelled to work and worked they were – in so many cases to death. In order to establish a secure means of supply to the most westerly of its forces, those in Burma intent on invading British-held India, the Japanese Imperial General Headquarters decided that the safest route would be overland, their transport ships proving only too vulnerable to the marauding U.S. submarines in the Pacific. But there was no existing rail link between Burma and its neighbour, Thailand. The British colonial powers had investigated the practicality of building a railway to join the existing railway networks in those countries which

---

[1] Fred Borch, *Military Trials of War Criminals in the Netherlands East Indies 1946– 1949* (Oxford University Press, 2017), pp.31–2.

would eventually link Bangkok and Rangoon, but had decided that the mountainous, inhospitable, jungle-covered terrain, broken by hundreds of streams and dry gaps, presented so many difficulties that the project was not undertaken. The route eventually taken, following that surveyed by the British, ran across the Bilauktbung range of mountains which forms the natural boundary between the two countries and reaches a height of more than 2,000 metres, as well as the Taungmyo range in Burma. In addition to having to blast or hew their way through solid rock, the workers also had to cut their way through thick malaria-infested jungle which covered 70 per cent of the route.

None of this would deter the Japanese. They would build that railway. To achieve this aim they would need a huge labour force and for that they had the Allied prisoners, as well as impressed and volunteer native workers – the 'coolies' as they were referred to in the medical officers' reports.

Altogether ten PoW working groups were established[2] and, in general, they were composed of the healthier, fitter men. In May 1943 two additional groups known as "F" Force and "H" Force were sent from Singapore to work on the line and these included a large number of men who were in poor physical shape.

These two groups, unlike the others, were controlled throughout by the Malaya PoW administration. Each group was organised as a self-contained unit. While supervised by Japanese internment camp representatives, internal administration was carried out by the PoWs themselves.

The purpose of these labour camps was to supply daily working parties as required by the Japanese's construction units, at which time the PoWs came under supervision of the units concerned. The task set for "F" Force was that of building a 50-kilometre stretch of the railway through the hilly and flooded jungle just south of the Three Pagoda Pass, under the command of the Japanese 5th Railway Regiment.

Stories abound of the atrocious treatment of the men who worked on the Thai-Burma railway, understandably labelled the 'Death Railway', particularly during the period known as the 'speedo' from June to October 1943 when the pace of construction was increased to meet a revised deadline for the completion of the railway. The majority of these stories were recorded after the war. The medical officers' reports included here from "F" Force were, however, compiled by the men in the

---

2   These were "A" Force, 3,000 men, sent to Burma; "B" Force, 1,487, Borneo; "C" Force, 551, Japan; "D" Force, 2,218, Eastern Thailand; "E" Force, 500, Borneo.

prisoner of war camps during the war. They were written with the aim of bringing to the attention of the Japanese authorities the conditions under which the prisoners were forced to live and work, in the belief that the government in Tokyo, while demanding the greatest possible exertions to build the railway, would not have approved of the manner in which this was undertaken. It is doubtful that these reports ever reached Japan and the commander of "F" Force, Lieutenant Colonel S.W. Harris, was ordered to destroy all copies. Fortunately, at least one copy survived, residing in The National Archives at Kew, London, under the reference WO 325/16.

That there were any such reports written in the first place is in itself remarkable. Such was the scarcity of paper, some camps could not keep accurate records, with those in charge of hospital wards having to write on long strips of bamboo – which could easily be washed off by a heavy monsoon downpour. In one instance, a Quartermaster had to write his ration issue on the shoulder blade of an ox!

With many of the reports being written by different officers, and it would seem at different dates and independently of each other, being as they were, in separate camps, there is a degree of repetition. This, though, helps to validate, or corroborate, their statements. Each one, in turn, adds something extra to the sum of the whole and taken together provides us with, at least, an impression of the suffering of the troops, though what they endured can never be fully appreciated by those who were not there.

In these reports we read of a seeming indifference to the suffering of the British and Australians, even by Japanese medical officers, of incompetence and neglect, as well as individual cruelty. This was certainly the opinion of a British medical officer who served in Changi prison and then in the PoW hospital at Kanchanaburi[3] as well as some of the working camps, but who was not part of "F" Force: 'To Japanese leaders, and those down the chain of command, PoWs were an inexhaustible supply of free labour and our health and lives were inconsequential … What I saw … was Japan's total contempt for sickness … sickness was equated with dishonour and shame … the justification for sending sick and starving men to work in sometimes appalling conditions may have been to make unworthy men more worthy.'[4]

---

[3]   Kanchanaburi was later chosen as the site of the cemetery for the graves along the southern section of railway, from Bangkok to Nieke.

[4]   Ken Adams, *Healing in Hell, The Memoirs of a Far Eastern PoW Medic* (Pen & Sword, Barnsley, 2011), pp.65-7.

Such was the Japanese approach to sickness that they reduced the ration issue to those too ill to work. So low was the calorific value of the food issued to those in hospital, that it was below that required for the maintenance of normal bodily metabolism. This meant that the patients were either killed by the disease or they slowly starved to death. As was put by Lieutenant Colonel Dillion in his main report, the Japanese issued starvation rations to the sick, 'on the grounds that this would drive them out of hospital quickly – which it did – to the cemetery'.[5]

Some indication of just what the Japanese expected from the prisoners was recorded by Australian Lieutenant Colonel Charles Henry Kappe, who wrote a highly detailed account of the activities of "F" Force:

'From 21st June working conditions had become worse and can only be described as barbarous.

'Men were being driven like cattle and were not returned to camp until as late as 2330 hours. The earliest that any party came in during the period 21-30 June was 2015 hours and the average time of return was 2130 hours. Men were soaked through with rain, tired, footsore and dispirited. After their meal they were often too weary to stand around the fires to dry their wet clothing, which by now was rapidly falling to pieces. Boots which had been in a poor state even before leaving Changi were becoming unserviceable and a great deal of men were forced to go to work bootless, resulting in numerous cases of trench feet, ulcers and other skin complaints.'[6]

The food ration issued to the prisoners was barely sufficient to keep them alive, consisting mainly of rice occasionally supplemented by beans and meat. Though some beef was 'on the hoof', the bullocks

---

[5] The speed with which illnesses could turn fatal was recalled by Dr Peter Hendry, 2/10th Field Ambulance: 'In Sonkurai … Beri-beri was the worst disease up there and it was dreadful in itself, but if you contracted that, it often became easy to get cholera or dysentery. I saw one fellow this particular day who had beri-beri and he was very bloated, then the next day he was emaciated with cholera – he was like a skeleton within twenty-four hours. Cholera was that quick and lethal and there was little to nothing we could do to stop it.' Pattie Wright, *The Men of the Line: Stories of the Thai-Burma Railway Survivors* (Miegunyah Press, Melbourne, 2008), pp.187-8. This was echoed by Charles Moore, recalling a private of the 2/26 Battalion A.I.F.: 'Most amazing, I was talking to Pte…… yesterday morning walking round the camp, he was admitted in the afternoon stricken with Cholera and died early in the morning.'

[6] Lieutenant Colonel C.F. Kappe, *Report on Activities of A.I.F. Contingent of "F" Force*, National Archives of Australia, NAA: A6238.

having been driven on the long march through the jungle with "F" Force, most was delivered to the camps in boxes. This boxed meat was often so decomposed as to be more liquid than solid and was heaving with maggots. So deficient in vitamins, fat and proteins was the food, beri-beri was widespread, and the men lacked the resistance to fight off disease. So desperate were the doctors to improve the diet of the prisoners they searched the jungle to find edible plants. In one instance the large 'hairy' leaves of an unidentified plant were boiled to create a stew – which was much appreciated by the men, even though they did not know what they were eating.

The Japanese side of the story, as one might imagine, paints a different picture, as is given in a collection of individual accounts, one by Captain Saburo Hasegawa, Adjutant of the 5th Railway Regiment, 2nd Railway Command Group, Southern Arm, and compiled by the World War II Remembrance Group. Hasegawa had been charged with setting up No.4 PoW Camp. He first met the Japanese officer responsible for "F" Force, Lieutenant Colonel Banno, on 11 April, as the British and Australian soldiers were marching to the camps that would become their homes, and, for many, their final resting places: 'It was humid and the sun shone down ruthlessly on the moving line of PoWs, who were panting in the heat. After the main group had passed, a small group came and sat down in the shade of the roadside staggering unsteadily. A tall officer was attending to a PoW who was lying down.' After introducing himself to Banno, Hasegawa asked the colonel about the state of the prisoners: 'They have been in bad condition since yesterday and worn out. I have left five men to rest in the rear,' replied Banno.

Hasegawa wrote that he drove his car to pick up the five exhausted men, who were being supervised by a Korean guard. 'I told them my purpose and put them in my car,' continued Hasegawa. 'They seemed to have recovered somewhat after bathing in wellwater in the village but were still staggering. The sun in the west was heating up the road, and I was sweating just sitting in the car, so it must have been terribly hot for the walking PoWs. As I wiped away my sweat, I saw several men resting where the tall Colonel was holding a PoW and giving him water with words of encouragement.

'"Don't go to sleep! Don't go to sleep! Just a little further to go."

'The man seemed to be suffering from sunstroke.

'"Mr Hasegawa, may I oblige you to take this man in your car …? He is not able to walk."'

Hasegawa goes on to heap praise on Banno: 'I was impressed to see him taking good care of the PoWs as if they were his own men. He was tall, always stood up straight and had something of the samurai about him.'[7]

The reality lay, quite possibly, somewhere between the opposing views. That the PoWs suffered tragically, and fatally, in conditions that almost defy description is without doubt, as the reports compiled here show, but much of the distress they endured was the consequence of the logistical breakdown which occurred as the construction of the railway advanced deeper into the distant jungle in the midst of the monsoon. Something in the region of 300,000 prisoners of war and civilian contract labourers (the coolies) were employed on the railway and its associated road, and from the beginning of the operation the Japanese were unable to keep this vast body of men supplied with adequate food, equipment or medical supplies – though, of course, the Japanese themselves were generally, or comparatively, well-fed.

The Japanese were very pleased with what was in fact a considerable achievement in constructing the railway. This was put into words by one of the officers of the Japanese 5th Railway Regiment, and someone who was referred to on a number of occasions in the medical officers' reports (and never favourably), Abe Hiroshi: '"Go into the jungle and build a railroad!" That was practically the only order we got in Burma. The jungle was incredible. It was deep, dark and dense, with giant trees like you wouldn't believe. There were no roads. There were no reliable maps, only a primitive chart made by the British army long before … We first surveyed the area on elephant while the weather was still good and recorded the basic topography. We felled trees and estimated roughly whether and where the track could be laid".[8]

As will be read in the postscript to this book, Lieutenant Abe was later tried for war crimes.

Exact numbers of those who died building the railway do not exist. It has been estimated that mortality was something in the region of 30 per cent, with the total number of deaths ranging between 80,000 and 100,000. "F" Force suffered the highest percentage of deaths of all the groups involved, with the Australians suffering losses amounting to 29 per cent and the British contingent a staggering 60 per cent. The significance of the medical reports is that this terrible death toll was very largely due to disease and inadequate nutrition – much of which could have been avoided. The story of "F" Force is a tale of dysentery,

---

[7] Kazuo Tamayama, *Building the Burma-Thailand Railway, An Epic of World War II 1942-1943* (privately published, 2004), pp.46-52.

[8] Haruko Taya Cook, *Japan at War: An Oral History* (The New Press, 1992), p.100.

malaria, beriberi, cholera and tropical ulcers more than it is of the building of a railway.

As far as possible, those reports are reproduced here largely verbatim. Long lists of medicines – both what was present and what was required – which form part of some of the reports, as well as some of the descriptions of medical treatments and extensive tables, have not been included for reasons of brevity. Likewise, for the same reason, some vertically arranged lists have been condensed. A few of these reports, particularly that written by Lieutenant Colonel J. Huston concerning tropical ulcers, are quite technical, but the details of such reports give graphic descriptions of these awful inflictions and the manner in which they led to rapid and terrible deaths. As can be seen, the names of some of the camps were spelt in different ways by different men and the use of capitals in names was common, though not universal. I have endeavoured to present these as they were written at the time and any deviation from the originals is not intentional. Some of the reports have faded over the years, and were typed in poor conditions with, no doubt, fading typewriter ribbons, and I have done my best to interpret them.

My father fought in Burma and was evacuated before the end of the war because he was incapacitated by disease. In 1946 he was discharged 40 per cent disabled, not through enemy action, simply because he had contracted many of the illnesses suffered by the men of "F" Force. In one of the medical reports compiled here, Captain T. Wilson wrote about the lasting effects of these diseases, and one of my earliest, and most unsettling memories is of my father lying in bed covered in perspiration and thrashing around deliriously during a bout of malaria - and that was many years after the war. But he suffered little compared to the unimaginable horrors endured by the men of "F" Force. I just hope I have done them justice in compiling these reports.

John Grehan

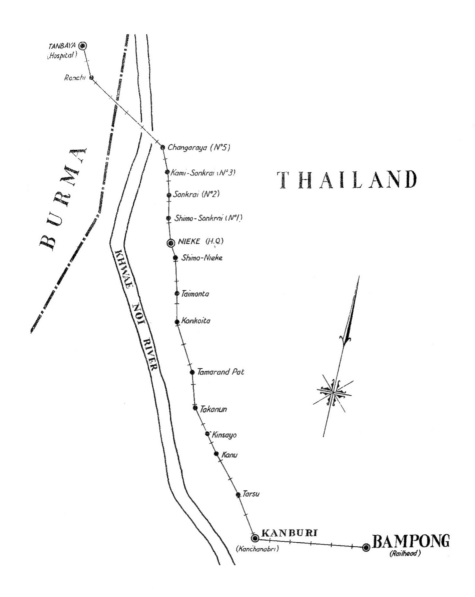

CHAPTER I

History of "F" Force

INTRODUCTION

1. In April 1943, a party of 7,000 PoW was sent from Changi, Singapore to Thailand. By the end of August 25% were dead and 90% of the remainder were sick. By December 40% of the whole force were dead and the move of the unfit remainder back to Singapore began; it was completed in April. The total dead was then approximately 3,100 or 45% in the one year.

2. This party was throughout the whole period under the charge of No.4 Bureau (Comd. Colonel Banno) of the Imperial Japanese Army (I.J.A.) Malayan PoW Administration, whose headquarters were at Changi, Singapore.

3. This account is being written in a PoW camp and is therefore confined to facts sufficient to establish a case and to describe steps taken by us to overcome our difficulties.

4. In order to keep the body of the report reasonably compact sufficient detail has been included only to make the general narrative clear. Further details must be obtained from camps and the evidence of individuals.

ORDERS

5. The orders received from the I.J.A. stated that:-

   a. The reason for the move was that the food situation in Singapore was difficult and would be far better in the new place.

   b. This was NOT a working party.

   c. As there were not 7,000 fit combatants in Changi, 30% of the party were to be men unfit to march or work. The unfit men would have a better chance of recovery with good food and in a pleasant hilly place with good facilities for recreation.

   d. There would be no marching except for a short distance

from the train to a nearby camp and transport would be provided for baggage and men unfit to march.

e. Bands were to be taken.

f. Gramophones, blankets, clothing and mosquito nets would be issued at the new camps.

g. All tools and cooking gear and an engine and gear for electric light were to be taken.

h. A good canteen would be available in each camp after three weeks. Canteen supplies for the first three weeks were to be bought with the prisoners' money before leaving Singapore.

i. The party would include a medical party of about 350 with equipment for a central hospital of 400 patients and medical supplies for three months.

j. The force was to include a HQ.

k. No Red Cross representative was to accompany the force, nor could any Red Cross money be obtained to take with the force. Facilities would, however, be given to communicate with Singapore for this purpose if need arose.

PREPARATION

6. Lieut-Col. S.W. Harris O.B.E., RA (Commander 18 Division PoW Area in Changi) was accordingly appointed by British H.Q., Changi, with concurrence of command A.I.F. to command the force, using 18 Div Area H.Q. as his staff. The A.I.F. contingent was to consist of 27 Inf Bde A.I.F., plus detachments, to bring the strength up to the required total, Lieut-Col. C.H. Kappe A.I.F., Commanding.

7. The A.I.F. contingent was to total 3,600 and the British 3,400.

8. The Force Commander with Major Wild had several interviews with Capts. Miyasaki and Tanaka (I.J.A. Offrs i/c at Changi) with regard to the force with special relation to sub-paras b., c., and d. above, i.e. work, fitness and marching. There was a special meeting with regard to Red Cross matters. At these interviews the actual figures of fit and unfit men were shown to the I.J.A. This showed that the A.I.F contingent would contain about 30% unfit for all duties. British contingent, however, would consist of not more than 50% unfit for heavy work and marching. It was also pointed out that even the so-called fit men in Changi had been in hospital as PoW for one reason or another and

2

were all without exception on the borderline of disease arising from lack of vitamins (especially B, B1 and B1 complex) in the diet and liable to recurrent breakdowns from this cause. This was, in any way, well known to the I.J.A. from continual representations from prisoners' H.Q. at Changi on the subject of the provision of a balanced diet and from our regular returns of sick.

9. In the light of the above instructions, H.Q. A.I.F re-examined all their men and reclassified as fit to go a number of men previously marked unfit. This classification was made, however, in the light of the Japanese instruction, which made it appear likely that the men accompanying the force would have a good chance of rehabilitation with good food.

   For the British contingent the problem was far more complex, as British PsoW were spread over four more or less independent areas. There was also to be considered the advantage of keeping units together rather than sending off detachments under strange N.C.Os and officers. The British soldiers were examined before selection, but the inspection did not amount to more than establishing fitness to travel.

10. It is conceivable that the I.J.A. in Changi believed themselves much of what they promised. In one particular item, however, this cannot have been the case. They stated that the purpose of the party was not to work. This must have been to their knowledge untrue and it is on them, therefore, that full responsibility for what followed must lie.

11. Orders were issued by the I.J.A. for the move of the force in thirteen trains, with Force H.Q. and all heavy baggage and medical gear in the first train. Later, at the last minute, this was altered; the first six trains were to be all A.I.F. and the later trains British. This displaced Force H.Q. and heavy baggage to Train 7 – a most unfortunate change which had far reaching consequences as will be seen later.

   If the medical and other essential gear had arrived with H.Q. in Bampong on the first train there would have been nothing to prevent it being moved up into the forward area before arrival of the troops and before the rains broke, rendering the roads impassable to M.T. The whole move was also put forward by two days thus making it impossible for the A.I.F. contingent to have their second cholera inoculation before leaving.

12. All ranks were glass-rodded by the I.J.A. and instructions

were issued for re-vaccination and inoculation against typhoid, plague, dysentery and cholera.

Owing to alterations in date the whole A.I.F. contingent left Changi after only one cholera inoculation and, owing to short issue of anti-cholera vaccine, part of the British contingent had no inoculation at all against this disease.

TRAIN JOURNEY

13. The force travelled to Bampong in 13 freight trains, leaving Singapore on successive nights in parties of 500-600. The accommodation was one steel box-car for approximately twenty-seven men. The journey lasted 4 to 5 days. Cooked rations of rice and vegetable stew, provided at various stations, were generally inadequate; drinking water was never supplied in sufficient quantities and this caused unnecessary hardship to men travelling in such overcrowded conditions during the heat of the day. In particular, most train parties received no food or water in the last twenty-four hours of the journey.[9]

RAILHEAD – BAMPONG

14. On arrival at Bampong the train parties were marched to the first staging camp, about one mile from the station. This camp was in a filthy state, having previously been used by native labour gangs. An I.J.A. notice posted at the entrance in English was entitled: "Camp Orders for Coolies and Prisoner of War". Accommodation consisted of large attap roofs resting on the ground without floors. Latrines, which were merely open trenches about six feet deep, were filthy beyond description and the whole area was as insanitary as

---

[9] Private Reg Twigg of the Leicestershire Regiment was on that journey: 'There was no toilet. We'd had no food or water since Changi … At first we peed through the slats, everybody negotiating with everybody else to change places for the purpose. Shitting was out of the question and I held on. Some of them couldn't, however. Dysentery rode that train with us and there were groans as men fought their way to a corner to shit where they could. Dropping shorts and pants was difficult and some didn't have time. The smell became indescribable, the overcrowding even worse as we tried not to stand in it.' Reg Twigg, *Survivor on the River Kwai, The Incredible Story of Life on the Burma Railway* (Viking, London, 2013), pp.130-1.

it could be. There was no water for washing and a bare sufficiency for cooking.

15. The "gunsoku"[10] guards at Bampong were in an even more excitable state than is usual among them when a move is in progress. Detrainment was carried out to the accompaniment of blows and the usual stream of conflicting orders. In the camp itself a "gunsoku" called Toyama [sic Toyoyama] on several occasions thrashed prisoners for no apparent cause, with the steel shaft of a golf club, inflicting more or less serious injuries on a number of officers and men.[11]

16. As each train arrived it learnt for the first time that the rest of the journey was to be made on foot, starting on the evening following arrival. Distance or the number of stages were not stated.

17. All heavy kit and stores, including medical stores and tools, belonging to the force, were dumped by order of the I.J.A. in an unfenced open space at the side of the road in Bampong, and no guard was allowed. When Force H.Q. arrived by Train 7, a further dump consisting of officers' boxes and valises and men's kitbags was in process of being formed at the roadside in front of the staging camp.

18. By this time, therefore, five train parties of the A.I.F. had already marched north of Bampong (the head of the column was already, in fact, 100 kms away) and the sixth party was due to leave that night. Nominally in control of this operation were Lieut. Fukuda and the interpreter Koriyasu, with their headquarters in Bampong. As each train commander, and, with the arrival of train 7, the force commander, objected to the march, Lieutenant Fukuda made excuse that it was unavoidable.[12]

---

[10] 'Gunsoku' is Japanese for a sergeant in the Japanese Army.

[11] James Boyle, 4th Motor Transport Company, 8th Division A.I.F. in *Railroad to Burma* (Allen & Unwin, 1990), called Toyoyama 'the curse of F Force, and was directly responsible for the loss of hundreds of lives as the result of his cruelty'.

[12] Fukuda Tsuneo's name appears numerous times in these reports. His attitude towards the prisoners was summed up during an interview with Major Bruce Hunt when the latter asked for co-operation in securing better hospital facilities, to which Fukuda replied: 'You use the word "Co-operation". You have no right to use that word. Co-operation is only possible between equals. You are not our equals; you are our inferior.' *West Australian Newspaper*, 29 November 1945.

Control on the way would, he said, be exercised by "another unit", and conditions were likely to be "cruel", but at the other end, they said, "we shall be able to be your friends again." The distance, however, was not disclosed and the impression given was that it would be about forty miles. Although the ordering of the marching was a breach of faith, the information available at the moment did not in any way foreshadow the rigours of the march to come. A march of 50 miles or so in short stages under reasonable conditions would have entailed hardship for some and some casualties, but it would not have been disastrous or impossible.

19. The maximum concessions which could be obtained following protests by Col. Harris were:-
    a. A few seriously ill men to be left in a Japanese hospital at Bampong.
    b. A few more in an extemporised hospital in the camp. Apart from these all men had to march.
    c. Medical stores and cooking containers were to be sorted out from the dump for priority of despatch by lorry to the destination.
    d. The dump itself to be put under guard (but this was removed by the I.J.A. shortly afterwards).
    e. Lieut-Cols. Harris, Hutchison and Dillon and Major Wild of Force H.Q. to go forward by M.T. to overtake the head of the column and take charge at Tarso, which was then understood to be the base camp of the final concentration area.

    It was also arranged that a rear party of Force H.Q. should remain at Bampong and come forward by lorry with Lieut-Col Huston, the S.M.O. of the Force when the last party left.

20. Permission to change Malay currency for Thai was refused. As a result, on the march the only means of buying extra food and, at camp, drinking water, was by means of selling to the Thais or I.J.A. guards personal belongings or kit which could be carried no further.

21. If Force H.Q. had arrived six days earlier by Train 1, in accordance with the original plan, it is probable that better arrangements could have been made, especially as regards medical stores and cooking containers. As it was, previous

train commanders had spent only a few hours at Bampong before marching out with their men, so that there had been no continuity of command there and consequently no chance of making proper arrangements for stores left behind. The I.J.A. had available for transport twelve Marmon lorries and one ambulance. On their first run north from Bampong those vehicles carried Japanese stores: few of them completed a second run and none a third, as the monsoon rains destroyed long stretches of the road, and after 20 May no wheeled vehicle was able to reach from the south the area in which the force was finally concentrated. As a result, all the heavy equipment of the force, which had been brought from Singapore by order of the I.J.A., including all heavy cooking gear and many smaller containers, all officers' and other ranks' kit not carried on the man, most of the tools and Red Cross stores, all reserve clothing including 800 pairs of boots, canteen goods to the value of $2,000 (purchased by the order of the I.J.A.) and three-quarters of the medical stores, was left permanently at Bampong and was not retrieved until the remnant of the force moved back to Kamburi seven months later, by which time a considerable portion had been looted.

THE MARCH

22. The march lasted for about 2½ weeks, over a distance of roughly 300 kilometres, covered in fifteen stages of about 20 kilometres each. Marching was invariably done by night, between 2000 hours and 0800 hours. Except for the first two stages the road was merely a rough jungle track, capable of taking wheeled traffic in dry weather only. Long stretches of it were corduroyed, which, with snags and holes, made marching in the dark difficult and dangerous. Falls, resulting in sprains and even broken legs, were frequent. Control on the march was virtually impossible as all torches had been confiscated during a military search at Bampong. At the same time, the fate of stragglers was uncertain, as Thais armed with knives hung on the tail of the column in certain areas, ready to strip off the equipment of any man who fell behind. It is probable that some at least of the twenty men still missing

from the force met their end at the hands of those bandits.[13]

23. Daily thunderstorms started on 30 April and the monsoon proper broke just after the earlier parties reached their destination. The later parties thus had to contend with even worse marching conditions. The road surface became slippery and treacherous and long stretches were flooded and even totally washed away. The night march now frequently lasted for fourteen or fifteen hours instead of twelve, and during the day's rest exhausted men had nowhere to shelter from the rain except on the sodden ground under trees and bushes. It was unfortunately the less fit British parties which had to contend with those worsened conditions, and this undoubtedly contributed to their already inferior physical state on reaching their final camps.

24. Even trained infantry in good physical condition would have found a march of this length and in these conditions an arduous one. But this force included men of all services and of every known physical category except A.1, for even those rated fit among them had for more than a year subsisted on an inadequate diet, with consequent weakness from malnutrition. In addition, there were the 2,000 and more unfit, included in the force as a result of the orders of the I.J.A. Hundreds of those were convalescents whose sole reason for being there was that the I.J.A. had guaranteed them a journey by rail and motor-transport to a comfortable

---

[13] RASC Adjutant Richard Laird's description of the march is related in his son's book *From Shanghai to the Burma Railway* (Pen & Sword, Barnsley, 2020), p.88: 'We were on unmade-up track and in the dark it was impossible to avoid the roughness of the track, which resulted in many cuts and bruises which later developed into tropical ulcers. Some nights it was so dark that we resorted to tying a piece of white cloth or towel onto our packs so that the man behind could have something to follow. We normally started our march at dusk and would arrive soon after daylight at the next staging camp (bivouac). All too often we were kept on parade all morning, sometimes up to twelve noon and frequently in full sun, to allow stragglers to catch up and for the Nips to get their figures right. At the end of that we had no more than a few hours before we were due to move out again in the evening, and during this time we had to get what food we could.'

camp where rest and good rations were assured. Among them were men suffering from beri-beri, post-diphtheritic hearts and other ailments, which rendered their survival impossible from the moment they were sent marching from Bampong. Those unfit men, the number of whom steadily increased, proved from the first a great strain on the fit, who had to help and even carry them from camp to camp. In addition, every party was burdened with as many small (3 and 6 gallon) containers and as much medical gear as it could carry. Thus, even those who were fit at the start of the march were seriously exhausted or themselves unfit at the end of it.

25. The staging camps were jungle clearings at the side of the road at about 20 kilometres distance from each other, generally (though not always) near water. Accommodation consisted of a cookhouse and open trench-latrines, and flies abounded; but of shelter there was none, except in two of the fifteen camps where tents were available for about 100 men only. These camps were under the command of junior N.C.Os of some I.J.A. movement control organisation, apparently unconnected with either the Malaya or Thailand PoW Administration. These men, whose behaviour was often harsh and unreasonable, evidently had orders to push the marching columns forward as fast as possible, and the greatest difficulty was experienced everywhere in obtaining to leave behind even the worst of the sick.

26. Food, which consisted of rice and vegetable stew, was supplied in insufficient quantities to maintain the strength of men engaged on such a march, and water was often short. At Kanburi staging camp drinking water had to be bought by the prisoners from a privately owned well.

    Lieut-Col. Harris tried to get this put this right, but the abuse was not [indecipherable stopped?] until after the last party of "F" Force passed though. When "H" Force arrived, however, some weeks later free water had become available there.

    From Kanburi Col. Harris sent back a letter to Lieut. Fukuda pointing out that a tragedy was in the making. This letter detailed the immediate steps necessary to avert disaster.

27. It was difficult for the men to obtain sufficient rest during the daytime halts at these staging camps; for, apart from the

lack of shelter parties were often required to carry water or perform fatigues for the Japanese. This could have been avoided if the I.J.A. had detached permanent fatigue parties of sufficient size at each staging camp, to close up on the force when the march was completed. Such parties could also have done much to improve the sanitation of the staging camps, all of which had previously been used by coolie gangs and which became progressively worse from day to day.

28. The strain fell particularly heavily on the Medical Officers and orderlies as they had to tend to casualties on the line of march and hold sick parades during the day's halt, not only for their own sick but also for the steadily increasing numbers left behind by previous parties. Also at every camp the day ended and the march began with an argument with the Japanese N.C.O. as to the number of sick men to be left. The end of this was always that seriously sick men, with blistered and ulcerated feet and such illnesses as dysentery, beri-beri and malaria, were driven out of the camp to join the marching party.

29. At Tarso the marching camp was of the usual type, but in the vicinity was the headquarters of both the I.J.A. Railway Engineers and the Thailand PoW Administration, with a permanent PoW camp and hospital, besides an I.J.A. hospital. When Advance Force H.Q. reached this staging camp (which, far from being the base camp of the force, proved to be at only one-third the distance to destination) Col Harris visited the HQ of the Thailand PoW Administration; but his reception there was so unfavourable and indeed offensive that it was evident a breach existed between the two administrations, presumably owing to jealousy at Malaya's retention of control over "F" Force during its stay in Thailand. There was ample confirmation later that this jealousy existed, and to it can be attributed some of the misfortunes of the force (such as uncompleted state of working camps (see below).

30. The proximity of the hospitals at Tarso gave rise to hopes that Force H.Q. would be able to secure proper attention and accommodation there for the more seriously ill. On the night of our arrival it was necessary to restrain the I.J.A. Corporal in charge of the staging camp from striking with a stick the sick men he had arbitrarily decided to send on the

march. From the A.I.F. party which arrived the following morning Major Wild took 50 sick men for inspection by the I.J.A. Medical Officer at Tarso, who told the Corporal that 36 of them were quite unfit to march that night. Later, a written order that these men should not be made to march was obtained from the Japanese M.O. and was conveyed by his Sgt-Major to the Corporal; but he chose to ignore it. The same evening the 36 men were paraded, and the Corporal ordered all but 10 of them to march. When Major Wild and Major Hunt AAMC, remonstrated, they were beaten with bamboos in front of the men, and a bone in Major Hunt's had was broken.[14] Finally, 17 of those sick 3 were carried back after covering a few hundred yards, and the remainder were as usual helped or carried by their comrades to the next staging camp. Among the latter was the Rev. Ross-Dean of the A.I.F., who died at the next camp shortly afterwards.

31. Similar scenes were being enacted daily at every staging camp along the road. Hundreds of unfit were being rendered seriously ill by this treatment and the whole force was being rapidly infected with malaria, dysentery and diarrhoea. In addition, the health and physique of the fit men also was deteriorating under the strain, so that they also rendered more liable to infection.

32. Finally, at Konkoita staging camp, after a fortnight's marching, every party was quartered in immediate proximity to hundreds of coolies, who were suffering from some intestinal disease, of which numbers sided daily. The whole area was heavily fouled and infested with a plague of flies. The I.J.A. pretended that the deaths were due to dysentery; it soon became certain that it was, in fact,

---

[14] This incident was witnessed by Tom McInerney, 2/29 Battalion A.I.F.: 'The Jap Corporal approached Major Wild with a large bamboo in his hand. We couldn't hear what was said, but Major Wild was hit in the face with the bamboo. Another Jap joined in and followed suit. Major Wild fell backwards as the Jap Corporal jabbed at the Major's genitals with the bamboo. They then attacked Major Hunt. Three Japs forced him to the ground then bashed him with bamboo. The dirty rotten scum beat him badly. He was not a young man. They bruised his skull, back, hands and arms.' *No Arguments*, by SX13097 Tom McInerney, pows-of-japan.net/books.htm. Bruce Hunt's own account of this incident can be read starting p.45.

cholera. Konkoita was the focal point of the infection which caused cholera to break out a few days later at all of the working camps to which the force was dispersed.

33. At Konkoita 700 A.I.F. of Parties Nos. 1 and 2 under Lieut-Col. S.A.F. Pond OBE 2/29 Bn A.I.F. (Lieut-Col. Kappe, Commander A.I.F. Contingent, was also in the camp but hoped to move forward), were halted and placed under the command of Lieut. Maruyama of the I.J.A. Engineers. This party of 700 was subsequently detached from the I.J.A. Administration of "F" Force and for all practical purposes came under the control of the Engineers until they re-joined the force at Nieke in December.

34. Lieut-Col. Banno, the I.J.A. Commander of "F" Force, made his first appearance at Tarso on 8 May in a lorry with the British officers of the Rear H.Q. On 9 May he took Col. Harris with them leaving the remainder three officers of Advanced Force HQ to follow on when the last party left Tarso. Two stages beyond Tarso Col. Banno suddenly ordered all the officers of the Rear H.Q. to dismount from the lorry with the medical stores which they were carrying to start a wayside hospital for the marching troops, while he proceeded up the road another 150 kilometres to Nieke with Col. Harris. This incredible action had serious results, as the services of Lieut-Col. Huston were thus denied to the force during the first critical six weeks, together with the consignment of medical stores, which could not be brought up later by road owing to the breakdown of the road in the monsoon and were not brought up even by river.

SHIMO-NIEKE – DISPERSAL TO WORKING CAMPS

35. Col. Banno arrived at Shimo-Nieke on 10 May by lorry, Col. Harris being the only PoW with him. This was to be the H.Q. camp. It consisted of two partially roofed huts and seven large unroofed huts in a partly cleared hollow in the jungle. There was a small natural stream to provide water for all purposes. The camp had previously been occupied by coolie labour.

During the next few days some I.J.A. stores arrived from Bampong and a small hut was roofed for Colonel Banno and his office. The roofed huts were occupied by the I.J.A. guards. No shelter whatever was supplied for PsoW – not even for a hospital, an M.I. Room or a cookhouse.

The first batch of troops arrived on 13 May (Party 3 and remains of Parties 1 and 2) and thereafter continued to arrive daily.

Thunderstorms by this time were a daily and nightly occurrence until the monsoon proper broke in Shimo-Nieke on 17 May and spread slowly northwards. From then until well on into September rain was incessant and heavy day and night. It was a rarity for more than four hours to pass without rain. There was one break of 24 hours in June and another in July.

36. The Force Comd protested to Col. Banno against the circumstances of the march and the lack of roofs. No satisfactory answer was received. The most obvious necessity was for a hospital for the sick as they arrived. It was already clear that the force would arrive heavily infected with malaria, dysentery, diarrhoea, with septic sores on feet and legs.

Col. Banno explained that only the H.Q. would remain at Shimo-Nieke. The remainder of the force (excluding the 700 A.I.F. left at Konkoita which was to be known as No.4 Camp) would be distributed to other camps which, he stated were all roofed. Distribution was to be:-

Changaraya (1Km from the Burma border)
10/12 km

Kami (Upper) – Sonkrai
7 Km

Sonkrai
8/10 Km

Shimo (Lower) – Sonkrai
10/14 Km

Nieke
8/10 Km

Shimo-Nieke
20/25 Km

Konkoita

13

Distribution

No.1 Camp ...	Shimo (Lower) – Sonkrai ...	2,400 Aust.
No.2 Camp ...	Sonkrai ...	2,000 Brit,
No.3 Camp ...	Kami (Upper) – Sonkrai ...	400 Aust.
No.4 Camp ...	Konkoita ...	700 Aust.
No.5 Camp ...	Changaraya ...	1,200 Brit.

H.Q. Camp & Base Hospital ... Shimo (Lower) – Nieke,
100 British, 200 Australians (100 HQ, 200 medical)

37. (The actual figures which had left Singapore are believed to have been: Australian 3,666; British 3,334)

    By the end of May movement had temporarily ceased but the numbers had resulted approx. as follows, including dead:-

No.1 Camp ...	Shimo-Sonkrai ...	1,800 Aust.
No.2 Camp ...	Sonkrai ...	1,600 Brit.
No.3 Camp ...	Kami-Sonkrai ...	400 Aust.
No.4 Camp ...	Konkoita ...	700 Aust.
No.5 Camp ...	Changaraya ...	700 Brit.

H.Q. and Hosp ... Shimo-Nieke (Nieke in June),
200 Brit. 200 Aust.
Still down the road, incl. drivers, cooks, sick, dead
566 Aust., 834 Brit.

OUTBREAK OF CHOLERA

38. On 15 May five cases of cholera were diagnosed by Capt. J.L. Taylor, MC, AAMC, a young M.O. who had not previously seen cholera, among the Australian party which had marched in from Konkoita on 14 May, having spent the previous day there. The seriousness of the outbreak was accentuated because the A.I.F. contingent and part of the British contingent were not protected against cholera.

39. The position at that moment was (from south to north) approx. as follows:-

South of Konkoita (but marching northwards ...
            Brit. – 3,034; Aust. – 766
KONKOITA (Cholera infection centre) ...
            Brit. – 300; Aust. – 900 (inc. 200 staging)
SHIMO-NIEKE   Aust. 1,000 including 5 cholera cases
SHIMO-SOMKRAI   Aust. 1,000
            Total 7,000

Over 800 Australians from the party with cholera cases were due to move from Shimo-Nieke to Shimo-Sonkrai on the 16th and similarly 300 British and 200 Australians were due to move from Konkoita to Shimo-Nieke that night, another party automatically moving into Konkoita from the south.

40. The Force Comd immediately saw Col. Banno and stressing the seriousness of the situation urged:-
    a) Immediate local arrangements for an isolation hospital
    b) Provision of vaccines to complete cholera inoculation
    c) Absolute necessity for not allowing further uncontaminated parties into Konkoita or Shimo-Nieke camps
    d) Cancellation of move of affected Australian party from Shimo-Sonkrai
    e) Col. Huston and his medical stores to be sent for immediately from Kanoi.

    Col. Banno agreed to a) and b) but did not act on c), d) or e). A definite negative was not given at the time but, that evening, orders for continuation of the move were issued.

41. As a result, camp to camp movements continued and the infected troops from Shimo-Nieke moved to Shimo-Sonkrai on the night of 16/17 May. One man actually fell out on parade with diarrhoea and died next day of cholera. Fresh cases arrived with each party from Konkoita and as infected troops moved on to Camps 2, 3 and 5 epidemic cholera broke out in each place.

42. As soon as news arrived from Camp 1 that cholera had broken out there, the Force Commander got Col. Banno to agree:-
    a) To send Major Stevens, S.M.O., A.I.F., and Major Bruce Hunt AAMC, from Konkoita. A similar request was later received from No.1 Camp.
    b) To send a letter of instruction to Col. Huston RAMC telling him to come forward as soon as possible.

The former was acted on at once and both officers arrived at Shimo-Nieke at 10 pm. Major Hunt with Capt. Taylor AAMC, some medical orderlies and six British soldiers who were fully inoculated and who volunteered for cholera nursing, went forward by M.T. at midnight with everything of use for fighting cholera that could be scraped together.

Major Stevens remained at Shimo-Nieke to control the base hospital.

The letter to Col. Huston was written by Col. Harris and sent by Col. Banno, but the I.J.A. private in charge at Kanoi refused to act on it and would not let Col. Huston move himself or his medical stores.

43. At another conference with Col. Banno the necessity for cholera vaccine, medical stores of all kinds, and the need for rest (to recover from the march) and a good protein diet were all emphasized. The necessity for getting Col. Huston and his stores forward was again stressed.

Col. Banno, who was obviously very worried, agreed to all points and produced for the sick six tins of milk from his private stock!

He did, indeed, produce cholera vaccine within about 10 days. In about a fortnight an irregular and inadequate meat issue was begun. Col. Huston arrived about six weeks later, but then on foot without medical stores!

LOWER NIEKE HOSPITAL

44. Some 400 seriously sick gradually accumulated at Lower Nieke. Some tents were issued, with I.J.A. instructions to put them up on bamboo roof-frames, instead of attap. It was found, however, that in this way they would not keep out the rain. Most of them were old British tentage, badly perished, and the pitch of the roof was, in any case, too flat using tentage as roofing. Accordingly, they were removed and set up inside the useless hut frames, in which way they gave reasonable protection. The I.J.A., however, insisted on them being put back on the roofs. This stupidity was later repeated at Nieke, in spite of visual demonstration of rain pouring through, just as if no tents were there at all.

In spite of difficulties, however, Lower Nieke hospital did good work. Stringent isolation of cholera cases and suspects kept the disease in check and by the time the hospital had been cleared to Nieke at the end of June, deaths from all causes had been only two officers and 32 men, of which 19 were due to cholera – a result achieved through unceasing effort on part of the mixed British and Australian hospital staff and of Capt. A. Barber, RAMC, on whom the bulk of the work fell.

45. On receipt of news that some parties of sick had been left in
     the neighbourhood of KONKOITA, Asst-Surgeon Wolfe, IMD,
     was send down to do what he could.

LATER STAGES OF CHOLERA EPIDEMIC

46. The cholera epidemic followed its usual course in all
     working camps. In Lower Sonkrai, the A.I.F. put out a
     tremendous effort to overcome their difficulties (especially
     to overcome the lethargy and weariness following the
     march) and succeeded in exterminating the disease when
     they had lost 110 men (6%) – a supremely creditable effort,
     especially on the part of Major Bruce Hunt, AAMC.
         At No.3 Camp the A.I.F. similarly stamped out the disease
     reasonably quickly. At Lower Nieke and Nieke (mixed camps
     under direct control of Force H.Q.) the situation was always
     in hand and deaths from cholera totalled only 26 out of a
     strength of 1,300.
         At Nieke the I.J.A. provided a small hut about half a mile
     from camp and an isolation hospital. It was effective,
     although difficult to supply with food and water. Cases,
     contacts and suspects were all segregated and Asst-Surgeon
     Wolfe took charge and lived there.
         On day, without warning, two Tamil coolies suffering from
     cholera were dumped at the isolation hut and left there for
     us to look after. As we were always attacking the I.J.A. on
     the international nature of the Red Cross we protested only
     on the grounds that this was an unfair burden on our
     already overtaxed medical staff and resources and one
     which the I.J.A. medical service should have properly
     borne. Five coolie cases in all were delt with, two of whom
     recovered.
         At Nos. 2 and 5 Camps (both British) the physical state of
     the men and the camp conditions were such that losses were
     more severe. Cholera deaths were:-
         In Camp No.2, strength 1,600 = 227 (14%)
         In Camp No.5, strength 700 = 159 (23%)

     The special difficulties of these camps will emerge as this
     report continues. By the end of June the cholera situation
     within the force north of Nieke was definitely in hand.
     Eventually the total deaths from cholera in the whole force
     were approx. 650 (or nearly 10%).

START OF WORKING CAMPS

47. To visualise conditions, it is necessary to remember that everything described took place in incessant rain, day and night. Camps, when occupied, consisted of huts without roofs for prisoners.

    At no camp were the I.J.A. personnel in charge of prisoners or the I.J.A. engineers without roofs for their huts.

    At Nos. 3 and 5 Camps, it was found on arrival that part of the accommodation was occupied by coolies who were already suffering from cholera. At those two camps the rations were at first issued to the coolies who cooked both for themselves and the prisoners. Although this was stopped in a few days, there was another certain source of cholera infection. At No.1 Camp, where Lieut. Fukuda was in charge, with an I.J.A. civilian interpreter Koryasu, a few days were allowed in which to set the camp in order. The advantage to be gained was largely nullified by lack of tools and the stupid insistence of Lieut. Fukuda on priority being given to non-essentials. It did, however, give the men a much-needed breathing space.

    At Nos. 2, 3 and 5 camps, no such break was allowed, and men were put on I.J.A. work at once.

48. There occurred at this time a minor horror which deserves mention. A party of 20 men under a Warrant Officer were sent from Shimo-Nieke to Nieke as advance party to form the new camp. These were actually taken off the line of march by the engineers before arriving at Nieke and put to pile-driving in the river. Fourteen days later, when Lieut-Col. Dillon came across them, it was found they had been pile-driving near Nieke daily from first light until 10 p.m. up to their armpits in cold, swift running water the whole time (except for half an hour for lunch) and driven with blows and sticks. They were then in a terrible state and only three were fit for any work at all. Strong representations resulted in cessation of their work, but they were too far gone, and all have since died.

49. In all camps, roofing was completed in the first two weeks by native labour, but the roofing material (attap) was so skimped that all the huts in all the camps leaked badly.

50. In Nos. 3 (A.I.F.) and 5 (British) camps, no arrangements existed for the isolation of cholera patients. All that could be

done was to collect them together in one party of the prisoners' huts. In No.3 Camp an isolation building was provided after about two weeks, but in No.5 Camp nothing was done until the cholera epidemic had almost spent itself.

51. In all camps the "hospital" consisted of merely normal huts with always twelve, and in some cases (No.2 Camp) sixteen to a bay (a bamboo platform 12 feet x 15 feet). No other hospital facilities whatever existed. Everything had to be improvised – bed pans from large bamboos, water containers from long bamboos, baskets from bamboo strips, bandages and dressings from shirtsleeves, trouser legs, mosquito nets or from banana leaves tied on by witheys, stretchers from bamboo and sacks, and many other necessary articles.

52. No light was provided by the I.J.A. and the best had to be made from light from fires in the gangways of the huts; but these, of course, made extravagant use of wood and gave rise to further difficulties in wood collection.

53. The huts were full of bugs. Lice were prevalent and the overcrowding soon gave rise to scabies which became universal among officers and men. Even those who worked in camp and had opportunity for daily washing were all affected. The spread of all other communicable diseases was also ensured by this overcrowding.

SHORTAGE OF STORES

54. Only a small quantity of the medical stores, Red Cross food (a small balance from the consignment received in Changi in August 42) and a few cooking utensils and food containers which had arrived at Bampong had been brought up to Shimo-Nieke.

Practically no tools were brought up – either belonging to prisoners or to the I.J.A.. The medical stores and the Red Cross food were stored by Force H.Q. at Shimo-Nieke and doled out to camps in small quantities on medical recommendation.

55. What cooking utensils and containers did arrive all went with the first parties to No.1 Camp, in the expectation of the arrival of further lorry loads. Even so, this camp was very poorly provided.

Each party had marched from Bampong carrying some containers and medical stores. As sick men accumulated at various staging camps, containers were forcibly taken by the I.J.A. from their later parties to maintain the sick and medical stores were used up in their treatment.

These later parties arrived at Shimo-Nieke therefore with very few or no containers and no medical stores.

56. As a result, Camps Nos. 2, 3 and 5 were formed with practically no containers and almost no medical stores. The I.J.A. provided very little except rice boilers (Koalis) which are heavy fixtures and therefore useless for food or water distribution to hospital or outside working parties.

In No.3 Camp (400 Australians), which was small and compact, close to its water supply with a cookhouse near the sleeping quarters, this lack was a serious inconvenience. In Nos. 2 (1,600 British) and 5 (700 British) Camps it was a disaster. The former had a cookhouse a quarter of a mile from the camp, and as the sick figures rose there were no efficient means of carrying food thence 800 yards to the main hospital and the isolation hospital yet another 400 yards.

Through the never-ending rain parts of meals were ferried all day by parties of officers and convalescents in the few buckets and containers available. No containers would be spared for use in the hospital for boiling water for sterilisation of utensils anywhere in camp, thus further ensuring the spread of disease.

In No.5 Camp the special difficulty was not he distance from the cookhouse but the fact that water had to be carried from one well over a long and bad patch to the hospital cookhouse and the camp – the results being much the same as in No.2 Camp. Sufficient containers were never issued by the I.J.A., even up to the end. There were few available in the "F" Force I.J.A. stores, and, in spite of pressure from our side, no attempt was made to obtain them from the Engineers, who had plenty. One hundred ordinary buckets would have eliminated most of our serious difficulties in this regard.

57. As regards tools, a few were carried by each marching party but, as in the case of containers, the later trains were denuded of these at staging camps. The I.J.A. brought up practically no tools for "F" force –which greatly hampered improvement work in the camp. In some camps it eventually became possible to borrow some tools from the Engineers, but then the process was so hedged with restrictions that it

lost a great deal of its potential value – until late September, by which time the damage had been done.

INTERPRETERS

58. Two of the four prisoner interpreters with the force were arbitrarily retained by N.C.Os of the I.J.A. organisation controlling the march at unimportant staging camps, and their services were lost to the force until it reassembled in Kanburi in December.

WORKING PARTIES

59. In all camps the I.J.A. Engineers demanded maximum numbers to work. The I.J.A. prisoners' administration adopted as a principle the calculation of figures as follows:-

Other Ranks

A. Hospital patients	-	
Hospital staff	-	
Camp duties	-	
Total A.	__	
B. Total camp strength	__	
B minus A	__	figures ordered for outside work

60. This did not allow for any sick in lines or convalescent. They had therefore to be kept in hospital if they were not to go out to work. The keeping of these men in hospital produced a delicate position; for the I.J.A. would not recognise debility, weakness, malaria, beri-beri and trench feet, as being incapacitating diseases.

61. If withholding numbers beyond a certain point the I.J.A. would themselves select men at random from the unfit or arbitrarily order out a further total number, e.g.:-
    a) Col. Banno himself did this more than once
    b) Dr. Tanio allowed men to be sent out though admittedly unfit and incapable of work
    c) Capt. Maruyama ordered (in writing) working parties to be augmented by sick
    It became our task, therefore, on the one side to struggle to obtain agreement to the lowest possible figure and, on the

other, to select men best able to stand a day's work to go out from the convalescents and "lines sick".[15]

62. In this matter, although continued and heavy pressure was maintained by us on the I.J.A. H.Q. for all-round reductions in working numbers, reasonable hours, and rest days, the struggle was largely an individual one in each camp – with varied and constantly varying success.

At force headquarters various reports and complaints were received from other camps and were invariably put to I.J.A. headquarters in the strongest possible manner. The interviews were often stormy and threats were frequently used by the I.J.A., mostly on the lines of cutting rations, to drive more men to work.

63. Referring back to the calculation of outside numbers, it will be seen that a great deal depended in each camp on the number which the I.J.A. would agree to being retained in camp for hospital staff and camp duties.

In one camp (No.2) the I.J.A. at first insisted on Red Cross personnel going out to work, but an appeal to Col. Banno had this decision over-ridden – one of the few promises he made and kept.

As the number of sick rose it became necessary in each camp to reinforce the Red Cross personnel with combat personnel to look after the sick.

This was done mainly by using convalescents. No.1 Camp (A.I.F.) pioneered the use of combat officers as ward-masters and for hospital registry work. This practice was an unqualified success and spread to all camps.

64. Less happily, No.1 Camp was forced by its I.J.A. officer into counting the number of combat officers in camp against the number of all ranks available for camp duties. Ostensibly this was "officers working to save their men". In fact, it was to the I.J.A., merely a means to increase the number for outside work.

---

[15] 'We saw a British soldier on crutches going out to work on the bridge,' recalled Tom McInerney. 'His legs were bandaged all the way up. He made up the numbers they demanded. His condition wasn't considered. A British doctor tried to substitute for him. He was beaten and kicked to the ground. One Jap never does it on his own, it's always two, three, or four. To retaliate would result in facing a firing squad.' Tom McInerney, ibid.

Once the principle had been established in No. 1 Camp pressure was immediately brought on other camps to fall into line. Previously in those camps fit officers had been working in camp but had been available in addition to the number of Other Ranks agreed for camp duties. The change also affected the amount of pay coming into camp.

65. In No. 4 Camp officers were sometimes made to work outside as ordinary labourers. In other camps they accompanied outside working parties only to supervise. There were one or two isolated incidents of officers being made to labour, but this was exceptional. One case occurred where an I.J.A. Engineer officer forced an officer to work at the point of a revolver. In another case an officer was sent to work for some days as punishment after torture.

66. The duties allowed in camp, apart from a small office, comprised men for cremation or burial, sanitation, cookhouse, wood collecting and wood cutting. As these were essentially jobs which required a particular aptitude and considerable proficiency combined with health and strength (especially in view of the minimum numbers allowed) in no camp was it found possible to organise any system of a day to day change-over to relieve men going out to work every day. As a result, men working outside worked on day after day until they fell sick and went to hospital. As already described, there was continual selection from convalescents to replace those going sick. As a result, there was no half-way; in effect a man was ill in bed or out at work, and the deterioration in health was rapid, general, and very quickly complete.

67. In camp also, multifarious duties had to be performed for both the I.J.A. and for ourselves. Ration drawing, fence making, draining, continual building for the I.J.A., hut repairing (the huts were rotten and constantly collapsing), double-bunking, basket making, collecting firewood for the I.J.A. cookhouse and guardroom, and many casual tasks. All these had, perforce, to be done by convalescents and by malaria patients on their better days, thus retarding and indeed often preventing recovery.

The situation would have been desperate enough even if the outside work had been a fair day's work, but inhuman slave-driving to which the outside working men were continually subjected made the situation hopeless.

OUTSIDE WORK FOR I.J.A. ENGINEERS

68. The working day started with reveille and breakfast in darkness at about 0600-0700 hours. Movement to and from meals for purpose of nature were all in pouring rain about the muddy, ill-sited camp. Breakfast consisted of ¾ pint of plain rice. Parade for work was at first light and then the I.J.A. Engineers took over. If the numbers were not up to demand there was a scene on parade, sometimes ending with the striking of officers in charge. The daily task of selecting the last few men to go out from a number of convalescents – really all unfit to go – was heart-breaking and a tremendous strain on those to whose lot it fell.

69. The party would be marched off to draw tools and then to the scene of work. This often entailed a considerable march of 5 to 10 kilos. Many men (in June up to 80 %) were without usable boots. Marching was always through deep mud with many snags in the way of rocks and sharp bamboo roots. Without boots it was difficult for men to keep their feet in many places.

70. The work itself was mostly very heavy – beyond the strength of an average fully fit man and far beyond the capacity of our starved and debilitated men.[16] Particularly

---

[16] Captain Ben Barnett, Adjutant 8 Division Signals, complied his unit's War Diary which refers to the nature and duration of the work the men were expected to perform: 'Removing mud from approaches to bridges up to 3 kilos from camp and replacing with creek soil. It was an extremely difficult walk along terribly muddy road to the job. Then continuous rain practically made the task impossible. Furthest men out did not get back to camp until about 2100 hrs. … Wet again, but still work parties required. Task making & levelling roads. Rain made it impossible to complete task in time. … One group of 4 men have to move [illegible] cub. Metres of earth per day 5, party of 2 carry 250 loads of earth. Work is in railway cutting. … Workers had lunch & tea out & were informed they would have to work through night until set task finished. They were eventually knocked off at 2245 hrs. …. Last men finished work in the dark at 2145 hrs. They had hazardous journey back to camp along frightfully muddy route. … Both parties out for evening meal despite assurance that latter party would be returning to camp. This party eventually kept at work until 0225 hrs on 14 Aug. Other party working until nearly 0300 hrs on 14 and back in camp just before 0400 hrs. … All personnel working on rock cutting today. Finished work about 2200 hrs.'

severe was the portaging of logs from the mountain side to the roadway and the pile-driving and tree-hauling for the big bridge at Sonkrai, which often entailed working in swift cold water up to the waist, sometimes even to the armpits. Obviously obeying instructions from their officers, the Engineer ORs in charge of parties drove the prisoners savagely with blows from fists, boots, sticks and wire whips.

72. Protests by our officers out on the work site often resulted in their being hit too. Visible resentment or objection were treated as mutinous and savagely punished.

73. It is necessary to emphasise that most of this continual beating was not disciplinary but was used to drive men as beasts to efforts beyond their strength.

73. All the time rain poured down, making conditions more unpleasant and work more difficult. On some tasks, men were often kept actively working (i.e. continually plying shovels, adzes, axes etc.) for three hours at a stretch without a second's break. A short interval, sometimes only a few minutes, was allowed for the midday meal – a pint of rice with a few beans.

74. Work continued until long after dark and then tools were collected, and the march back began – a nightmare performance in the mud, rain and darkness. Tools had to be checked in and this was frequently made an excuse for further harsh treatment and delay. With the best will in the world it was very difficult to collect or check tools in the darkness at the scene of work where small parties were distributed over a large jungle area.

75. At last the party would arrive back in camp at 2200 hours or even later, tired, worn out and dispirited. Numbers had again to be checked before they were dismissed to eat their evening meal (1 pint of rice and ½ pint of some form of vegetable stew) and turn into their sleeping quarters – 2 feet by 6 feet, or less, per man – to get what sleep they could before the next day's agony started.

76. Those who were sick had to be examined by fire-light. With these working conditions, starvation diet and with cholera, dysentery, diarrhoea, malaria, beri-beri, tropical ulcers and trench feet rife, it was not long (by the end of June) before the total number of men working outside camps from the whole force (originally 7,000 strong) was 700.

EFFORTS TOWARDS AMELIORATION – FAILURE OF I.J.A. ADMINISTRATION

77. The fight to break out of these evil conditions was from our side unceasing, prosecuted with every means in our power, and very slowly met with a measure of success.

78. Basically, the I.J.A. attitude depended on orders from Tokyo (with an alleged message from the Emperor) that the railway was to be finished at all costs. Secondarily, it was generally held that prisoners had no rights whatever and that prisoners from the "unconditional" surrender of Singapore, in particular, were I.J.A. chattels, and were outside the provisions of any international agreement. In addition, the I.J.A. rank and file were pumped full of lying propaganda of the bad treatment of I.J.A. prisoners by the Americans and of all Eastern races by the British, e.g. the Japanese newspapers published illustrated statements:-
    i) That the British cut off the thumbs of Indian mill workers to prevent competition with Lancashire!
    ii) That the Americans in Guadalcanal laid Japanese wounded out in rows and deliberately ran tanks over them!

79. From our own side action was continually and urgently demanded with regard to:-
    a) Starvation diet. Full details are given in the Medical Report
    b) Lack of medical supplies except cholera vaccine and a minimum and precarious issue of quinine.
    c) Inhuman working conditions.
    d) Lack of containers, tools and clothing, especially boots and blankets. Only 60% had blankets on leaving Singapore.
    e) Impossible working numbers.
    f) Bad accommodation, especially for hospitals.
    On all of these points a continual bombardment was kept up in all camps by letter and interview, and by Col. Harris at Force HQ to Col. Banno. Appeals were made in writing to General Arimura in Singapore, to the International Red Cross at Tokyo, and to the Japanese Government.

80. It is no part of this report to minimise the local Japanese difficulties; the situation was as follows:-
    In May railway construction was several months behind schedule and the orders from Tokyo for its speedy finish

entailed working through the monsoon, mid-May to mid-September.

By 20 May the road south of Shimo-Nieke had ceased to be practicable for M.T. or bullock carts and there was no hope re-establishing it for use.

In order to maintain a railway labour force of PsoW and coolies in "F" Force area it was therefore essential to keep open the road thence northward into Burma. In May this road was merely a track cleared through the jungle. Through lack of foresight no steps had been taken to weatherproof it before the monsoon broke.

81. The task of keeping it open by corduroy work for about half its length, and the building of bridges and culverts, was therefore essential to the maintenance of labour for the railway in the area. Even with the work done it remained a precarious means of communication traversable at irregular intervals only by six-wheeled lorries with non-skid chains.

82. The I.J.A. Administration of "F" Force failed utterly to cope with the situation:-

a) "F" Force itself had in the forward area about six Marmon Harrington lorries in bad condition and without non-skid chains. These lorries could have been put into good order if the I.J.A. had allowed us to do so or had done it themselves. They took neither of these courses in spite of much urging. Chains could have been obtained from Bampong, Singapore or Burma, or made up in the big Engineers' workshop at Nieke. This was not done. As a result, the lorries were completely wasted. When taken out they broke down and became bogged – necessitating digging and hauling by convalescent men, who were called to the rescue. The effect on "F" Force was that for transport it remained at the mercy of the engineers and had to subsist on whatever they chose to spare. As the supply of labour from "F" Force was poor, the engineers made things as difficult as they could and a vicious circle of failure was established, which the I.J.A. Administration failed to break.

b) With the seasonal rise the river from Bampong became, by mid-June, navigable for motor-boats right up to Nieke. This line of supply was used by the I.J.A. engineers and by the local Thai shopkeepers. It could equally well have been used to bring up food, clothing and medical stores and take down the sick. Nothing was done in spite of continual urging by us.

c) With a properly concerted plan the road could have been organised so that regular convoys from Burma could be passed through. No such plan existed, and labour was frittered away in disjointed work, much of it useless and ill-conceived.

d) As pointed out earlier, the forcing of convalescents out to work, plus lack of food, clothing and accommodation rapidly reduced the amount of PoW labour available.

e) The failure to evacuate the sick used up a lot of effort, in all camps, which could have been usefully employed on the road.

f) The continual brutal treatment of working parties by the I.J.A. engineers, long hours and no holidays for months on end, further reduced the labour available.[17]

RESPONSIBILITY

83. Col. Banno himself always expressed sympathy on the question of brutal treatment and told us again and again that he had seen the Engineer officer and that brutality would cease and shorter working hours would be arranged.

In practice, he was overruled, and conditions did not improve until September.

He himself, however, had a hand in sending unfit men to work, and he continually approved of the wicked practice of issuing a starvation ration to sick men in hospital, on the grounds that this would drive them out of hospital quickly – which it did – to the cemetery.

84. In Thailand there appeared to be a military command under

---

[17] Lieutenant Jim Bradley wrote of the treatment meted out by the Japanese engineers: 'There were daily beatings of officers and men at work, sometimes even into unconsciousness. The object of these was to urge sick and weak men to physical efforts far beyond their remaining strength. Kicks and slaps were commonplace, and men were driven with wire whips and bamboo sticks throughout the day. If anyone worked badly, or appeared to be slacking, they were sometimes made to stand holding a rock or large piece of wood above their heads. If they let it drop, they were beaten.' James Bradley, *Towards the Setting Sun, An Escape from the Thailand-Burma Railway, 1943* (J.M.L. Fuller, Wellington, 1982), p.53.

whom was (amongst others) a Thailand PoW Administration, responsible for other PsoW already in Thailand. The I.J.A. Engineers appeared to be independent of the Thailand Administration and to be the paramount authority in the "F" Force area.

"F" Force continued to be administered by the Malayan PoW Admin in Singapore, and Col. Banno was the local representative of that organisation.

The Singapore office failed (if it ever tried) to intervene effectively to improve the conditions of "F" Force.

Whether the headquarters was properly informed by Col. Banno is not known but what evidence we have seems to show that it was so informed.

IJA ADMINISTRATION WITHIN THE FORCE

85. The I.J.A. Administration within "F" Force attained a standard of inefficiency which is almost beyond description. A cadet officer (Onishi, promoted 2/Lt in Dec 43) who was responsible for "Q" and pay, appeared to us to be mentally deficient. It is probable that much can be put down to the uselessness of this individual, but he was working right under the eye of Col. Banno and the result of his muddling was plain to see and was continually the subject of complaint by us in all camps. With the exception of Lieut. Wakabyashi, those in a position to have things put right did not do so. This especially applies to Colonel Banno.

An opportunity to compare Lieut. Onishi's work compared with that of another quartermaster similarly placed. In November, when "F" Force returned to Kanburi, it shared a camp with part of "H" Force – also under Malayan PoW administration. Although Kanburi was a land of plenty, supplies to "F" Force were never more uncertain, and greatly inferior to supplies to "H" Force.

The issue of rations to "F" Force was never on a fixed scale, but was on an iniquitous "present" system, by which we were at the mercy of dishonest store-keepers. Peculation among the Korean gunsoku in charge of stores was universal. This was pointed out again and again to Colonel Banno and Lieutenant Onishi.

They constantly asserted that the ration issued to the PoW was the same as that issued to the I.J.A. This was a flagrant lie. Very often, and for long periods, the PoW ration was not half that drawn by the I.J.A. in rice, and in other commodities was similarly on a reduced scale. For example, in Nieke (Col. Banno's own camp), when one bullock was killed, half the dead weight was taken for forty I.J.A., leaving the poorer half, consisting mostly of bones, for 1,000 PoW This was pointed out to Colonel Banno and Lieutenant Onishi more than once.

On the "A" side, matters were mainly in the hands of a civilian interpreter, Mr. Saji. His attitude towards the PoW varied from time to time, but his authority derived only from the idleness of the officers over him.

The I.J.A. were entirely dependent on us for records, but it was clear that some effort was directed to obscuring the real position from Tokyo; e.g. all deaths from dysentery were reported as from "diarrhoea" to save office work, the former being a disease that demanded special reports. This interpreter often acted in that capacity at interviews with Col. Banno and Lieut. Onishi and others. Sometimes (as in the matter of pay) he was most helpful; at other times he took an extreme anti-PoW attitude.

86. Again and again we pressed the question of Japanese international obligations under the '06 and '07 agreements and asked how they thought Japan would be able to explain things away. The answer always was that a victorious Japan would not need to explain to anybody, and this appeared to summarise the attitude of all Japanese officers except Lieut. Wakabyashi.

THE BURMA HOSPITAL PROJECT

87. Shortly after arrival at Shimo-Nieke, Col. Harris pointed out that no amenities existed for the establishment of a base hospital and suggested that all sick should be evacuated immediately to Tarso or Bampong. He also pressed to be allowed to visit all camps as soon as they were established. This was refused, but on 27 May, Col. Dillon was allowed to accompany Col. Banno on a flying visit to Nos. 1, 2 and 3 Camps.

88. As a result of information then collected and information received from No.5 Camp, Col. Harris again saw Col. Banno on 2 June and again stressed the seriousness of the situation, pressing for the immediate evacuation of the bulk of the

seriously sick (about 3,000) to Bampong. Col. Banno stated it was impossible while cholera continued and that it would still be impossible to do such an evacuation by road, even after the monsoons. Col. Harris then urged that it should be done by river as soon as the water was high enough.

This project was considered at length by the I.J.A. and on 23 and 24 June, Col. Harris was allowed to visit all four camps forward of Nieke and reported to Col. Banno upon his return. His report of the deplorable conditions, especially in No.5 Camp, is attached. The I.J.A. at last produced another project to open a hospital in Burma.

89. Orders were eventually issued for the evacuation of a staff and 1,700 patients to a camp at Tanbaya in Burma by road and rail through three staging camps to be established at Changaraya (No.5 Camp), Kando, and Ronshi. The I.J.A. gave assurances that the hospital would be provided with medical stores and good rations. Road and rail movement tables, which were perfect specimens of their kind, were issued by the I.J.A. and on 30 July the advance party of staff moved. Thereafter followed the normal Japanese administrative mess. In no single instance were the movement tables adhered to and the journey was carried out under most distressing and inhuman conditions, which added greatly to its unavoidable hardships to the sick. These additional hardships were due to no other cause than Japanese inefficiency and callousness and sometimes active and bestial cruelty. Evacuation to Burma dragged on through August and was not completed until September.

90. The selection of patients to go was exceedingly difficult. It was no good sending those that would not survive the journey; on the other hand those who were not sent would surely die if retained in our working camps. The patients themselves were almost without exception eager to take their chance and go.

The selection was of course made without pre-knowledge of the unnecessary evil conditions under which the journey would be made. Forty-three out of the 1,700 patients died on the journey.

91. The Tanbaya hospital itself consisted of a hutted camp without light or water or any special amenities. The amount of medical stores issued were infinitesimal and rations were ay all times poor, being particularly deficient in Vitamin B,

which was vital to the treatment of the patients (debilitated from dysentery, malaria and tropical ulcers), practically everyone of whom suffered from beri-beri in one form or another.

Approximately 750 patients died at Tanbaya, or about 45% of the total.

92. This outcome was a bitter disappointment, but at least the remaining 55% were saved from inevitable death in the working camps. On one point, the I.J.A. kept its word – Tanbaya was not called upon to supply outside working parties. Convalescents were thus at least given a chance to recover if and when they had managed to survive their actual illness.

The story of the hard struggle against disease and death at Tanbaya by the medical staff, headed by Major Bruce Hunt, AAMC, is given in detail in the report on Tanbaya Hospital (attached)

Lieut-Col. G.T. Hutchinson, MC, RA (GSO I, 18 Division) was appointed Administrative Commandant of the hospital camp and his report is appended.

REORGANISATION NORTH OF NIEKE

93. No sooner had the move of the advance party to the Burma Hospital started than an order was received to close Nieke, Shimo-Sonkrai and Changaraya and to re-group at Sonkrai and Kami-Sonkrai in such a way that each camp could provide approximately the same number of working men: a figure of 800 from each camp was mentioned. Patients and staff for Burma were ordered to remain in the old camps until moved. The men who were so ill that they had not been selected for Burma were also to stay. Most of these were expected to die. This order was received at 1400 hrs on 2 Aug and the move was ordered to be completed on the following day. It involved marching through rain knee-deep in mud, carrying all personal kit, cooking and medical gear and with all patients other than those booked for the Burma Hospital or too ill to be sent there.

Col. Harris protested strongly against the order. He pointed out that the Burma project catered for only half our sick, the remainder (about 1,700) would be left on our hands, and apart from the difficulty and inhumanity of moving them, the figure of 800 working men from each camp was beyond all possibility: about half that number might with difficulty be found.

In the end we were forced to carry out the move. All sick (except those mentioned above as remaining) had to be got out of bed and marched to the next camp. We did obtain the slight concession that these sick should stage at Shimo-Sonkrai and Sonkrai on successive nights on the journey to Kami-Sonkrai. This arrangement was, however, broken forthwith by the I.J.A., and they were forced to march straight through. There is no doubt that a number of the deaths which occurred subsequently at Kami-Sonkrai were directly attributable to this march.

94. In order to balance the number of working men available at the two re-organised forward camps it was necessary to create mixed camps of fitter Australians with the less fit British.

95. Kami-Sonkrai, commanded by Col. Kappe, A.I.F., had as its I.J.A. Commandant Lieut. Fukuda.[18] This remained until the end a disgraceful camp from the point of view of the I.J.A. responsibility and had during August, September and right through October a very heavy death roll. The other camp, No.2 at Sonkrai, was at first an even worse case, but after the general clearance of the bulk of the worst patients by death (averaging ten a day throughout August), and by transfer to the Burma Hospital, the situation greatly improved. To this camp also was posted Lieutenant Wakabyashi, who was the only Japanese officer with whom "F" Force had to deal who showed the slightest glimmerings of humanity or understanding of his responsibility towards the PsoW under his charge.

96. About 20 Aug. Lieut. Wakabyashi came to Col. Harris and stated that he had orders from Engineers H.Q. that unless

---

[18] 'On 10th August the sorry spectacle of nearly 200 light duty and no duty men being forced almost to crawl to work in the pouring rain was witnessed, and yet the same day Fukuda demanded that next day 200 British troops be included in the work party, which was to be further increased to 600. There was another instance on 10 August, where a man who had collapsed on the job was not permitted to return to camp, and was forbidden to take his mid-day rice because he had not worked.' See Lieutenant Colonel C.F. Kappe's report on "F" Force, National Archives of Australia, A6238.

the working figure produced by both camps was doubled, all prisoners, sick as well as fit, would be turned out into the jungle to fend for themselves, thus making room for coolies who could work to be brought in. This threat also applied to Kami-Sonkrai. To his credit must be said that Lieut. Wakabyashi was obviously thoroughly ashamed in having to repeat this order.

A few days later the Colonel commanding the Engineers visited Sonkrai and Lieut. Wakabyashi created an opportunity for Col. Harris, with Col. Dillon and Major Wild, to approach him on the subject direct. The attitude of the Engineer Colonel was at first most unencouraging, but after great perseverance, Major Wild, speaking for Col. Harris, managed to shame him into allowing us to retain part (about two-thirds) of our accommodation, leaving the remainder available for fresh labour. It is emphasized that the project of turning us out into the jungle was a real one and would have been carried out if it had not been for the interview, in spite of the fact that the monsoon was in full flood. It is a grim recollection that we were able to promise to make available a third of our accommodation only by taking into consideration the number of deaths which would inevitably occur in the next few weeks.

97. About 20 Sept., the monsoon started to peter out and conditions began to improve, which improvement was maintained at a slow rate until the force was finally withdrawn to Kanburi en route to Singapore in November.

CANTEEN SUPPLIES

98. Canteen supplies were at all times in very short supply. There was one small shop across the main river from Nieke, from whence the goods had to be ordered and brought up by elephant to Sonkrai. They were distributed thence to the two forward camps, volunteer parties of officers and men carrying forward the goods the remaining four miles to Kami-Sonkrai.

FINANCE

99. (a) Officers.
When the force left Singapore, the officers had been paid up to the end of February. They did not receive pay for March, April and May until well on into June. In the meantime the

only money possessed by the force was its central fund, amounting to some $12,000, but as none of this was changed into Thai currency, it was useless. Throughout the period in Thailand officers continued to receive pay at $40 or $50 a month, 40% of this being deducted for the purchase of extra food for hospitals under schemes which varied as the situation altered.

(b) Combatant O.Rs.

Working pay was paid to men who worked. It averaged about twenty cents per day per working man, or one-fifth of the prevailing rate to coolies working under identical conditions. Here again the practice varied from time to time and in different camps, but as a general rule some system of pooling by camps was in force.

c) Red Cross O.Rs.

These drew rates varying from $10 to $20 per month. They were allowed to draw their full pay, as the burden on the hospital staffs was tremendous and it was felt the little extras they could purchase with this money helped to keep them fit to work and thus the camps benefitted more than if the money had been pooled.

RETURN TO SINGAPORE

100. In November, the force was moved back – first to Kanburi over the Thai railway and later by Bangkok-Singapore railway to Singapore. The arrangements for the first part of the journey were disgraceful, no attempt being made to provide reasonable amenities, food or water for the fit or sick, and fourteen men perished on this journey. The arrangements for the second part had not improved since April and were as described previously.

Residue hospitals were left in Burma and Kanburi and finally returned to Singapore in May 44.

MORALE

101. As may be imagined, under the terrible circumstances displayed in the foregoing report, the bonds of discipline and morale were stretched to breaking point – but they never quite broke. If they had, probably not one man would have returned alive. The Australian half of the force suffered 28% deaths while the British half suffered 61%. The reasons for this difference may be summarised as follows:-

a) The Australian officers and men were all members of one volunteer force with a common emblem and outlook. The British portion was a heterogenous collection of men of all races and units, many of whom found themselves together for the first time.

b) The average physical standard of the small volunteer Australian force was incomparably higher than that of the mixed force of regular soldiers, territorials, militiamen, conscripts and local volunteers who formed the British half. As will be noted from the earlier paragraphs referring to the selection, it was possible for the A.I.F. to maintain a higher standard of fitness for selection for this particular force than could the British half.

c) The A.I.F. had among it a higher proportion of men who were used to looking after themselves under "jungle" or "bush" conditions.

d) The Australian contingent was fortunate in completing its march and occupying its working camps before the monsoon broke.

e) It so happened that at the main Australian camp there was a Japanese officer of the PoW Admin in charge, whereas at Sonkrai and Changaraya there were only military auxiliaries of Private rank and in the latter cases therefore the local Engineers were able to give free rein to their brutality.

Report to Military Police

102. At Kanburi the Military Police visited the camp after Col. Harris had left for Singapore and demanded a report on conditions in Thailand. The PoW Admin, represented at that moment in Kanburi by Lieut. Fukuda, were aware that the request had been made and demanded that a copy should also be given to them.

Col. Dillon and Major Wild prepared the report which follows and handed it over. This report has never been answered or challenged. We did, however, receive orders to destroy all copies of it; which, of course, was not done. It will be noticed that it is stressed in the opening paragraph that it is neither a complaint nor a protest, but a statement of fact. These were included only to evade the rule which the PoW Admin had made that complaints and protests would only be handed to it.

Appendix I

REPORT BY LIEUTENANT COLONEL J. HUSTON, SENIOR MEDICAL OFFICER, "F" FORCE

Introduction

The following medical report deals with conditions leading to the death of over 3,000 British and Australian Army Prisoners of War between April 1943 and April 1944. These belonged to "F" Force, a party of approximately 7,000 men – half Australian, half British. It was taken, under the care of Lieut-Colonel Banno, Imperial Japanese Army, from Changi, Singapore Island, to work on the construction of the Burma-Thailand road and railway in the vicinity of Three-pagodas Pass. The main body of survivors returned to Changi in December 1943 leaving only the very sick, with their attendants, at Tanbaya, Burma and at Kanburi, (Kanchanaburi) Thailand. The survivors of these "hospitals" re-joined at Changi at the end of April 1944.

(J. Huston)
Lieut-Colonel, R.A.M.C.
Late S.M.O. "F" Force

MEDICAL REPORT ON "F" FORCE
Prisoners of War for period April 1943 – April 1944

Preliminary Information
At the beginning of April 1943 information was received at Changi, Singapore, that a force of 7,000 PoW would move by train at an early date. The orders stated that the food situation at Changi was difficult, but this would be better at the new destination, that it was not to be a working party and that it would include 30% unfit men who would have better chances of recovery as the new place would be situated in low hills with good facilities for improving their health. Bands, lighting sets, all tools and cooking gear were to be taken. Canteens would be available after the first three weeks. There was to be no marching except from trains to adjoining camps and transport

for baggage and unfit would be provided. A medical party with equipment for 400 patients and three months medical supplies were to be included.

The personnel had been P.O.W, since the capitulation of Singapore to the Japanese on 15.2.42. The anticipated effects of the ration supplies to prisoners by the I.J.A. had been reported to their Headquarters in writing by the British and Australian Medical authorities at Changi at the beginning of March 1942. It was then pointed out that the diet was deficient in proteins, fats and vitamins, and that it was too low in quality to support health and that serious diseases such as beri-beri and pellagra would follow if the defects were not remedied. These ill-effects had appeared for many months at Changi before the departure of "F" Force, a large majority of whose personnel had been in hospital once or many times with dysentery or pellagroid manifestations (glossitis, stomatitis, pellagra skin, burning feet, partial amblyopia, and granular cornea) or scabies and infected skin conditions. Diphtheria was rife. Many men were thin and undernourished after periods in hospital. Diet centres where better food was provided from Canteen and Red Cross sources, had improved the condition of these men, and many of the recovered were included in the force. They were fit enough to move by train to the better conditions promised.

The medical store at Changi was already depleted of many useful stores because of supplying forces of PoW who had left previously and the consumption of large hospital populations there and in working camps in Singapore. Consequently Emetine (100 grains), Diphtheria antiserum, Sulphonamide drugs, Sulphur, Magnesium sulphate, all very important drugs, were produced in negligible quantity. Blankets (twenty very old and worn), mattress covers, bedpans and urine bottles were inadequate. Small quantities of meat extract, tinned milk and meat were taken. Units of the force took their carefully saved Red Cross rations where those existed.

The force consisted of approximately 3,500 Australians and 3,500 British troops. The whole party was submitted to anal swabbing and blood (thick drop) examination before departure by I.J.A. Vaccination against Smallpox, inoculation against Dysentery, Plague, Cholera and Enteric were given in two doses in weekly intervals under Area managements. In some cases, these were not completed owing to alterations in the train programme.

Train moves

Personnel were moved by lorries from Changi, and entrained in all metal rice trucks at Singapore. 28-9 men were packed in each truck. A Medical party, including one or more Medical officers and a box of medical requirements, were taken with each train. These were adequate for the journey which lasted five days. Thirteen trains moved the parties. As each train load of 600 arrived at Bampong Thailand, kit which could not be man carried was dumped. Each party was marched to a nearby transit camp and was detailed to march the same night or the following night carrying all that could be carried. The camp at Bampong was insalubrious, the forerunner of worse places to come. No troops staged more than twenty-four hours, and all were fatigued after 5 days cramped in hot trucks with poor meals at infrequent intervals. Medical parties moved with each trainload, leaving the sick in a bamboo hut to be taken care of by the next incoming party until the following day. On orders of O.C. "F" Force Lt. Col. S.W. Harris O.B.E. R.A., I stayed after arrival in train nine to see to the disposal of the sick unable to march up the road.

When the whole force had passed through there remained some 50 seriously ill men. Much negotiation resulted in five of the worst dysentery patients being removed to a Japanese hospital in the neighbourhood (these were well treated) and the others were carried in loaded ration lorries two marches up the road to Kanchanabri (KANBURI). These included acute-pleurisy and pneumonia, a fractured femur, etc., and all were ill. They were cared for by Major Rogers AAMC and party who remained behind at this camp until the return of "F" Force at the end of November 1943 when a total mortality of one for the whole period was reported. These were Fortune's Favourites, the mortality of the upcountry camps far exceeded this figure.

The medical stores of the Force were dumped with all other equipment at Bampong; it was difficult to locate the most important articles. I was able to get my hands on about twelve panniers of drugs and equipment and move these in the two lorries with the sick when the last party left. Meanwhile each road party took such essentials as were at hand and could be carried. Valiant efforts were made to take as much as possible.

At Bampong I represented the great necessity of getting forward the main medical equipment to Lt. Col. Banno, the Japanese officer in charge of "F" Force; he said it would be sent within a few days. He accompanied the two lorries and after leaving the fifty sick at Kanburi, we went on to Tarsu and spent the night. Next morning, we were joined by Lt. Col Harris who had preceded us. When some 15 Km beyond Tarsu, near Kanu, Col. Banno stopped and ordered me to take the medical panniers and form a wayside hospital for the marching men of the Force. It was pointed out by Col. Harris and myself, through an interpreter, that as Senior Medical Officer it would be better for me to go ahead to make medical arrangements at our final destination. Major W.J.E. Phillips R.A.M.C. who had been ill at Bampong was with us, and we told Col. Banno that we could leave him there to make a hospital. Col. Banno's mind was made up. Both Major Phillips and I were left with the medical panniers and a Japanese medical orderly who produced a very rat-eaten inner lining of a small marquee – this was to house the hospital for the sick.

We carried the equipment to a bamboo patch beside a stream by the road and dealt as best we could with the sick arriving each morning after their night-long march. Rations were poor, marching parties were exhausted and had to sleep in the open and there were many sick with dysentery, diarrhoea and an enormous number of blisters and sores on feet and legs. There was a daily battle with the accompanying guards who wanted to make the maximum possible numbers march up the road. Between preparation and taking of food, and having feet attended to, muster and roll-call, the marches averaged 3 hours sleep at this camp. There was no shelter except the hospital "tent" which sheltered the men – most of them were rained upon with monotonous regularity as the monsoon had broken. Major Phillips was sent off with one of the later parties which were made up of men who had been sick at other stages of the road and were being hurried forwards to catch up with the main body. Officers and men were for the most part unfit, many of them wretchedly so.

By the end of May I received a note from Col. Harris that cholera had broken out in the camps where "F" Force were located and that the I.J.A. ordered movements to camps to continue. He asked me to come up as quickly as possible as Col. Banno had sanctioned this, and to send up any stores suitable for dealing with cholera. I packed a pannier with such funnels, tubing, needles, sodium chloride, camphorodyne, and potassium permanganate as were with me and despatched them with directions by an on-going lorry. I repeatedly asked all Japanese in the vicinity assisted by the interpreter with "H" Force HQ nearby, but nobody would, or could, allow me to proceed. The excuses were that the roads were impassable, or it was not within their jurisdiction to allow the move. If Col. Banno or his staff sent a written order, this useless delay could have been obviated.

Finally, at the beginning of July – two months after arrival, I was allowed to go back to Tarsu by barge with 30 sick men who had been in the camp for weeks; they were left in the charge of Major Agnew and after two days interrogation by the Japanese P.M.O. on cholera, Indian epidemics etc., I was sent to Tankanun by boat, delayed 8 days there and marched to Nieke by Korean guards, arriving at "F" Force HQ in mid-July.

9 Medical panniers were taken from me by I.J.A. at Kanu, these contained, among other stores tinned milk, soup, beef etc. for invalids. I was allowed the 3 remaining panniers as far as Tarkanun and arrived at Nieke without these (these finally arrived a month later).

It may be mentioned that conditions in Tamil and British camps in the Kami area were utterly distressing. Coolies, stricken with cholera or dysentery were ordered out into the jungle by their guards and there left to die. A British camp (O. C. Lt. Col. Warren, Royal Marines) was almost knee-deep in mud, including the hospital huts; their employers made nefarious demands for labour, there was a shocking sick rate. The mortality for June 1943 was 104 out of approximately 650 strength (including only two cases of cholera)[19]

These notes describe conditions of the march. The reports of other medical officers relate similar experiences.

---

[19] British doctor Robert Hardie recorded the following description of the coolies' camps: 'They are kept isolated from Japanese and British camps. They have no latrines. Special British prisoner parties at Kinsaiyok bury about 20 coolies a day. These coolies have been brought from Malaya under false pretences – "easy work, good pay, good houses!" Some have even brought wives and children. Now they find themselves dumped in these charnel houses, driven and brutally knocked about by the Jap and Korean guards, unable to buy extra food, bewildered, sick, frightened.' *The Burma-Siam Railway: The Secret Diary of Dr. Robert Hardie, 1942-1945* (Quadrant Books & Imperial War Museum, 1983), p.109.

Appendix II

STATEMENT BY
ASSISTANT-SURGEON B. WOLFE, I.M.D.

Three to four days after the completion of the march and arrival at Shimo-Nieke, I proceeded under instructions from Lieut-Col. S.W. Harris, with four medical orderlies, to Konkoita.

After marching all night in heavy rain, through mud and without food, the party arrived at Konkoita the following morning. There I found nineteen patients crowded into one tent on the river bank. Of these, nine were cholera cases and the remainder untreated malaria and bad ulcer cases. These personnel had been without attendants or treatment for some days and the tent was in filthy condition and full of flies; the cholera cases defecating and vomiting where they lay, their comrades being unable to help them.

My party began work immediately segregating the patients, cleaning up and giving what little treatment was available, and I went and interviewed the senior I.J.A. MO at the camp, pleading for drugs, food, shelter and/or conveyance to our own camp. He gave no help, even refusing conveyance, and when I remonstrated with him, pointing out that all the patients would die if no assistance was forthcoming, he said: "We must all die some day" or words to that effect.

The party remained at Konkoita for some days, the Japanese giving us plain rice only during that time and refusing us permission to communicate with PoW drivers passing the camp daily.

With the aid of a common metal funnel provided by a Tamil coolie, the rubber tube of my stethoscope and a needle I had in my possession, I managed to keep the patients alive by administering intravenous saline.

Eventually I obtained permission, after refusal by the Japanese to make bullock carts available, on the grounds that they would become contaminated, for myself and the four orderlies to move the nineteen patients to one of our own camps.

42

The Japanese, however, still refused permission for me to communicate first with such camp.

We left the camp with five stretcher cases, cholera cases having to be half dragged along by men who were already carrying stretchers, and others doing their best to hobble along on their own. The Japanese sent no guards as they were too afraid of becoming infected through contact with the party.

In stages of about 100 yards, we eventually reached a point about one kilo from the camp, and out of sight of it, where I hid the party in the jungle and improvised shelter for patients, and sent an orderly to obtain assistance from the nearest camp which was under the command of Lieut-Col. C.H. Kappe A.I.F.

On reaching this camp, the orderly made his way in stealthily through the back of the camp, as admission to the camp was prohibited. He contacted Lieut-Col. Kappe, Lieut-Col. Pond and Capt. R.M. Mills, who immediately made available one officer and fifty men with stretchers, food, water, and a few drugs and they managed to bring my patients to the camp where they were cared for.

I am greatly indebted to these officers and men. Were it not for their prompt assistance we would have been completely stranded.

(Signed) P. Wolfe
Asst. Surgn, I.M.D.

Appendix III

REPORT OF BEATING UP OF INTERPRETOR OF NO. 5 PoW CAMP, THAILAND, 27 JUNE 1943

On the evening of 27 June while at the 115 Kilo Camp, I and Lieut. Raw were invited by the No.1 Nipponese Engineer to come to his hut for coffee and a hot bath. This hut was about 50 yards from the British officers' hut and there had never been any question of its being out of bounds. While there I received a message from the PoW Camp Commandant 2/Lt. Kanada to report to his HQ when I returned. This I duly did. Asked where I had been I said that I had been having a bath in the Engineers' hut. I was at once accused of being out of bounds and without more ado beaten ferociously with sticks by 2/Lieut. Kanada and other Nipponese soldiers. The Nipponese interpreter told me that I had been trying to escape. After about half an hour of this bashing, I was made to stand to attention with my left foot right up against the fire and was told I would have to stand there for five hours. Every now and again I received further blows and if I staggered, I was always made to resume with my left foot touching the fire. I fell once or twice but was always beaten to my feet again. Lieut. Raw was summoned, but no action was taken against him. Major Gairdner (British C.O.) was summoned and confirmed that no word had been said placing this hut out of bounds. After some two hours I was permitted to depart (at 2400 hrs). Both my eyes were black and swollen and I had several cuts and bruises over the head and shoulders. My left leg had burns on the foot and all up the calf.

Following on this I was made to work for four days, axing trees, carrying stores and digging latrines in spite of the medical officers declaring me unfit for it. At the end of that time I could not put my left foot to the ground without very great pain and was allowed to be admitted to hospital. The ulcers developing from my burns healed up at the beginning of September.

Signed
R.G Fletcher, Lieut.

CHAPTER 2

Extract of Report by Major B.A. Hunt, AAMC

MARCH.

The march was long and extremely arduous – it laid the foundations for the widespread debilitation of the force which played a major part in increasing the death rate from infectious diseases (Cholera, Malaria and Dysentery). The march was always done at night. The average distance covered was about 23 k.m. and the majority of the troops covered 14 such stages aggregating about 300 k.m. "Rest nights" were given at Camp 2, Camp 4, Camp 7, and Camp 9, but many who had been left behind for a night on account of illness were unable to take advantage of these, being compelled to press on and endeavour to join their parties. After the first two marches which were along a highway the roads were bad and usually very bad – the moon gave no assistance for most of the march – rain was frequent and conditions on really wet nights were nightmarish. Owing to the appalling road conditions many of the marches lasted 10-14 hours with only very short halts. Little rest could be obtained at the staging camps, especially by the medical personnel, most of whose time was taken up in attending to the sick from their own and previous parties and in dressing the hundreds of blistered and ulcerated feet which were brought to their attention. There was no shelter at any of the camps apart from improvised bivouacs, and heavy rain frequently made these ineffective. Every possible endeavour was made by M.Os. to protect the sick against the weather, with, however, only moderate success.

Food was poor – it consisted almost solely on rice and onion water. At the first three staging camps it was possible to purchase supplementary foodstuffs, but thereafter these facilities ceased.

Treatment of the troops, and in particular the sick, by the I.J.A. guards varied from march to march and from camp to camp. At some camps the M.O. was subject to much interference, and at several places men with active malaria or with dysentery or with large infected ulcers on their feet were compelled to do a whole night's march, to the great detriment of their health. One such episode, the details of which are still fresh in my mind, is worth recording. At Camp 5 (Tarso) I was informed that all sick had to be submitted for inspection to the I.J.A. M.O. who was stationed about ½ mile away. The total of sick on this occasion, derived from men from my own and previous parties, was 37 – 27 with infected feet, 10 with malaria or dysentery. The Japanese officer agreed that none of these men were fit to march but the corporal of the guard only gave permission for 10 to remain. A further interview with the I.J.A. M.O. by Major Wild (interpreter) and myself confirmed the previous advice and produced a letter of instruction from the MO to the corporal. This also was resultless [sic] as was a further visit from Major Wild to the M.O. later that afternoon.

At the time scheduled for parade I fell in the 37 men apart from the main parade, and Major Wild and I stood in front of them. The corporal approached with a large bamboo in his hand and spoke menacingly to Major Wild who answered in a placatory fashion. The corporal's only reply was to hit major Wild in the face. Another guard followed suit and as Major Wild staggered back the corporal thrust at the Major's genitals with his bamboo. I was left standing in front of the patients and was immediately set upon by the Corporal and two other guards – one tripped me while the two others pushed me to the ground. The three then set about me with bamboos, causing extensive bruising of scull, back, hands and arms, and a fractured left 5th metacarpal bone. This episode took place in front of the whole parade of troops. After I was disposed of the corporal then made the majority of the sick men march with the rest of the troops.

At Camp 6 I was again struck and some of my patients rejected – these were only occasions on which I personally received violence at the hands of the guards. It was the general practice of M.Os to march at the rear of the column to succour the stragglers and to endeavour to prevent any possible molestation of these by the guards – I saw such threatened on a number of occasions as sick men were hurried along, but the intervention was usually successful, and I never saw a blow struck under these circumstances.

The chief disabilities which manifested themselves during the march were:-

1) <u>Senility and Cardiac weakness</u>. All these cases were left behind at Camp 2, and I believe that many of them were forced along the road with fatal results.

2) <u>Dysentery</u>. Became increasingly common as the march progressed (I myself was held up for a day at Camp 9 by a very acute attack of Bacillary Dysentery).

3) <u>Septic abrasions of the feet</u>. Many of the boots were ill-fitting and very many of the men were totally unaccustomed to marching.

4) <u>Fevers</u>. Were of lesser frequency and importance until arrival in working camps.

CHAPTER 3

Report on PoW Camps 1, 2, 3, and 5 Visited 23 and 24 June 1943

To: Colonel Banno
Officer Commanding
British and Malayan PoW Camp
THAILAND

Sir,
I have the honour to enclose a report on the four forward PoW Camps I visited on 23 and 24 June 1943.

While I fully appreciate the difficulties our local I.J.A. administration are faced with, and appreciate the fact that Colonel Banno and his administration are doing everything they can on our behalf, at the same time there are certain outstanding needs that are of vital necessity for the health and welfare of the troops under my command. Unless immediate action is taken to deal with these needs the opinion of my senior medical officers is that a great number of lives of these PoW will be unnecessarily sacrificed.

I found in all camps that the morale of the PoW troops was good and improving.

I wish to press for:-
1. An increased ration scale to contain more vitamin B content i.e. towgay and beans, and also for an issue of cooking fats. Also for the supplementation of rations by the establishment canteens and local purchase. The medical officers consider this the most important need and state that unless this is done there will be a high incidence of deficiency diseases, and men recuperating from cholera, dysentery, malaria and debility diseases generally will have no chance of recovery and becoming fit for work.

2. Shorter working hours for the road parties so that men can have an opportunity to wash themselves and their clothes. If working parties could return by 1830 hours this would meet the case. A regular holiday for working parties in all camps is also necessary.

3. A stoppage of beating and ill-treatment of working parties by I.J.A. Engineers. At No.1 Camp this is particularly in evidence. Every day men are being beaten and there are constant cases of face-slapping of officers.

4. No ill or unfit men to be included in outside working parties.

5. A sufficient number of tools to be made available for Camp Hygiene purposes.

6. The supply of buckets and containers for all camps and particularly for Camps Nos. 5 and 2, where they are most urgently needed.

7. I am most grateful for the supply of quinine which has been made available for all camps as malaria is greatly on the increase. Mosquito nets are a crying necessity.

Recently I put forward a consolidated request for drugs and medicines. I trust that steps are being taken to procure these as they are of vital necessity.

I also put forward a written request to be allowed to get in touch with the nearest representative of the International Red Cross. I should be glad if you would advise me what is being done in this matter as we are in urgent need of his assistance. I have a prescriptive right to apply for access to an International representative under the Hague Convention.

Camp No.1
Morale of the troops is good. Camp Hygiene and sanitation satisfactory. The Camp Commandant presses for:-
1. A fuller ration scale, supplemented by a canteen.
2. Shorter working hours for road working parties and a regular holiday.
3. Cessation of ill-treatment by I.J.A. Engineers of officers and men on road parties.

4. Road parties in this camp were tested on "piece work" by the I.J.A. Engineers, and their work was found satisfactory. Could this principle be established and the men allowed to work under their own officers?

Camp No.2

Morale of troops good. Camp hygiene and sanitation fair. The Camp Commandant would be grateful for:-
1. An increased scale of rations supplemented by a canteen.
2. The attapped huts across the roadway from his camp (at present occupied by about 50 natives) to be made available for 200 of his troops, as accommodation in his camp is badly overcrowded.
3. The river to be made available again for bathing and washing purposes. At present the water carry is a long one and there are only a few men and containers available for this duty.
4. The I.J.A. Administrative Sergeant is constantly overruled by the I.J.A. Engineer officer. Can this be remedied please?

Camp No.3

Morale of the troops very good and the Camp Commandant expressed satisfaction with his working conditions.

Camp No.5

Conditions in this camp are deplorable. British PoW are living in close proximity to Burman labourers and camp hygiene is impossible. The ground is waterlogged and it is not possible to construct adequate latrines and refuse pits.

The I.J.A. Engineers insist on every available man going out on working parties. There are insufficient men for carrying out hygiene and sanitation. The water carry in this camp is a long one and there are NO buckets or water containers available.

I feel strongly that this camp needs all the help possible from our own I.J.A. Administration. There is a high incidence of sickness, disease and death in this camp. This high incidence of disease will continue until conditions are improved.

I wish to make the strongest representation that in all camps, but this one in particular, only fit men are taken out on working parties, and that buckets and containers be supplied to them as soon as possible.

CHAPTER 4

Report of Conditions of Prisoners of War in Thailand May to December 1943

<u>Introduction</u>

The representative of the I.J.A. Military Police has requested a frank report to be made on the recent conditions of PsoW in Thailand with suggestions for the improvement of conditions for PoW generally.

Accordingly, this report is made in two parts: I Facts and II Suggestions.

Part I is neither a complaint nor a protest, but a statement of facts, all of which can be substantiated by officers who were present.

The suggestions in Part II are made in the sincere hope that the conditions of PoWs will improve in future, since it is our firm belief that our recent experiences have not been in accordance with the policy or intentions of the Imperial Japanese Government in Tokyo or of the Japanese Red Cross, who cannot have been aware of the actual state of affairs in Thailand.

I. FACTS

1. In early April orders were issued to prepare 7,000 Ps.o.W. for a move by train. The orders stated that:-

    a) The reason for the move was that the food situation in Singapore was difficult and would be far better off in the new place.

    b) This was <u>NOT</u> a working party.

c) As there were not 7,000 fit combatants in Changi, 30% of the party were to be men unfit to march or work. The unfit men would have a better chance of recovery with good food and in a pleasant hilly place with good facilities for recreation.

d) There would be no marching except for a short distance from the train to a nearby camp and transport would be provided for baggage and men unfit to march.

e) Bands were to be taken,

f) All tools and cooking gear and an engine and gear for electric light were to be taken.

g) Gramophones, blankets, clothing and mosquito nets would be issued at the new camps.

h) A good canteen would be available at each camp after three weeks. Canteen supplies for the first three weeks were to be bought with prisoners' money before leaving Singapore.

i) The party would include a Medical party of about 350 with equipment for a central hospital of 400 patients and medical supplies for three months.

2. As each trainload arrived at Bampong they were informed to their astonishment that a march of several days was to be carried out by all men, including the 30% unfit. All kit that men and officers could not carry was to be dumped at Bampong. This amount to the equivalent of about 15 railway truck loads of stores and baggage.

3. The March, in fact, was one of 300 kilometres in 15 stages and lasted 2½ weeks. Marching was at night along a rough jungle track (except for the first two stages) and as all torches had been taken from all PsoW during a search at Bampong, control by PoW officers and N.C.Os. was difficult or impossible.

4. After the first stage the unfit men became increasingly ill and were a heavy handicap to the other men, who were at first fairly fit but rapidly themselves became ill and exhausted as they had to help and even carry the increasing number of men who were unable to walk unaided.

5. Conditions at the staging camps were:-

    a) At no stage was overhead cover provided except for a few tents (for 100 men) at one camp. The weather was variable, and the rainy season started while the march was in progress.
    b) Food supplied was generally very poor and in many cases consisted of rice only.
    c) Water was short at many camps and at Kanburi drinking water had to be brought by the prisoners from a privately owned well. Col. Harris protested but the matter was not put right.
    d) No proper arrangements existed for retaining sick at these camps and men who were absolutely unfit to march (owing to disease and weakness) were beaten and driven from camp to camp. Officers, including medical officers, who begged and prayed for sick men to be left behind were themselves beaten at many camps. In one particular case, a Japanese medical officer (a lieutenant) ordered the I.J.A. corporal in charge of Tarso staging camp to leave thirty-six men behind as they were too ill to move. The corporal refused to obey this order, although it was repeated in writing, and a British officer interpreter (a major) and an Australian doctor (a major) were severely beaten when they protested. A bone in the doctor's hand was broken. Of these sick men who were compelled to march nearly all have since died, including an Australian chaplain who died at the next camp. (The Japanese medical officer had particularly said that the chaplain should not march as he was an elderly man with a weak heart and was already at the end of his strength.)
    e) The men marched all night, as a rule from 7 p.m. to 7 a.m. They had to perform camp duties, get their meals and wash during the day and so had very little rest.

6. Medical

    a) Such medical stores as had been hastily selected at Bampong and carried by hand with the marching parties were rapidly used up and the march continued with no medicines at all.

b) Dysentery and diarrhoea broke out in all parties and
exhaustion was general. Ulcerated feet occurred in large
numbers, due to sick men with blistered feet being forced
to march on day after day.

7.   At Konkoita the marching parties were quartered in the
same camp as a Thai labour corps, who were suffering from
cholera. The infection was picked up by each of the thirteen
parties of marching prisoners.

8.   On 15 May cholera broke out at Shimo-Nieke. Col. Harris
(Commander of the PsoW) immediately reported to Col.
Banno, and requested that the movement should cease until
the outbreak was under control and that Konkoita Camp
should be at all costs not used by further parties.
Unfortunately, Col. Banno was unable to comply with this
request and, as a result, cholera was spread into all five
camps occupied by the force.

9.   Only a very small quantity of the medical stores at Bampong
was later brought up by lorry (over three-quarters of it was
still in Bampong when the force returned to Camburi [sic] in
December). The I.J.A. were unable at this stage to produce
any medical supplies whatever* but Col. Banno gave us six
tins of milk of his own property.

10. By the end of May about 5,000 men had been distributed to
several different camps. These camps consisted of huts
without roofing, although the rainy season had now fully
started, and rain was falling heavily day and night. The
camps were not fully roofed for some weeks, during which
time the men had no proper shelter; consequently, deaths
from pneumonia were numerous.

11. In spite of the above conditions, the general state of exhaustion
of the men, the presence of epidemic cholera in all camps, and
practically universal malaria, diarrhoea and dysentery, the
men were put to work by the Engineers at once.

12. Maximum numbers of men were taken out to work every day.
This left insufficient men in camp for sanitary duties and for
nursing the sick, while disease of every kind increased rapidly.

In some camps Red Cross personnel were forced to go out to work on the road, but this was quickly stopped by Col. Banno.

13. In several camps a great scarcity of tools made improvements to sanitation difficult or impossible. The tools which the prisoners had brought from Changi, and which were part of the heavy baggage in Bampong, were never brought up.

14. It was clear to all prisoner officers that if the Engineers continued to take all fit men and convalescent men to work every day there would soon be no me at all fit to work. In fact, the Engineers were rapidly destroying their only available source of labour.

    This aspect was explained to our own I.J.A. Headquarters, who clearly agreed but were apparently unable to prevent the Engineers doing as they liked.

    The task in front of the Engineers and the need for speed were fully understood by us, but the destruction by the Engineers of their only available labour was just as bad from their point of view as ours.

    A little common sense on the part of the Engineers could, early in June, have saved the situation for us and for themselves.

    Unfortunately for us, this short-sighted policy continued, and by the end of June only about 700 for heavy work. Of the remainder, except for Red Cross personnel, and a small number of administrative personnel (including officers), all men were lying ill in the camp hospitals.

15. By this time, the road from the South was impassable and to the North was difficult, and the scale of rations fell below the level required to help sick men back to health. It has been said that we were on the same rations as the I.J.A. soldiers, but this is not true and can very easily be proved.

    The rations of men in hospital were fixed at far too low a scale.* * In our opinion this was a great mistake and we continually said so to the I.J.A.

    There seemed to be an idea that the lack of pay and rations would drive men out of hospital, but this, of course, would happen only if the men were not really ill. There was, however, no deception about the illness of our men and men were dying in large numbers.

16. As the health of the men grew worse the demands of the Engineers were more and more difficult to meet, and their treatment of our weak men while at work became more and more brutal.

   The work was often beyond what could reasonably be expected of fit men and it was certainly beyond the strength of our weakened men. This especially relates to the carriage of heavy logs. It was noticed where Thai or Burmese labour was used two and three times the number of men were used.

   It became common for our men to be literally driven with wire whips and bamboo sticks throughout the whole working day. Hitting with the fist and kicking also occurred frequently throughout the day. It is emphasised that this beating was not for disciplinary purposes but was intended to drive unfit men to efforts beyond their strength.

   * except cholera vaccine and quinine, which were always supplied as required.
   **250 to 300 grms of rice and a small quantity of beans per day.

17. The hours of work were also excessive. Fourteen hours a day was a common occurrence and work went on day after day for weeks on end and [the men] never had a chance to wash themselves or their clothes.

18. In some camps where the number of fit men fell below the Engineers' demands, the Engineers themselves came into the camp and forced prisoners out of hospital to work.[20] Except in isolated instances officers were not made to work

---

[20] There are far too many stories of the sick being driven out of hospital to join the working parties. One such example, which occurred on 16 August, was related by Lieutenant Charles Henry Moore, 2/26 Battalion A.I.F: 'After having out every available fit man to work, the Japs demanded 50 men for camp work which was impossible without using hospital patients. Toyama [*sic*] came up and demanded 50 men be produced or else whole camp to go on ½ rations. We were forced to take some bed patients out to make up the numbers as the Senior Medical Officer decided it was better to do this than have the rest of the serious cases cut down to half rations which would be detrimental.' C.H. Moore, 1963, *The Ill-Fated "F" Force*, pows-of-japan.net/ article.

outside camps but the Engineers often used the threat that officers would be taken to work if more men were not turned out from hospital.

19. At Songkrai, where conditions were probably worse than anywhere else, the I.J.A. Engineer officer in charge, Lieutenant Abe, himself came into the Officers' quarters and, asking to see the six officers who were most seriously ill (of whom three subsequently died), said, "unless 150 more men are produced for work tomorrow I will send my soldiers to take these officers out to work". This Engineer officer was conspicuous at all times in failing to stop brutal treatment of prisoners by his men when it happened in his presence.

   Of the 1,600 men who originally went to Songkrai Camp in May 1,200 are already dead and 200 more are still in hospital, of whom many are not expected to recover. Many petitions and appeals were made to Lieutenant Abe but he treated them with contempt.[21]

   The result would have been much worse if it not been for the arrival of Lieutenant Wakabayashi (of the Malaya Prisoner of War administration) in Songkrai Camp at the beginning of August. From the date of his arrival the situation in that camp gradually improved.

20. By July more than half the force were without boots and this caused a large number of poisoned feet and "trench feet", from continual work in the wet.

   Blankets were not issued as promised (at Changi) to the men without them. (Later in August some blankets and sacks were issued and more in Kamburi in November).

   Clothing issues were negligible. Issues of medical stores were totally inadequate. Bandages and dressings were seldom issued, and only in very small quantities. For hundreds of tropical cases, dressings were improvised from banana leaves, and bandages from sleeves and legs cut from

---

[21] Richard Laird wrote the following about Abe Hiroshi: 'Lieutenant Abe was a real bad one, not just the usual Bushido attitude, but really vicious as well … In general I did not feel vicious about the Nips, but I certainly did about this one.' Laird, op. cit., p.97.

men's shirts and trousers. Consequently, many limbs had to be amputated unnecessarily and many patients died.

21. By the end of July the road from Bampong was still impassable but although the river was open to traffic and was in use by the I.J.A. and Thai shopkeepers, our medical and other stores at Bampong were still not brought up. This was in spite of our repeated requests.

22. It was during the foregoing period that several men, sometimes alone, sometimes in groups, disappeared into the jungle. Some probably had some idea of escaping and some undoubtedly only left so as to die in freedom rather than in captivity by disease and ill-treatment. The men on the whole were in despair. The choice in front of them seemed to be death from disease, or never-ending toil and brutal treatment at the hands of the Engineers.

    Their officers were unable to protect them in spite of all their efforts. One party of officers, seeing their men dying and ill-treated all around them, and in despair of being able to get any redress from the I.J.A., attempted to escape so as to let the world know what was happening to the prisoners and obtain help from the International Red Cross.

    This party failed, as was inevitable. Five perished from privation in the jungle and the remaining four were recaptured.

23. In August a hospital was established in Burma and about 2,000 men were sent there. Unfortunately, the rations were still deficient of the necessary vitamins and 800 men died. Nevertheless, the Burma hospital did great good for there was not Engineer work and therefore many men had a chance to get well slowly.

24. From August onwards things improved at Songkrai but did not improve much at Kami-Conkrai [sic]. As late as October, for instance, the Engineers there were blasting in a quarry just behind the prisoners' hospital in such a way that rocks and stones fell on the hospital huts at each blast. The huts were crammed full of patients, many of whom were in a dying condition. (About 8 a day were dying). All patients were terrorised, many were hit and more or less seriously

injured, and one man had his arm broken and subsequently died from the combination of the injury and his previous sickness. This went on for over a week before representations by the I.J.A. officer in charge of the camp were successful in stopping it. Blasting continued but in such a way that rocks did not fall on the hospital, thus showing that the previous practice was avoidable.

In this camp also the latrine used by several hundred Tamil labourers was within ten yards of the prisoner officers' quarters. The Tamils had suspected cholera and smallpox at the time.

25. In all camps the accommodation was totally inadequate. Men slept actually touching each other and as a result skin disease infection was 100% throughout the force. Except in Sonkrai most officers were as badly off as the men.

26. The move back to Kanburi took place in November but the men were in such a state that (although the worst cases were left in Burma) forty-six died on the train journey and 188 more in the first three weeks in Kanburi, in spite of better food and living conditions.

It is certain that several hundreds more will die in the next month or two from the result of their treatment in Thailand.

27. Our own guards on the whole treated us well. Face slapping of prisoners of all ranks was discouraged by the I.J.A. officers but was still fairly common. It nearly always arose from a language misunderstanding and was not in itself serious, although it makes the maintenance of discipline very difficult for the prisoner-officers when their men see them being slapped by young Japanese privates. Similarly, when the men are slapped and beaten it merely breeds resentment and bad feelings, which will last long after the war.

There are some guards, however, who seem incapable of any task without losing their tempers and hitting prisoners.

The most flagrant case is that of a Gunsoku, Toyama, who claims to be a well-educated man. At Bampong he hit officers and men of every party with a heavy steel-shafted golf club. He cut one Major's head open, badly damaged another Major's arm and severely hurt many others. The cause of these assaults was never known. Later, at Shimo-Songkrai and at Kami-Songkrai camps he habitually hit officers and men on every possible occasion for no just cause. He has an ungovernable temper and is apparently uncontrollable by his own officers, especially senior officers. Such a men should never be allowed to be in charge of prisoners.

28. There were many cases latterly in which our own guards prevented Engineers from maltreating prisoners.

29. It may be thought that some of the above report is exaggerated. It is, however, only the barest outline of a period of intense hardship suffered by a party of prisoners of war.

   If proof is wanted it is surely sufficient to point to the fact that of the 7,000 prisoners who left Changi, in April, now, in December, about 3,000 are dead. 3,000 more are hospital patients or convalescents, of whom hundreds more will die in the next few months from the result of the hardships they have undergone.

30. We know from letters received from England and Australia that it is believed there that prisoners-of-war are being well treated by the Japanese. If the actual facts regarding Thailand were known abroad, the news would be greeted with indignation and amazement.

II. SUGGESTIONS

General

We ask firstly that we should be treated in accordance with the letter and the spirit of the Geneva and Hague Conventions, particularly those of 1906 and 1907, both of which were ratified both by Britain and Japan.

   It has been suggested that the unconditional surrender of Singapore places the prisoners from Singapore outside the terms of the Hague Convention. This is obviously not so.

   The position of any prisoner who is captured on the field of battle is clearly that of unconditional surrender, but no one would suggest that he is not covered by the Convention. How then can the nature of Singapore's surrender (which was correctly made at the written request of General Yamashita 'in order to avoid further useless loss of life on both sides and especially the lives of civilians in the city') put the garrison of Singapore outside the terms of the Convention?

Detailed suggestions

The following detailed suggestions are all consequent on this general one.

1. "Doctors and Red Cross personnel are not prisoners of war and should not be treated as prisoners." (Genera Convention, 1906, Article 9)
2. "Prisoners should be humanely treated." (Annex to Hague Convention, 1907, Article 4).
3. "Work should not be excessive." (Annex to Hague Convention, 1907. Article 6).
4. "Prisoners should be treated as regards rations, quarters and clothing on the same footing as the troops of the government which capture them." (Annex to Hague Convention, 1970, Article 7).

Note 1. All the above were broken in Thailand.

Note 2. As regards rations, it is not enough to fix a scale of rations; the essential is that the rations should reach the prisoners. It is suggested that the military police undertake the duty of seeing that the scale of issue allowed does in fact reach the prisoners.

Note 3. As regards quarters and clothing it should be remembered that officer prisoners pay for their quarters.

5. "Officers must not be employed for labour." (This equally applies to being threatened with labour). (Annex to Hague Convention, 1907, Article 6).
   There were not many occasions when officers of this party were made to labour, but it was known to all of us that hundreds of officers in other parties were forced to work as labourers on road and railway construction in organised

gangs. This treatment of officer prisoners of war is without precedent in the whole history of modern war, besides being a direct breach of the Hague Convention. It will not be forgotten or forgiven for a hundred years.

6. "Red Cross representatives should be allowed to visit PoW camps." (Annex to Hague Convention, 1907, Article 15).

   No representatives were allowed to visit us in Thailand.

7. "Proper arrangements should be made to collect deceased's' effects." (Annex to Hague Convention, 1907, Article 14).

   This has not been done and many effects have, as a result, been lost.

8. "Soldiers should be respected and taken care of when sick." (Geneva Convention, 1906, Article 1).

   This was often broken in Thailand.

9. Games, entertainments, reading, educational classes and lectures should be encouraged to keep up morale.

10. Arrangements for letters to and from home should be improved. Letters arriving are a year old and we have not been allowed to write a single letter home, but only a few lines on a postcard twice in two years.

Prisoners of war in all belligerent countries in Europe are allowed to write as follows:-

Officers: Two letters and two postcards each month.
Other Ranks: One letter and one postcard each month.

CHAPTER 5

Report on No.2 Camp (Sonkrai)

Trains Nos. 7, 8 and 9, totalling 900 all ranks, arrived at SONKRAI on the morning of 20 May 1943 after a march of 315 kilos.

The camp consisted of three huts, approximately 150, 200 and 250 ft. long. The I.J.A. guards, PoW officers and W.Os, were quartered in the smallest hut; the other two, which were roofless, being occupied by O.Rs. Adequate latrines were already in existence, as was also a cookhouse, but "kawalis"[22] had to be installed before a meal could be prepared. Only twelve containers (six gallon) were brought up, this shortage, which was never remedied, causing endless difficulties.

The 21 May was spent clearing up the camp. Large quantities of tree toppings and scrub being removed from between huts.

On the 22 May 600 men were sent out to work on the railway. On the final stage of the march the men had marched for five consecutive nights, becoming in most cases quite exhausted, and had the I.J.A. given the men a few days rest on arrival there is no doubt that the subsequent death rate would not have been nearly so high.

On the 23 May, Lt-Col Pope with 700 men of Trains Nos. 10 and 11 arrived, bringing the camp strength up to 1,600. Lt-Col Pope assumed command of the camp, but on 6 June relinquished it owing to ill health to Lt-Col. A.T. Hingston. Lt-Col. Pope subsequently died in Burma.

Cholera broke out on 23 May and by the end of the month sixty-three deaths had occurred. The monsoon was approaching, and rain was falling daily, but it was a fortnight after our arrival before the Burmese finished roofing the two large huts. This lack

---

[22] Frying pans.

of roofing caused great hardship to the men, who, coming in wet from working parties, were never able to dry their clothes and this constant living and sleeping in wet clothes and bedding undoubtedly reduced their resistance to disease.[23]

As more and more men fell sick from cholera, dysentery, beri-beri, fever, and a form of trench foot, it became increasingly difficult to find the number demanded by the I.J.A. for working parties, and as the weeks passed an increasing number of sick men had to be turned out to work until finally 65 to 70% of working parties consisted of sick men.[24] Repeated representations were made for the reduction of working parties without effect, the difficulty being that there was only a Sergeant in charge of the I.J.A. administrative party, whereas there was a Lieutenant in charge of the Engineers, who overruled all objections, flatly refused reductions, and threatened that if working figures demanded were not produced, his men would go into the huts and fetch the sick out themselves.

---

[23] Lionel de Rosario described No.2 Camp in his book *Nippon Slaves*: 'The clearing of the camp was covered in a thick carpet of black mud; the attap sided huts had no roofs ... The huts were 100 metres long and six metres wide, constructed of bamboo with attap panels in the walls. There was an opening in each wall but no roof, and the floor, as outside, was a mud bath. There was a central aisle with sleeping platforms each side, raised 75cm above the ground and made of bamboo slats'.

Padre J.N. Duckworth called Songkurai 'the horror hell of Prison Camps': 'Our accommodation consisted of bamboo huts without rooves. The monsoon had begun and the rain beat down. Work – slave work – piling earth and stones in little skips on to a railway embankment began immediately. It began at 5 o'clock in the morning and finished at 9 o'clock at night and even later than that. Exhausted, starved and benumbed in spirit we toiled, because if we did not, we and our sick would starve. As it was the sick had half rations because the Japanese said, "No work, no food." Then came cholera. This turns a full-grown man into an emaciated skeleton overnight. 20, 30, 40, and 50 deaths were the order of the day ... The Japanese still laughed and asked, "How many dead men?" We still had to work, and work harder. Presently, come dysentery and Beri-Beri disease bred of malnutrition and starvation. Tropical ulcers, diphtheria, mumps, small-pox, all added to the misery and squalor of the camp on the hillside where water

By mid-June the ration situation, never good (the main ration being rice and onion or bean stew) had deteriorated to such an extent that a party of fifty men had to be sent to No.5 Camp to collect rations, the bullock carts used having to be pulled by the men themselves as the bullocks were exhausted and the road was impassable to lorries. The I.J.A. also ordered that the sick men were to be reduced to two meals daily, the working men continuing to receive full rations. This was done partly in an endeavour to force more men out to work and partly due to ration shortages.

On 7 June two parties of five and eight ORs escaped. The larger party was recaptured in September, but nothing has since been heard of the smaller party. Little excitement was shown by the I.J.A. over this escape.[25]

The last, and 201st, death from cholera occurred on 16 June, but as the cholera cases decreased the dysentery, fever and ulcer cases increased until there were over 1,000 men sick in

flowed unceasingly through the huts at the bottom.' From Padre J.N. Duckworth "A Japanese Holiday", which was broadcast from Singapore to London on 12 September 1945. See britain-at-war.org.uk/ww2/Death_Railway/html/songkurai.htm.

[24] Major Cyril Wild wrote of this: 'Every morning the same grim spectacle was repeated in the various camps of parading men for work at first light. Emerging from their crowded huts or leaky shelters in the pouring rain, even the fitter men appeared gaunt and starving, clad in rags or merely loincloths, most of them bootless and with cut and swollen feet. In addition, some 50 or 60 sick men from "hospital", leaning on sticks or squatting in the mud, would be paraded to complete the quota, and would become the subject of a desperate argument between the officers and the Japanese engineers. Sometimes all of these, sometimes only a part, would leave the camp hobbling on sticks or half carried by their comrades'. James Bradley, Cyril Wild, The Tall Man Who Never Slept (Woodfield Publishing, Bognor Regis, 1997), p.62.

[25] The story of the larger group, which was recaptured, was told by Peter Jackson in his book Sacrifice, Captivity & Escape (Pen & Sword, Barnsley, 2012). The others – a total of seven, not eight – were Sergeant Ian Bradley, his brother Corporal Bernard Bradley, Sergeant Jimmy Singleton, Corporal 'Taffy' Ellis, Joe Dawkins and James Hedley, a Singapore resident and member of the Singapore Volunteer Army Reserve.

lines or hospital, which figure remained constant until the evacuation of sick to Burma. On 20 June Lieut. FUKUDA[26] addressed the officers and informed them that the high death and sickness rates were due to bad camp sanitation and to the fact that the men did no P.T. At the beginning of July Lieut. ABE and an I.J.A. medical officer inspected the hospital, and, in spite of protestations by our M.O., ordered 50 more sick men to be sent out on working parties. The death rate was then 230.[27]

A camp duties figure of 171 had been agreed to by the I.J.A., but, owing to their excessive demands for working parties, some of this total, which included a sanitation squad, cooks, water carriers etc., had to be sent on I.J.A. work and replaced by sick men, until finally, except for a few cooks, the camp was worked entirely by sick men. The position finally became so acute that for some weeks officers were carrying all rations to the hospital and isolation camps, no fit men or sick men strong enough to carry full containers being available.

On 5 July eight officers and one O.R. escaped, four being subsequently recaptured, the others dying in the jungle. All officers had their kit searched, their money confiscated and were confined, under guard, to their quarters without food for thirty-six hours. The O.C. Camp was told that if another escape

---

[26] Around this time there was an incident related by Lieutenant Clive Moore: 'A pick was found to be missing and as a result the Officer in charge of these tools was forced to stand up in the blazing sun all day outside the Jap Guard House, or, until the pick was found. By nightfall the pick was still missing, so the Major in charge of our group was called to the Jap Hut and told by Fukuda that if the pick was not found by daylight, every man would go without rations for 24 hours. Every body was pulled out of bed at 0100 hours (1 a.m.), and searched but still no pick found. Next morning we were allowed to give breakfast to 330 men going to work on the Railway and light diet to 700 hospital patients, but the other 800 men in camp had to starve for the day unless the pick turned up.

'Fukuda then issued an order that all men left in camp were to be concentrated in 3 huts and no movement outside was allowed. The pick was found under a heap of bamboo beside a hut at 1100 hours (11 a.m.) and returned to Fukuda, but it made no difference as he now wanted the man responsible. As this was well nigh impossible to find we continued our punishment until, at 4 p.m., he suddenly decided he had been satisfied and the ban was lifted.' C.H. Moore, op. cit.

occurred, he would be shot, as he was considered responsible by the I.J.A.

Cases of ill-treatment of men by I.J.A. engineers were frequent, representations to Lieut. ABE being totally ignored as also were requests for the reduction of the number of men demanded for work and of the number of working hours – the men leaving for work at daybreak and invariably returning soaking wet after dark.

The rations improved slightly in the latter half of July, but were always inadequate, except for rice for working or sick men. The container and cooking pot situation steadily deteriorated as 'kawalis' wore out and were not replaced by the I.J.A.

On 2 August, Force H.Q. moved up from NIEKE and Lieut-Col. Dillon took over command of the camp.[28]

That the death rate in No.2 Camp was so much higher than in other camps may be attributed to the following reasons:-

1. Exhaustion of the men from the long march and the failure of the I.J.A. to allow any time for them to recuperate before being made to work. Many of them were sick or on light duties before leaving Changi. No "rest days" were allowed, work going on for seven days out of seven days for month

---

[27] There was often little point in the Japanese driving helplessly sick men out to work. This is revealed in *World War II Experiences of WX 17634 Pte W. Holding*: 'Men with ulcers on their legs were going out to work. They were helped to go out and laid down till it was time to go back to camp – the numbers had to go out!' www.pows-of-japan.net/books.htm.

[28] Lieutenant Arthur Godman, though part of "H" Force, was at Nieke: 'The accommodation at Nikki into which I was sent consisted of old, torn Indian Army tents. My particular tent was the outer cover of a tent and had several tears in the canvas through which the rain came. Inside the tent were two *changs*, one on each side, about three feet off the ground. When it rained – as it seemed to do every day – the ground was muddy and sometimes flowed through the tent … We were crowded into the tents, with each person having about eighteen inches of *chang* on which to sleep. It was impossible to lie on your back … We slept alternately head to foot so your head was between two pairs of feet. Before going to sleep you had to decide which was the least dirty pair of feet.' Arthur Godman, *The Will to Survive, Three and a Half Years as a Prisoner of the Japanese* (History Press, Stroud, 2002), p.93.

after month, plus constant ill-treatment by the I.J.A.
engineers whilst at work.

2. Living conditions. Overcrowding in unroofed huts;
   insufficient rations; no canteen for the first 2½ months, and
   men's clothes wet for days on end.
3. Working conditions. Men often worked up to their waists in
   water long hours, being made to lift excessive weights and
   the forcing out of sick men to work.
4. Absence of drugs, antiseptics and dressings; men's shirt
   sleeves, old clothes and even banana leaves being used for
   the latter.
5. That a I.J.A. Sergeant only, was i/c of the Administrative
   party, whereas in all other camps there was an officer. This
   sergeant, although he did his best, was unable to obtain any
   relief or concession from the Engineer officer, who insisted
   on his demands for men being met, which prevented much-
   needed work on latrines, cookhouse, camp improvement etc.
   being carried out.
6. Tools. These were in the hands of the engineers. Cutting
   tools for cookhouse and cremation wood were often
   unobtainable and were issued late and had to be returned
   early.

It is not possible to obtain complete figures of the number of
deaths, but it is estimated that between 1,200 and 1,300 out of
the original 1,600 all ranks forming this camp are now dead –
their deaths being entirely due to the conditions under which
they were forced to live and work by the I.J.A.

CHAPTER 6

Report on No.3 Camp
3 June 1943

1. <u>Sick.</u>
   Strength: 392
   Sick:

Cholera	2
Dysentery & Diarrhoea	97
Fever	49
Beri-Beri	5
Septic Sores	15
Others	2
	170

2. <u>Site.</u> A very bad site; water runs into camp from all sides and lies there. There is no drainage.

3. <u>Cholera.</u> There has been one death and there are now two cases. No building exists for segregation, and the two cases are in the hut with the rest of the men.

   There is no medicine or medical equipment to deal with the sick. The following are urgently required:-
   A building in which cholera cases can be segregated.
   Buckets for use with cholera and other patients.
   4 bottles of cholera vaccine to complete first inoculation.
   10 bottles of cholera vaccine to complete second inoculation.
   Hypodermic syringe to give inoculations.
   Disinfectants.
   Quicklime.
   It is reported that the coolies cholera hospital is using as a latrine a small stream which flows into the one used by the prisoners for washing.
   Coolies are dying every day of cholera.

4. Accommodation. In addition to a building for cholera patients, more accommodation is required for the main party. There are now 9 men to each bay on each side of the hut. There are 8 officers who are paying a large sum for this accommodation.

More attap is urgently required to roof more huts.

5, Mosquito nets, mats and blankets. None have yet been issued. As a result, malaria is rife.

6. Clothing. Many men are without boots with soles. 150 pairs are required at once, and 200 more pairs within a month.

Shorts and socks are now beyond repair and a general issue is necessary. Officers need their suitcases and bed-rolls left behind at Bampong.

7. Food. Adequate on the whole but lacking Vitamin 'B'. Rice polishings, vitamin 'B' tablets or injections must be produced to make good the deficiency. More cooking pots and a big container for boiling water is needed.

8. Containers. Extra cooking pots are also required to enable separate cooking for the sick.

9. Canteen. No facilities exist for purchase of local supplies.

10. No arrangements have been made to change Malayan-Japanese money. No arrangements have been made for working pay.

11. Office. No office facilities, paper or pencils are available. Keeping of rolls is impossible.

12. Relations with I.J.A. Good. The I.J.A. NCO in charge gives all assistance but has little or nothing with which to help.

13. All fit or unfit men except 11 cooks and duty men, 4 cowmen, the commanding officer, all other combatant and non-combatant men go out to work daily.

At least [number indecipherable] are required for camp sanitation all day.

Non-combatants should not be sent out to work.

A system is required by which every fit man gets one day's rest in seven.

14. Conclusion.

    a) Unless immediate action is taken today a general outbreak of cholera will occur in this camp.
    b) Unless the other points noted are carried out, no men in this camp will be fit for work in a few days.
    c) If the I.J.A. are unable to meet requirements then help should be sought from the neutral representative of the International Red Cross, quickly.

(signed) F.J. Dillon
Lieut. Colonel

Afternote
5th June 1943

Since writing the above, six cases of cholera have developed, and there has been another death, with two more expected.
    a) The I.J.A. N.C.O. in charge has promised to arrange for segregation of cholera patients.
    b) All work has been stopped.
    c) Col. Banno has delivered some lime and disinfectants.

CHAPTER 7

Report on No.4 Camp

Headquarters Camp
10 June 1943

Sir,

The following report from Mr WOLFE on conditions at No.4 P.o.W. Camp is submitted as requested. I should be grateful if the remaining British personnel at KONKOITA, which I understand consists of 11 cooks, could be transferred as soon as possible to No.4 Camp, as the conditions at KONKOITA seem deplorable.

I am most grateful for the prompt delivery of quinine yesterday, which will do much to assist the malaria patients at No.4 Camp.

I have the honour to be, Sir,
Yours faithfully
Lieut-Colonel
Commander

The Commander,
Prisoner of War Camp
Imperial Japanese Army

REPORT ON NO. 4 CAMP

1. <u>KONKOITA</u>
On 26 May 10 sick men were brought by lorry from KONKOITA to this Headquarters Camp. Of these, one man died on the way and two more died soon after admission to hospital. As the report of these men was that the other sick left at KONKOITA were in a terrible condition without medical attention of any kind, Colonel BANNO kindly gave permission for Assistant-Surgeon WOLFE to go to KONKOITA with a small

party. Mr WOLFE arrived at KONKOITA on the evening of 28 May. The Japanese guard did not allow him to visit the sick until the morning of 29 May; there were 3 cases of cholera, 1 case of malaria, 3 of dysentery and 3 of diarrhoea. These 10 men had been lying helpless for several days in one tent. They had no medical attention whatsoever. There were no sanitary arrangements of any kind. The cholera patients were vomiting and defecating on the ground and the flies were everywhere. Hundreds of coolies were isolated in neighbouring huts, and numbers of these were dying every day, apparently from cholera.

Mr WOLFE saw the Medical Major of the Imperial Japanese Army at KONKOITA immediately to report the 3 cases of cholera. He asked for a truck to bring the sick to Headquarters Camp, but this was refused. He offered to hire bullock-carts with the patients' money, but this was not permitted. He asked the Medical Major on 3 separate days for medical supplies but was given nothing except a little disinfectant for his hands. He was told, "If they die, they die".

Finally, on 2 June, Mr WOLFE and his party carried the sick away from Konkoita in the rain, and put them in a bamboo grove beside the road while he sent an urgent message to No.4 Camp. A party of 40 Australians then came and carried the 10 sick (also 5 sick cooks who had been working at KONKOITA) to No.4 Camp where they received proper treatment.

2. NO. 4 CAMP

All men who could work marched out on 8 June, except 30 fit men left for camp duties. Lieut-Col. POND has stayed behind in command. Malaria has been rampant, 25 to 30 new cases daily. Sick men left behind are approximately: malaria 140, dysentery and diarrhoea sixty-five, cholera 11 cases (in isolation). In addition to the 30 fit men, there remain 1 Medical Officer and about 17 medical personnel. Total about 350 men.

Medical supplies should be sufficient, thanks to the very prompt delivery of quinine tablets yesterday.

Rations are a great problem, as meals recently had to be reduced to two, of rice gruel, daily.

CHAPTER 8

General Report on Conditions at No.5 Camp (Changaraya)

1. Before leaving NIEKE Camp I was told by Major Wilde, the interpreter, that the I.J.A. Colonel was fully alive to the state of health of the men, and to the necessity for three days complete rest on arrival at the new camp, in order to settle in and rest the men before working parties would be expected.

2. On the evening of 27 May, the first party – 'A' Group (383) under the command of Major [blank] reached the camp and were housed in No.1 Hut, with the officers in a small room in the I.J.A. N.C.Os hut next door. These huts were fully roofed. At 2100 hrs 'B' Group (318) under my command arrived in the pitch dark, having been held up for one hour at No.1 Camp. Accommodation was eventually found under what roofing existed by putting 200 men into 7 bays 12 feet by 15 feet, and the remaining 110 with 'A' Group.

3. <u>Cookhouse</u> – This was found to be in use by 500 Burmese coolies with whom we were expected to share – which turned out to mean that we were allowed to use it when the Burmese did not want it, the natural result being that the mid-day meal on the first day was eventually served at 1700 hrs.

4. <u>Rations</u> – These were drawn from the I.J.A. NCO i/c of the Burmese cookhouse, and it was found that both our own and the Burmese rations were issued in bulk to this cookhouse, so that we were given what they did not want.

5. <u>Cooking utensils</u> – No utensils of any sort were issued to us on arrival and all our cooking had to be done in the Burmese containers and rice "qualies".

6. <u>Wells</u> – There are two wells, the one near the cookhouse containing very dirty water fit only for washing the body and clothes. This was being used by the Burmese cookhouse for cooking water. The other is some 500 yards away by a very bad track, but excellent water.

7. <u>Containers</u> – only 4 x 6 gallon containers managed to arrive in camp with the two parties and these were the only means of drawing water and cooking stews.

8. On the morning of 23 May I made immediate representation to the I.J.A. for a) Separate Cookhouse b) water containers and buckets c) two 65 gallon oil drums, of which I could see several not in use in the camp d) better accommodation for the men e) blankets f) other cookhouse utensils and g) lime for the cookhouse and latrines.

9. As a result of these representations, I was given permission to build myself a cookhouse alongside that of the Burmese and was issued with12 qualies (two broken) and some wicker rice baskets and have since received a few wooden buckets which can be used for issues to the troops. Rations are now drawn separately but are issued to the cookhouse at the discretion and whim of a completely incompetent I.J.A. Korean 3rd Class private. 18 bullocks were also issued for the week, which have been consumed and have been a godsend. The rations to date have consisted otherwise of rice, onions and salt fish and we have been assured for the past ten days that onions were the only vegetables available. However, yesterday our man was sick and the [blank space] did the issues and was surprised when we said we did not want only onions. He told us he had plenty of beans, peas etc. which we could have had all along if he had known we liked them. These are now being received. Although they admit there are plenty of buckets in the camp they are on charge to a different unit and cannot therefore be issued to us. We have received one 65-gallon drum which has a leak in the seam one-third of the way up. This is now used as a reservoir at the hospital, catching rainwater.

10. Over the period of the next five days further accommodated was attaped, and the men were able to spread out to about 10 a bay. Incidentally, as an example of their inconsideration, at midday on the day following our arrival the officers were

ordered out of their present quarters into one of the barrack blocks which was still roofless and the attap was actually put on the roof while and after the officers moved in a downpour of rain. The following morning when 400 men were out on a working party, I was ordered to move the whole of 'A' Group and one company of 'B' Group out of their quarters at five minutes notice, again into quarters which had not been roofed. A certain amount of roofing had now been done, but for the next two days we were again squashed up to about 16 to a bay. The roofing in accommodation for 200 is still not complete.

11. As regards all other stores, I invariably got the same answer that they are coming up from the rear and we will have to wait.

12. In spite of the assurance I received before leaving NIEKE, I was ordered to send out on a working party all fit men of 'A' Group the morning after arrival at 0900 hours. 300 paraded and were worked until 2000 hours.

13. That night (the second in camp) we had our first case of cholera. This resulted in an issue of five small bags of lime and a visit from an I.J.A. doctor, also the erection of an isolation hut to accommodate about eight cases.

14. The general sanitation of the camp when we arrived was nothing short of unbelievable filth. The Burmese had thrown all their unwanted rice and other food all over the camp and particularly near their own huts. Incidentally, there were parties of Burmese in every hut in our area, including those occupied by my own men, and had "shat" indiscriminately everywhere. The flies were a menace; remains of slaughtered animals and skins were in the undergrowth all around the cookhouse in every degree of decomposition.

Latrines are on the whole good, but shortage of lime renders it difficult to keep them clean. They are some way from the huts and have paths to them, which makes it difficult to get to them in these dark nights.

It must be remembered that 80% of the men arrived in camp with diarrhoea. This resulted in a further menace of the men following the example of the Burmese and shitting indiscriminately in the undergrowth at night. Some undoubtedly could not get to the latrines in time, others were just lazy, as they have been throughout this crisis.

The following steps have, however, been taken to improve conditions and a marked improvement has resulted throughout:-
a) All undergrowth has been cleared between huts and the vicinity of the cookhouse.
b) The Burmese have been made to clear up the mess in their area and are firmly dealt with by the I.J.A. when seen throwing food about.
c) A limited amount of lime is now available for the latrines and the cookhouse.
d) A railed path has been made to one latrine.
e) Night latrines have been erected between the two huts and are being used by the men.
f) General drainage of huts and paths is in progress as and when men are available.

15. Representations were made the third day to the engineer officers of the I.J.A. to give me two days off working parties, partly to give the men a rest, and partly to get the camp in order. I was told that they would get a rest later on but not yet. However, after the fifth day of work, I was given the men for one day. This did help enormously in the camp, but I am afraid was little or no rest for the men.

16. Meanwhile cholera was getting a grip and other sick were increasing at an alarming pace until it came to the time when I could put only 200 men on working parties.

17. I again appealed to the engineer officer to let me have some of the fit men for work in camp and the reply that I received was that I was not producing enough for him, and that I would have to turn out the sick 'B' men as well the next day.

18. That day (4th June) the I.J.A. Colonel i/c PoW Camps arrived with two sacks of lime and some other disinfectants. I told the Interpreter of our requirements, such as buckets, lime and blankets – also another M.O. The Colonel ordered that all work would cease until all men in camp were fit again. I also sent down to the base a note that Lt. Col. Harris which I had written two days before and was therefore rather out of date, but had no time to rewrite, by the British driver.

That night at 11 p.m. I was sent for by the I.J.A. engineer officer and told that the Colonel had only referred to work on the railway and not to work on the road which must continue and that I might keep 15 fit men in came next day but the rest must work. I appealed against this order as it did not fit in with the spirit of the Colonel's remarks. However, he compromised by making me give him 80 O.RS, the following day he took 30 and today 100.

19. On the 3rd June the I.J.A. doctors again arrived complete with glass rods and stabbed all diarrhoea and dysentery cases. On the 4th a list of 61 names was sent in of men they said were cholera positives and were to be isolated immediately. This was done but only three of these so far have been admitted to the Cholera Ward.[29]

20. There were only 4 R.A.M.C. in the party on arrival, of which 2 have since died of cholera. Seven other Orderlies from Roberts Hospital were with the unit. This was the basis with which we had to start, since when over 80 O.Rs have volunteered to work in the wards, of which through sickness, death and complete exhaustion, only 20 are now available for work. No further volunteers can be obtained even after continued appeal by Company Commanders and others, and I have now been reduced to ordering the cholera suspects to act as orderlies. The work done by the medical staff and volunteers cannot be too highly praised. They worked themselves to a standstill cheerfully expecting any moment to be a case themselves. The M.O., Capt. Emery, has been suffering for the last 4 days from malaria and diarrhoea but has carried on throughout, even on one day from his bed in the M.I. Room next to the Dysentery Ward. A convalescent bay has now been established, which is rapidly filling up – which speaks for itself.

21. Disposal of dead has been a great difficulty, owing to the weather and complete absence of petrol. However, up to

---

[29] Captain Harry Silman, a Medical Officer with the 9th Northumberland Fusiliers, saw the cholera ward on 3 June: 'I have been over to the cholera centre. It looks like a scene from a film, completely unreal. There is a long, dark, attap hut, with over a hundred thin skeleton-like beings, writhing on the long platform, vomiting and passing motions where they lie. Groans and cries are the only noises to break the silence. Two or three orderlies with masks over their mouths were giving intravenous injections of saline, using Heath Robinson contraptions. About nine corpses lay outside covered with blankets and groundsheets, and a little distance away, the smoke of the pyre where the corpses are burning could be seen.' war-experience.org/events/the-thai-burma-railroad.

yesterday, all bodies were disposed of by fire, but yesterday 10 bodies had to be buried. Burial again has its difficulties as graves fill up with water at two feet and it is lucky if rock also is not encountered. Yesterday a pit three feet deep was dug, the bodies put in and then a high mound of earth and rock raised above it. This was the only method found to be feasible.

22. Four officers have been taken with cholera, one, Lieutenant Furze R.E., has died, two are well on the way to recovery and the fourth, Capt. Turner A. & S. H.[30], is still in the balance. Of the other fifteen officers, with the exception of myself and Adjt. (Lieut. Fletcher), only two officers are really fit to do any heavy work, malaria and diarrhoea being the main causes of trouble. Similarly, very few N.C.Os are still at work.

23. Miscellaneous. A box of medical stores was received from Force H.Q. on the 3rd, containing anti-cholera serum and some antiseptics and bandages, all most useful. The serum was given as injections to medical orderlies who asked for it. A further box was received on the 6th, brought on foot by an A.I.F O.R., who also brought a reply to my letter to Col. Harris. He took back with him a further report from me, stating my immediate requirements. Although a second M.O. had been promised, he has not yet turned up.

24. A bottle containing an antiseptic solution is kept in each Company for disinfecting hands after any chance contamination. Also, two troughs of antiseptic solution are placed in each hut for use at any time, particularly after Benjo[31] by the troops.

25. A steriliser is kept by the cookhouse, which is useful when it is in action, but great difficulty seems to be met in keeping the thing going.

9 June 1943

A further stool examination was carried out this morning by the I.J.A. 480 men were examined.

At last, after almost daily application, permission has been given for us to keep and use as water containers empty oil tins from the ration issue. Three are now in use, two in the cholera

---

[30] Argyll and Sutherland Highlanders.
[31] When someone has used the toilet, in this case the latrine.

ward and one in the dysentery ward. Also, ten rice sacks have been given to us permanently. These have been issued to the convalescent cholera ward. All further sacks emptied from rations may be retained on loan, to be returned when a blanket issue is made. Similarly, a second 65-gallon oil drum has been received and is kept at the cookhouse for boiling drinking water. A marked decrease in cholera admissions over the past three days looks hopeful.

Although a second doctor was promised four days ago, none has yet materialised. One more bag of lime was received last night. 50 men daily are still going out on working parties.

An issue of pumpkin has been received, sufficient for four meals, also thirty-eight head of cattle.

Rain has averaged between 18 and 20 of the 24 since our arrival, mud everywhere and our drainage is only in its infancy. Far more men are required for making paths than I can produce.

Permanent daily fatigues are required ... which eat up men: cremation 12, hospital water 8, hospital wood 6, cookhouse water 8, cookhouse wood 6, sanitation 6, herdsmen 5, cooks 20, medical 46.

Signed
Gairdner, Major
7 June 1943
O. Commanding, No.5 Camp

CHAPTER 9

Tanbaya Hospital

Kamburi
Dec 1943

1. At the end of June a project for the establishment of a
    hospital in some locality where food was readily available
    was put to the I.J.A. This was examined and a
    reconnaissance in Burma was carried out by the I.J.A.
    Medical Officer. However, nothing materialised and the
    project was shelved indefinitely. Nevertheless, at the end of
    July it was suddenly resuscitated and became a *fait accompli*
    almost immediately.

    The hospital was to accommodate twelve hundred and fifty
    patients who were to be drawn from two categories (i) men
    who would not recover from their present illness within two
    months, and (ii) old men with a permanent disability or
    unsuited for heavy work on the "road". The allotment of
    patients to camps was:-

NIEKE	250
SHIMO-SONKRAI	500
SONKRAI	350
KAMI-SONKRAI	50
CHANGARAYA	100

    The move was to be carried out by M.T. in flights of 250 with
    nightly stages at CHANGARAYA, KANDO and RONSHI. The
    I.J.A. would allow a medical staff of only 8 officers (including
    one assistant-surgeon) and 130 ORs with an administrative
    staff of 4 officers and 51 ORs. Any additional personnel
    required were to be drawn from the convalescent patients.
    The advance party moved off at a bare 12 hours-notice and
    the patients were to follow the next day. As will be seen later
    neither the move or the allotment of patients to camp went
    according to schedule.

2. On 30 July 43 the advance party consisting of all the administrative staff and eight officers and thirty-six other ranks of the medical staff, assembled at CHANGARAYA, which they reached by route march. The remainder of the medical staff was to be spread over the flights of the patients whom they accompanied. Both the administrative and medical staffs were drawn from all the camps. The advance party had to drop off at the staging camps – Kando and Ronshi – one medical officer, three medical orderlies and ten administrative personnel to look after the patients in transit.

The executive order for the advance party to move was delayed and did not reach the camps until some time after the working parties had left. Consequently, there was some difficulty in collecting the ear-marked personnel. In fact, the detachment from SONKRAI had to be completed from semi-fit men who were in camp and two of them collapsed on arrival at CHANGARAYA and eventually died.

Next day the move to KANDO was made by M.T. Here the party was housed for the night in a hut already occupied by coolies. The move to RONSHI was carried out by route march and M.T. The staging party was dropped off and six men including the two mentioned in the previous paragraph had to be left behind sick. The march – a distance of fourteen kilos – began at 04,30 hours in the pouring rain and pitch darkness and was most arduous. Eventually RONSHI was reached and here the party stayed for thirty-six hours and were occupied in repairing a hut, which was to house the patients in transit. TANBAYA was reached on 3 Aug by route march as the railway was not working, owing to a bridge having collapsed in the floods. During the march, which was along the railway line, it poured the whole time.

3. It had been decided to adopt a somewhat novel system of command, which in practice turned out very satisfactorily. Lt-Col C.T. Hutchinson MC, RA, was appointed Administrative Commander, while Major Bruce Hunt, AAMC, was nominated O.C. Hospital. The former was responsible for all outside activities and personnel employed outside the hospital, also for rollcall returns and finance, while the latter's domain was inside the hospital, including the discipline of the hospital personnel and patients. To assist the O.C. Hospital officers were appointed to act as wardmasters.

Above: Suffering from dysentery, members of "F" Force are pictured relieving themselves during a break from the train journey from Singapore up into Thailand. (Australian War Memorial; P02569.184)

Below: Cholera hill, an isolation hospital for members of "F" Force suffering from the disease at Shimo Sonkurai No 1 Camp. To the right of the hospital tents is a make-shift operating table where amputations, treatment for tropical ulcers and autopsies were done. (Australian War Memorial; P02569.189)

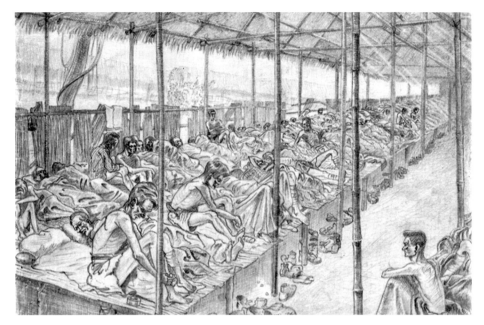

Above: The hospital camp that was established at Kanchanaburi when the railway line construction had been completed. Men of "F" Force were brought back to these camps on stretchers off river barges or the railway. This is one of five surviving drawings by Gunner James Joseph French. (Australian War Memorial; ART92689)

Below: Another of James French's drawings which, as with the previous one, gives some kind of indication of conditions in the hospitals, once again at Kanchanaburi. (Australian War Memorial; ART92690)

Right: A partially healed tropical ulcer on the shin of one of the prisoners. (Australian War Memorial; P01433.028)

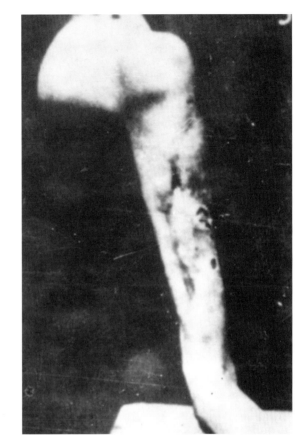

Below: The feet of one of the prisoners suffering from beri-beri. In this case his feet are badly swollen, making standing difficult and walking very painful. (Australian War Memorial; P01433.029)

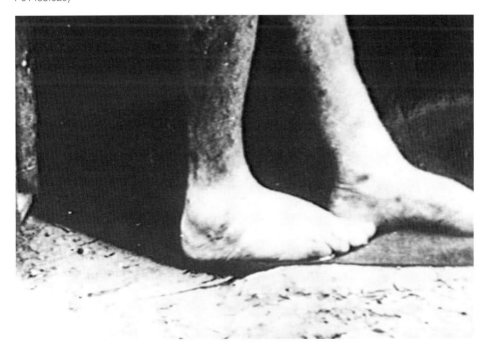

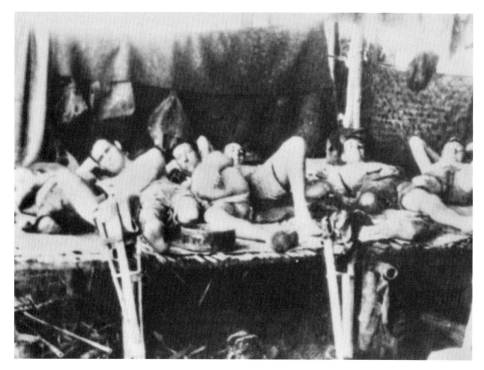

Above: Believed to have been taken in 1943, this photograph is of an amputation ward at one of the hospitals. Most of these men had legs amputated because of uncontrollable tropical ulcers. (Australian War Memorial; P00761.012)

Below: A 1942-dated photograph of prisoners of war transporting attap, a roofing thatch made from palm fronds. (Australian War Memorial; P00406.013)

Above: Three 'fit' workers at Shimo Sonkurai No 1 Camp, standing outside the camp hospital. From left to right they are believed to be Bruce Pearce, Oscar Jackson and Reuben Niles Pearce, all of the 2/30th Battalion AIF. Pearce is unable to fasten his shorts because his stomach is swollen with beri-beri. (Australian War Memorial; P02569.192)

Below: Tropical ulcers forming on the lower legs of two unidentified members of "F" Force. (Australian War Memorial; P02569.191)

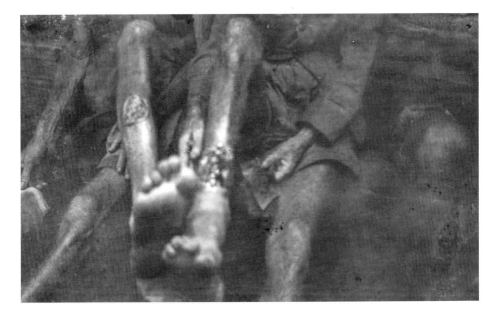

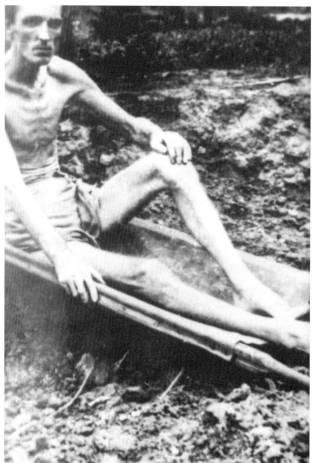

Left: Gunner J.P. Bradley showing the effects of malaria and beri-beri. He had suffered six bouts of malaria in six weeks, three of which were without quinine. During this period, he was only able to complete one day's work and was kicked by a Japanese soldier who broke his ribs. (Australian War Memorial; P01433.024)

Below: An indication of the gruelling type of work undertaken by the men of "F" Force, with these Australian soldiers carrying railway sleepers. (Australian War Memorial; P00406.026)

Above: A mess parade for PoWs at a camp on the Burma-Thailand railway. In theory, the Japanese ration scale for prisoners on the railway included 680 grams of rice, 520 grams of vegetables and 110 grams of meat or fish per man per day. In practice, these figures were seldom achieved during the railway construction period of 1943. (Australian War Memorial; 128455)

Below: An all-too familiar scene – the funeral of one of the many thousands who did not survive the terrible conditions in Burma and Thailand. (Australian War Memorial; P00406.031)

Left: Colonel Cyril Hew Dalrymple Wild pictured in the witness box at the War Ministry Building Courtroom in Tokyo on 11 September 1946. He was a War Crime Liaison Officer who testified for the prosecution that Japan violated Siam's neutrality, also to the mistreatment of prisoners of war by the Japanese in the trial of twenty-seven ex-leaders of Japan. He was killed the next day in a plane crash on his way to Singapore. (National Archives, Harry S. Truman Library)

Below: A 30-metre stretch of the Thai-Burma railway, constructed from original rails and sleepers, can be seen in the UK at the National Memorial Arboretum, Alrewas, near Lichfield, Staffordshire. This remarkable relic was transported from Thailand to the UK in 2002 by HMS *Northumberland*. (Author)

4. The camp, which was adjacent to the railway, had been an old camp which had been allowed to fall into a bad state of disrepair. Secondary jungle had grown up all around. The actual site itself was dry considering it was in the middle of the monsoon. One hut and the cookhouse were roofed in, the remaining huts were in the process of being roofed and otherwise repaired. In the roofed huts the advance party, together with the I.J.A. guards, were housed. Other huts were occupied by coolies employed on the railway and on the repair of huts.

The camp consisted of seven huts each a hundred metres long, with attap sides and roof and a wide bamboo platform to take two men, with a gangway along one side. Each of the huts were scheduled to take two hundred patients. In addition, there was a smaller hut to hold eighty patients and this had two platforms with a gangway down the centre. Later, when the establishment of the hospital was increased, a small camp the other side of the railway line and occupied by I.J.A. railway personnel and coolies was made available. Here there were two big huts, a smaller hut, and in addition, a small hut which was used as an operating theatre and chapel.

When the hospital was finally established, the layout was:-

Ward I	Administrative personnel
Ward II	Malaria and beri-beri patients
Ward III	Dysentery patients
Ward IV	Malaria and beri-beri patients
Ward V	Malaria and beri-beri patients
Ward VI	Dysentery patients
Ward VII	(Medical (non-dysentery) patients
Ward VIII	HQ officers and stores (Q.M. dispensary etc.)
Ward IX	Tropical ulcer patients
Ward X	Tropical ulcer patients
Ward XI	Officer patients

Latrines were the usual open trench type, and the majority were the old existing ones, only two new ones being provided.

The camp lay on either side of the railway line and about a hundred yards from it. The actual precincts of the camp were fairly clear of trees, though the jungle was quickly reached. It did not, however, have that confined feeling prevalent in the working camps. An outcrop of low hills a mile and a half to

SKETCH OF TANBAYA HOSPITAL

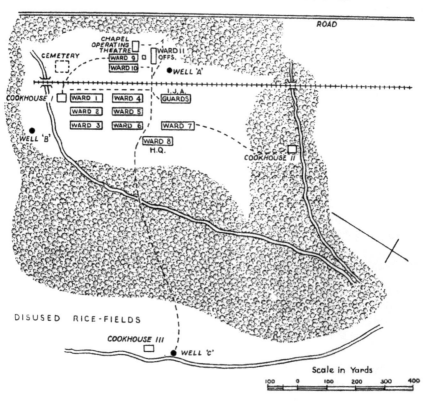

two miles away made a pleasant view. The camp was bounded on three sides by two small streams, which eventually joined at the north-east corner of the camp. One flowed almost past the cookhouse and provided the water supply for the camp. The fourth side of the camp was bounded by the THAILAND-MOULMEIN road. Towards the outcrop of hills and a thousand yards from the camp was a largish stream flowing in a north-westerly direction.

5. As soon as the advance party arrived the usual administrative difficulties began. There were no tools available for camp maintenance, let alone camp improvement had it been possible to start on it. Indeed, the only wood cutting tool available for the first few days was an axe carried all the way from THAILAND by one of the advance party. The coolies living in the camp fouled the whole area and that

added to the difficulties of the hygiene squad. Requests to have the coolies moved to the other end of the camp were negatived. Malaria took its toll and, in order to provide the fatigues required by the I.J.A., the officers, including medical officers, had to be employed on carrying and chopping wood for the cookhouse, which was shared by the I.J.A. The fatigues on which the medical personnel had also to be employed consisted of ration drawing and carrying, construction of a hut for the I.J.A. guard, and even clearing ground to make a thirty-yard rifle range. The carrying of sacks of rice was a heavy physical strain on the men.

Tools were always short and improvisation was necessary. At one time in the early days no cross-cut saw was available, though the part-time use of an I.J.A. pattern two-handed saw was permitted. Apart from what was brought by PsoW, the maximum tools available were one cross-cut, part use of another, two axes, two shovels, one pick and eight chunkels[32]. Nothing in the way of wire or wire cutters for the maintenance of huts or latrines was forthcoming. The shortage of cutting tools was most acute when the daily death rate was high, as all bodies had to be cremated[33].

Cooking utensils too were always a difficulty, especially containers for cooked food, which were never sufficient. As water had to be boiled for drinking, sterilisation of eating utensils and for medical purposes, each ward had to be issued with some containers, This reacted unfavourably on the distribution of food, so much so that at one time meals were being served continuously from 0730 hours to 2130 hours and sometimes later. About the middle of September Force HQ sent down a number of containers of various descriptions and it was then possible to feed the camp in two shifts for each meal. At one time the rice qualies were each being used to cook eighteen boils.

[32] A chunkel is a form of hoe.
[33] Though cremation was the usual way of disposing of the diseased bodies, in some camps burial parties were so overwhelmed with the number of dead that mass graves were dug to dispose of the dead. Sears A. Eldredge, *Captive Audiences / Captive Performers, Music and Theatre as Strategies of Survival on the Thailand-Burma Railway 1942-1945*, https://www.digitalcommons.macalester.edu.

Water was obviously to be the problem of the camp. The stream at the south-east corner of the camp was originally allotted for all purposes. When it was pointed out that as soon as the rain stopped this stream would quickly dry up, the I.J.A. replied, "You won't be here then." However, on 13 Oct. the supply suddenly dried up and the cookhouse had to be moved, this time to the other stream to the north of the camp. This source of supply also failed a week later and again the cookhouse had to be moved, this time to the big stream. Although both these moves meant a longer carry for the cooked food and uncooked rations, the manpower and containers involved were less than those necessary to carry the water to the cookhouse. There was at this big stream a pump house with a gravity tank, which was connected to a stand-pipe in the camp. All that was required was a lift and force pump. This, however, was not available. To save the long carry of water to the wards two wells were brought into use, but for these the I.J.A. provided neither buckets nor ropes. Requests to purchase these on behalf of the camp were met with the reply that these were unprocurable. Again, PsoW property was employed.

6. The basic ration lacked Vitamin B content and this was clearly proven by the increase in beri-beri, amongst both the patients and the fit men. Representations resulted in an improvement and the bean ration was increased somewhat. It was not until 13 Oct., when it was pointed out that a hospital camp five kilos away drawing from the same supply depot was receiving a surfeit of beans, that the supply could be considered as adequate. On 19 Oct. rice polishings were issued – at first on a scale sufficient for berberi patients but later the issue was increased to allow for a good ration to be made to each individual.[34] Incidentally, it might be added in passing that these polishings were the best ever seen to date in any camp. The meat issue was on the hoof, though latterly dried meat in boxes was issued. From time to time prawns

---

[34] Rice polishings is the bran layer of rice rubbed off in milling. It consists of outer skins of the grain and also includes the embryo. It contains an abundant supply of the vitamin B and is consequently used to eliminate certain deficiency diseases such as beri-beri and pellagra (https://www.bspittle.wordpress.com, Changi Notes).

were issued in lieu of meat. These scalded made a pleasant variety in the diet. The meat issue was spasmodic and averaged out at about two ounces per head. At no time could a ration scale be obtained from the I.J.A. Odd quantities of sugar, flour and cooking oil were received, but these commodities were so small they could only be used for special diets. Tea was insufficient for a general issue. Vegetables in the first place were mainly runner beans, loofahs and egg-fruit, but latterly sweet potatoes and ordinary potatoes were issued. The amounts received varied and at times there was almost a glut, so much so that it was possible to produce a riceless meal occasionally by making a big issue of potatoes. At other times again there was almost a shortage. The various representations on rations were usually verbally, though they were referred to in letters on medical subjects.

7. Canteen facilities were practically nil. Parties of six men were allowed to be sent to ANAQUIN – five kilos. away – to buy, but the amount they could carry back was obviously insignificant compared with the requirements and the necessity for an I.J.A. pass made it impossible to buy bullock carts for the carriage of purchases. Traders were allowed to come to the camp, but their visits were spasmodic, and their supplies limited to smokes, gula and bananas. Eggs in sufficient quantities were unobtainable, and cost 25 cents each. The cost of cooking oil was prohibitive, being over two hundred rupees for four gallons, and beans, if procurable, were about 80 rupees a 100-pound sack.

In the evenings, talks, sing-songs and general knowledge quizzes were organised in the wards. There was no site suitable, if it had been desirable, to hold any form of centralised entertainment. To the speakers and organisers a tribute is due and their efforts were greatly appreciated.

8. Patients began to arrive on 8 Aug. The first batch had staged at RONSHI and, owing to damage to a railway bridge, they were forced to trek over two kilometres where the trains were operating. This in itself was sheer cruelty, as the majority of cases were suffering from tropical ulcers. No further parties arrived until 21 Aug. when the railway was through again. Parties then arrived daily in batches of varying numbers, the smallest party being thirty odd while the largest was over a hundred and eighty. Parties staged at CHANGAYARA and KANDO. Ronshi was not used after the

first party. The journey was made by M.T. and rail and was a severe strain on the patients. The trip from KANDO took anything between twelve and eighteen hours, with long periods without food and long waits at the debussing and entraining point, where there was no shelter from the rain or shade from the sun. Patients were herded into closed or open trucks and as many as fifty-four in one closed truck is recorded. As the majority of these cases were suffering from tropical ulcers and/or dysentery the atmosphere in the trucks bears no description. Deaths en route were not infrequent and as many as eight in one party were found to be dead on arrival. Patients arrived in a sorry state and the lack of clothing and bedding was appalling. Some had only a cloth around their waists.

The time of arrival of parties varied between 2000 hours and 0800 hours. As the only light in wards was from fires the organisation for reception was distinctly hampered.

The last party arrived on 7 Sept. bringing the strength of the camp, including staff, up to 1,776, while during the intervening period there had been 148 deaths. The number of patients from working parties bore no relation to the original plan, since owing to the high death and sickness rate at SONKRAI, the I.J.A. changed the allotment. The numbers from each camp worked out at:-

Ex NIEKE	159 British	138 A.I.F.	total 297
Ex SHIMO-SONKRAI	3 British	320 A.I.F.	total 323
Ex SONKRAI	752 British	406 A.I.F.	total 1158
Ex CHANGARAYA	146 British	–	total 146
Totals	1,060	864	1,924

In these figures the staff have been included.

Patients were suffering from a combination of dysentery, recurrent malaria, tropical ulcers, beri-beri and scabies.

9. The change of environment and the belief that better food would be available coupled with the knowledge that no "work on the road" was awaiting them as soon as they became convalescent, did a lot to improve the moral of the patients. Alas, the disillusionment that followed, quite neutralised any good that may have been done. True, there was no work awaiting convalescents, but the knowledge that no drugs to

cure the dysentery were available, that there were no dressings for tropical ulcers and nothing to combat beri-beri had an adverse psychological effect on the patients.

Nevertheless, the spirit and cheerfulness of the sufferers under such circumstances is to their undying credit. The unselfishness and willingness to help each other in any capacity was most marked.

There was no attempt made to segregate British and Australians. The camp was treated as a single unit and personnel put in wherever they were best fitted, irrespective of whether they were "English" or "Aussie". The harmonious cooperation between orderlies and patients was most marked. If any reorganisation of wards was necessary, requests were frequently made that a party of "cobbers", invariably containing some British and some Australians, be allowed to remain together. Indeed, it would be true to say that many lasting friendships have been made.

A number of patients arrived at TANBAYA undernourished and debilitated. Some suffered from the delusion that they could not eat rice. In view of the small calorific value of the ration it was essential that every scrap of food should be got into the patients. Consequently an "Eat your rice" campaign was started, in which everyone was encouraged, and indeed forced, to eat all their meals – time being no object.

Malaria was prevalent and many primary infections were recorded. The frequency with which relapses occurred was alarming and had a debilitating effect on patients, especially sufferers with dysentery and tropical ulcers. It also had a serious effect on the personnel available for camp labour. Owing to overcrowding in huts there was a general distribution of skin diseases, especially scabies. The resultant irritation caused loss of sleep and also secondary ulcer formations. Oedematic beri-beri was prevalent and severe cardiac beri-beri caused many sudden deaths. With the lack of emetine, the gradual distressing and inevitable wearing away of the dysentery patients was pathetic.

Owing to the change of plan for the despatch of patients the surgical instruments did not arrive until the middle of September. Prior to this some emergency amputations had to be carried out with certain instruments loaned by an A.I.F. Hospital five kilometres away and an ordinary hand-saw borrowed from the I.J.A.. In all, about forty amputations were performed. The results were most disappointing, only about four surviving. This low figure can in no way be attributed to medical skill, but rather to the fact that patients' vitality was low and that they lacked any power of resistance.

10. Drugs were always inadequate and repeated representations were of no avail. Quinine was short for a period and at the beginning a full treatment could not be given. Later this was improved and sufficient was always available. When a suspected cholera case died the I.J.A. issued sufficient serum to inoculate all the permanent staff and other key men against cholera and plague. No sulphur was available for the treatment of scabies and no drugs or dressings for the tropical ulcers. Emetine and B.1 were, of course, not forthcoming, except on one occasion and in minute quantities.

A colonel of the I.J.A. Medical Service visited the camp on 25 Sep and a plea for drugs brought forth a promise of sulphur and potassium permanganate for the tropical ulcers. These, however, were not forthcoming. In addition, a prescription of powdered charred yak bones for the dysentery patients was given.

At the beginning of November, a small supply of drugs was received including 12lb of sulphur and sufficient emetine to treat six patients. The former was a godsend and had a marked effect on the incidence of scabies. The I.J.A. produced on repayment a quantity of muslin, which was of the greatest value for bandages.

11. About the end of September there were indications of a move back to SINGAPORE, but it was not until mid-November that anything concrete became known. A return called for by the I.J.A. showed that there were 117 patients unfit to take a railway journey of fifty-six hours and 176 patients who would have to be moved on stretchers. Eventually the I.J.A. ruled that no stretcher cases were to be moved and that a plan for the organisation of the hospital with those remaining was to be prepared. It was then made known that the destination was to be KANBURI and, later, SINGAPORE.

The move began on 19 Nov in parties of 200 on consecutive nights till the night of 24 Nov, when the final party of 132 left. The journey varied from 72 hours to 132 hours, with long halts en route. Like all other journeys it was most uncomfortable. Closed and open trucks at a scale of thirty-three to a truck were used. Food as usual was spasmodic and insufficient.

Major M.D. Price, R. Sigs, was left in command with Capts. E.J. Emery RAMC and F.J. Cahill AAMC, as medical officers. The details were:-

	British		A.I.F		Totals	
	Offrs	ORs	Offrs	ORs	Offrs	ORs
Medical Staff	2	23	1	29	3	52
Administrative	2	16	2	27	4	43
Patients	3	139	-	76	3	215
Totals	7	78	3	32	10	310

*Includes one Assistant Surgeon

Of the patients approximately 85 were suffering primarily of dysentery and approximately 65 primarily from tropical ulcers. The predominate disease amongst the remainder was beri-beri. Medical opinion considered that the deaths within the ensuing two months would be approximately 90 – 100.

12. The total number of deaths, including dead on arrival, up to 1430 hours on 24 November was 665, representing about 45% of the British and 21% of the A.I.F. population of the camp. Deaths in the main were attributable to dysentery, both amoebic and bacillary, tropical ulcers, beri-beri and malaria. Undernutrition and lack of essential vitamins very greatly increased the mortality rate from these diseases.
13. The I.J.A. Administration after the arrival of Lieut. Iraiwa, about 22 Aug was in the main sympathetic and helpful within the limits of its power. The hospital was still under the control of Colonel Banno at NIEKE. The British method of paying compliments was accepted and this had a marked effect on the morale of the prisoners. A gift of cigarettes with tea and margarine was most acceptable.
14. On the whole, Tanbaya Hospital was not the success it was hoped it would be for the two reasons: (i) lack of well-balanced diet and (ii) complete lack of drugs. A tribute must be made to the zeal and energy of Major Bruce Hunt and all his medical staff – both officers and other ranks. With their professional knowledge the task set them to cure the patients must have seemed hopeless, but never for one instant did

they despair and were always at pains to do anything in their power at any time day or night to alleviate suffering.

It must be placed on record that the patients themselves bore their illnesses with great fortitude, helped both themselves and their comrades in a thousand and one small ways, when the[ir] end came, expressed their gratitude for what had been done for them and passed on like heroes.

Administrative Commander
Lt-Col C.T. Hutchinson, MC, RA

CHAPTER 10

Medical Report
Tanbaya Hospital
Aug 1 – Nov 24, 1943

I INTRODUCTORY

It was on 29th June that the I.J.A. first intimated that it was intended to establish a hospital in Burma to receive men of "F" Force who would be incapable of work for at least two months. Rolls for a 2,000-bed hospital were prepared, but on 8th July it was announced that the idea had been abandoned. On 21st June fresh orders were issued to prepare rolls, this time for a 1,200-bed hospital. Lt.-Col. S. Harris commanding "F" Force had appointed me OC Hospital on 1st July and on 24th July I was sent into Burma with Lt. SAITO to examine the hospital site. I returned on 29th July and on 30th July left with the advance party for Burma.

II GENERAL COMMENT

When the proposal for a hospital camp was first mooted hopes ran high that this would be the means of saving hundreds of lives. This was particularly the case amongst hospital patients who by reason of their illness might be regarded as eligible for selection for Burma. There seemed reasonable grounds for this enthusiasm, as the I.J.A. had given assurances that no work would be demanded from the camp. Moreover, a further statement had been made that necessary drugs and dressings would probably be supplied.

The records contained in the war diary indicate that the hopes at first ascertained for the success of the camp were not realised. A death rate of 660 (with a probability of a further 90-100) out of a total camp entry of 1,924 is a profoundly disappointing result. The reasons for the huge death rate are set out below. It is a melancholy reflection that in November there was almost as much enthusiasm to leave Burma as there had been in July to go there.

III FACTORS CONCERNED IN THE HIGH DEATH RATE

A.   actors Antedating Tanbaya

(i)   State of Disease. Very many patients were in such an advanced state of their disease on their arrival in Burma that even with the best hospital facilities in the world recovery would have been impossible. This applied particularly to patients from Sonkrai camp (No.2), from which it is believed that evacuation of all very sick patients was practically compulsory.

(ii)   State of Nutrition. Apart from the state of their diseases, the emaciation of many of the patients gravely prejudiced their chance of recovery. In part this was due to poor rations at the working camps but in part it arose from the failure of the medical officers in certain of these camps to insist on the consumption by their patients of the full daily ration. In many cases of dysentery, liquid diet had been presented over an unconscionably long period, resulting in practical starvation of the unfortunate patient. Apart from the emaciation, long-standing deficiency in intake of vitamins A, B, B1 and B2 and C also greatly lowered the patient's ability to combat his disease.

(iii)   Effects of Journey. The journey was made under very arduous conditions. An inadequate number of fit men was available to help sick patients on the way. Food was poor and long exposure to rainstorms and severe jolting for hours on end were the lot of all. Under these circumstances many patients whose fate hung in the balance had their last chance of survival taken away by the strain of the journey.

B.   Factors Operative at Tanbaya
(i)   Diet. So far from the diet being better in Burma than at the working camps it was for a long period considerably worse, as will be seen from a study of the ration issues set out in

the war diary. Rice was in general adequate, but every other essential was grossly deficient. In particular, until the bean ration was raised from 1/3 bag to 1 bag on 22 September, the diet contained practically no vitamin B whatever. Innumerable protests and requests for rice polishings and for more beans were made to the I.J.A. but always met [the] reply that rice polishings were quite unobtainable, and that there was a great shortage of beans, which were being reserved for the camps further from the railhead. In this connection it is interesting to note that when on 10th of October we learned that "A" Force Hospital Camp 5 kms away had been receiving an adequacy of beans, since its formation in July, and pointed this fact out to the I.J.A. camp commander he raised the bean issue from 1 bag to 2½ bags forthwith. It is also interesting to note that from 26th October onwards regular issues of rice polishings were made to the camp. Had these two steps been taken earlier in the camp's history, it is my considered opinion that upwards of 100 lives would have been saved.

The deficiency in vitamins A and C undoubtedly produced a marked lowering in the resistance of tissues to infection, thereby increasing the frequency and severity of ulcers, furuncles, impetigo, pemphygus and other cutaneous infections. Deficiency in protein produced a lowering of general vitality as also did the deficiency in calcium.

(ii) <u>Drug Shortage.</u> Until 5th November no drugs were received from the I.J.A., and then even the supply was pitifully small and inadequate. In particular, no particular therapy was available for the treatment of amoebic or bacillary dysentery, the major killing diseases in the camp. There was no idoform or other drug suitable for local treatment of the numerous tropical ulcers. No sulphur (a common, cheap and easily procurable product) was available to treat scabies until 5th November, by which time the whole camp was infected, with much secondary suppuration[35] and ulcer formation. Dressings were woefully deficient and many mosquito nets had to be sacrificed to dress the enormous

---

[35] This is the forming or discharging of pus.

ulcers. No iron was available to build up the anaemic patients and no concentrated B1 was available for the numerous severe beri-beris.

(iii) <u>Malaria.</u> Tanbaya was an area where malaria of a particularly severe type was hyperendemic. Eighty-seven deaths are shown as being due either wholly or partially to malaria, but beyond this the disease had a debilitating effect throughout the camp, where its incidence reached practically 100%. In most cases, malaria caused marked deterioration in the condition of patients suffering from ulcers or dysentery.

IV SYSTEM OF ADMINISTRATION

The system of administration adopted at Tanbaya differed in several respects from that customary in military hospitals. In part these differences were dictated by local necessity, in part they were devised as possible improvements. Lt. Col. Hutchinson, as Administrative Commandant of the camp, was responsible for such services as cooking, securing wood and water, hygiene, canteen, and pay. Major Hunt as OC Hospital was responsible for all medical treatment and for the administrative control of all medical personnel, whether professional or amateur, and of all patients. This subdivision of authority worked very smoothly and I should like here to pay my tribute to Lt. Col. Hutchinson, for his loyalty, his unfailing tact and his untiring efforts in the interests of the patients and the camp as a whole.

Details of medical administration were as follows: Patients were segregated as far as possible according to their complaints; this facilitated treatment and prevented cross-infection. Thus one ward was devoted solely to dysentery, one ward to pure dysentery and ulcers combined with dysentery, two wards to ulcers, and three wards to general medical diseases, chiefly malaria and beri-beri. Each ward contained in the earlier stages approximately 190 patients and was under the control of a wardmaster. The wardmaster was a combat officer, usually of company commander status or above; he had as assistants an assistant wardmaster, usually a subaltern, two NCOs, who acted as C.S.M. and C.Q.M.S. respectively and a clerk. The wardmaster was responsible for nominal rolls, for discipline, for hut cleanliness, for messing, for canteen supplies and in general for everything which took place in the ward except such matters as involved technical medical knowledge or skill. He had, in addition, through the medical officers or senior nursing N.C.O. supervisor control over the activities of the nursing orderlies in regard to their non-technical functions.

This system of wardmaster control, first devised in Shimo Sonkurai camp and further extended in Burma, proved of the greatest possible assistance in running the hospital. Discipline and general ward efficiency were very much better than they usually are under N.C.O. control, in particular messing functioned much more efficiently and with much less complaint than is usually the case. I was particularly fortunate in having a very able body of wardmasters; they worked, ate and slept in their wards and were completely devoted to their duties and to the interests of their patients ...

The wardmasters' conference, attended also by OC Hospital, Registrar and Messing Officer, was held daily at 1530 hours; this proved the most satisfactory means of keeping the wards in close touch with camp policy.

In view of the shortage of drugs all requisitions were checked and countersigned by OC Hospital before completion. This took place at 1500 hrs and permitted of a just distribution of drugs between the various wards and also of the conservation of necessary supplies.

As patients in the various wards improved and became fit for camp duties they were sent to the "labour exchange" where they were vetted by OC Hospital and then assigned to various sections of the hospital according to the requirements of the different departments.

V STAFF

Although the number of RAMC and AAMC personnel at Tanbaya was at its highest 142, very many of these men arrived as patients and either died at Tanbaya or remained as patients during their stay in Burma. Nine members of the RAMC and eight members of the AAMC died at Tanbaya, and five RAMC and nine AAMC were left behind as seriously ill patients when the bulk of the camp moved in November. The maximum number of the Hospital Corps personnel available for duty at any one time was 62 and the number generally varied between 40 and

50. Under these circumstances it was necessary for the greater part of the nursing work to be done by volunteers from none-medical units, and the steadfast devotion to duty of these men under circumstances of much difficulty and discomfort is worthy of the highest praise. Many of the volunteers showed a marked aptitude for the more technical branches of nursing and in some cases were as good if not better than many of the professionals.

VI DISEASE

Four diseases dominated the clinical picture. These were in the order of mortality which they produced, dysentery, tropical ulcers, ber-beri and malaria.

(i)   Dysentery. In the absence of facilities for bacteriological or sigmoidoscopic examination it was impossible in most cases to differentiate between amoebic and bacillary dysentery. Clinically, however, I formed the impression that the former disease predominated, and autopsy and the results of treatment of five cases by emetine in November (this was all the emetine we ever received) tended to confirm this impression. The dysentery wards were amongst the most tragic places in the camp. Many of the patients put up a most gallant struggle, forcing their rice down day after day and week after week in an heroic effort to stay alive until adequate facilities for treatment arrived. Dysentery alone caused 114 deaths and in association with other diseases played a part in killing 334 men. In many cases an attack or a recurrence of dysentery was the terminal factor in carrying off patients suffering from beri-beri and ulcers.

(ii) Tropical ulcers. These were of very great frequency and in many cases of horrifying severity. Huge area of skin, flesh, and in some cases bone were eaten away and the skin appeared to possess little or no resistance to the infecting organisms. Ulcers followed small scratches or cuts with depressing frequency and not a few patients died of ulcers which actually developed in the camp ...

The lower extremity and in particular the region of the tibia was the site of selection for the formation of ulcers. They could and did however occur in almost any area of the body, as for example, trochanter, over the lower spine, in the groin, over the scapula, on the elbows, wrist and fingers. A few cases responded strikingly to the application of sulphanilamide or idoform, and had these drugs been available in anything like adequate amounts much life could have been saved. In the absence of these drugs simple dressings with eusol or saline two or three times a day provided the best results, which however in many cases were bitterly disappointing. Amputations were performed in about 60 cases ... but here also the results were in general disappointing owing to the poor general condition of the patients and owing to the frequent occurrence of severe secondary sepsis in the stump. It was noticeable that an attack of dysentery or malaria caused considerable deterioration in the conditions of the ulcer which hitherto had progressed quite favourably. Ninety-two patients died of ulcers alone, and one hundred and five of ulcers complicated by other diseases.

(iii) <u>Ber-beri</u>. Beri-beri was widespread throughout the camp. At one time there were upwards of 600 patients showing clinical manifestations of the disease. It was also more severe than any which I had previously seen in a PoW experience of two years.

A further complication which caused much loss of life in beri-beri   patients was the frequency with which the grossly oedematous[36] patients developed a rapidly spreading gangrene in their water-logged extremities. This complication was almost invariably fatal. Many patients remained oedematous for several weeks and in such cases cardiac deterioration generally accompanied or followed on the oedema.

Cardiac beri-beri was both common and severe. Practically every clinical abnormality ever recorded in cardiac beri-beri was observed at Tanbaya. Hearts were enlarged both to the right and the left, chiefly the latter ... Cyanosis and other signs of congested heart failure were relatively infrequent. Sudden death, frequently occurring in the middle of the night, was not uncommon.

---

[36] An excessive accumulation of serous fluid in the intercellular spaces of tissue.

Administration of vitamin B intravenously saved a certain number of lives when cardiac emergencies occurred, but this, as of all other valuable drugs, supplies were grossly inadequate. Beri-beri alone killed 68 men; in a further 260 cases beri-beri was one of the causes of death.

(iv) Malaria. Malaria was practically universal throughout the camp and in August and September relapses were very frequent as, owing to shortage of quinine supplies, it was not possible to give quinine treatment longer than 7 days. After the end of September supplies increased considerably and it was possible to increase the course from 24gm daily for 7 days to 32gm daily for 12 days, accompanying the latter with plasmoquine 0.02gm daily. After this step was taken there was a marked fall in the incidence of malaria relapses. Microscopic examination conducted by the I.J.A. showed the relative frequency of BT and MT[37] infection to be approximately 2:1. One of the outstanding clinical natures of the malaria at Tanbaya was the high degree of resistance to quinine. In many cases of undoubted malaria the fever did not come under control until 6, 7, or 8 days after the commencement of treatment. A number of patients were observed to relapse on the 10th or 11th day of treatment while still taking 32gm of quinine daily. Finally every person who had either been protected from malaria in Thailand by suppressive atebrin had clinical malaria in Burma, although continuing to take atebrin regularly. Ten people were thus affected.

Cerebral malaria occurred in about thirty cases, many of which responded satisfactorily to parenteral quinine. Haemoglobinuria was seen half-a-dozen times, but no true case of blackwater fever occurred.

(v) Typhus. A 14-day fever clinically resembling typhus in many respects was observed in about 40 cases. No rash and no escher[38] was seen, but previous experience of this disease left me in little doubt as to the nature of the fever. Serological confirmation of the diagnosis was, of course,

---

[37] These are Benign Tertian and Malignant Tertian.

[38] An eschar is a piece of dead tissue that is cast off from the surface of the skin.

impossible. The typhus was in general relatively mild and only two or three cases succumbed.

(vi) <u>Catarrhal Jaundice</u>. About fifty cases of this disease was seen, all mild and non-fatal.

(vii)<u>Respiratory Disease</u>. Coryzas were frequent but only about half-a-dozen pneumonias were seen, two of which were followed by empyaemia[39].

(viii) <u>Scabies</u>. Scabies spread steadily from the formation of the camp onwards and by November when the first supply of sulphur arrived it was almost universal. Scabies, of course, had a high nuisance value but in addition to this it gave rise to much secondary infection and in some cases to severe ulcers which resulted fatally. Treatment was instituted immediately on the arrival of the sulphur in early November, cooking oil being used as a base. Much improvement naturally occurred in the scabies, but the sulphur came far too late to prevent the hundreds of cases of impetigo which caused much distress throughout the camp.

<u>(VII) RECORDS</u>.

The register of deaths is contained in the War Diary. The camp roll contains an entry of the disease from which the various patients suffered during their stay at Tanbaya with a view to giving each individual patient some record of his ailments, and entries made by medical officers were made on both British and Australian paybooks. Where paybooks had been lost cards or bamboo slips were issued on which the appropriate particulars were inserted. Every man who left Tanbaya should have had with him a full record of the illnesses from which he suffered in that camp.

<u>(VIII) EVACUATION</u>.

As early as September strong representations were made to the I.J.A. that many hundreds of patients would not survive a long

---

[39] Pockets of pus that have collected inside a body cavity.

railway journey. As a result of these representations considerable leniency was allowed in the selection of patients to travel. Much care was taken with this selection, and as a result, of the 900-odd patients who left Tanbaya for Kamburi only two failed to survive the arduous five or six days' journey.

A staff of 102 was left behind in Burma to look after 218 patients. Of these patients approximately 85 were suffering from dysentery and approximately 65 from ulcers; the majority of the remainder had beri-beri. If conditions prevailing in November persist, and if patients are evacuated in February, as seems probable, I anticipate a mortality of 90-100. This would include about 60 dysenteries, 15 ulcers and 15 beri-beris.

(IX) CONCLUSION.

The Burma hospital camp, for reasons stated above, could not be regarded as a success. Its partial failure, however, was much mitigated by the efficient work of the administrative staff, by the devotion to duty of the wardmasters and the professional skill and knowledge displayed by some of the medical staff.

> (Sgd) Bruce Hunt, Major
> A.A.M.C.
> Formerly Cmd. Tanbaya Hospital

CHAPTER 11

Report by Assistant-Surgeon Wolfe, IMD

Left Singapore on No.7 Train. On march from Bampong carried out duties of M.O. as Capt. Silman was ill and remained behind at about fourth halt. Medical duties were difficult owing to

1. Shortage of drugs, dressings and orderlies (only 2 untrained orderlies were available owing to others having dropped out).
2. Arduous conditions on the march. Medical personnel had to treat sick left behind by former party soon after arrival at camp. On completion of this they had to attend to the sick of their own party. In addition had to treat sick all along the route of march and consequently had little time to rest between marches.

Arrived lower Nikki late May. The following day Cholera broke out and an isolation ward was immediately established. I worked in this ward until the arrival of two more medical officers. The next day, under orders from Col. Dillon and Col. Harris, I and four nursing orderlies proceeded to Konkoita. On arrival there I saw a horrible scene. In one tent on the bank of the river fifteen patients were lying helpless. Eight of these were suffering from Cholera with nobody to attend to them. The whole area was polluted with infected stools and vomit, and full of flies. A report was made to the Japanese Medical Officer (Major) who removed us to the coolies' Cholera camp. In spite of repeated requests this officer refused to give us any transport to move the patients to hospital. He also refused to give any drugs or adequate accommodation (most of us were left out in the rain). I treated these cases with M & B, EnNO4, and saline by a transfusion set improvised from stethoscope rubber and funnel. These drugs were soon exhausted and I sent an orderly with an urgent appeal for help to 2/29 Bn. A.I.F. camped at Timonta, 7 miles away. An officer was sent next day with necessary drugs etc., I then received orders from Col Harris to proceed to Timonta to relieve Capt. Mills (MO) who was ill. I could not leave my patients and go to Timonta, so I suggested that all of us, including the patients, should go to Timonta. The Japanese MO refused permission for the move.

On 5.6.43 eventually after a great deal of representations from 2/29 Bn., I was told I could take all my patients to Timonta. No transport was provided. I raised subscriptions amongst ourselves and promised to pay for the hire of 2 or 3 bullock carts. This was refused. We improvised bamboo stretchers and carried 5 stretcher cases, 2 men carrying a stretcher. The rest of the patients had to struggle along somehow. It was impossible to carry the patients very far in the rains and boggy roads. Col. Dillon had told me that on the authority of Col. Banno I would get all the necessary help at Konkoita from the Japanese hospital. The Japanese MO not only refused to give me any help but treated me most callously and only smiled when I remonstrated to him that we would all die there if we were not given drugs, help and transport. He did not seem to care. Fortunately, there were no sentries and we managed to get out of the camp area and hide ourselves in the jungle. I then send an orderly to Timonta with an appeal for help. The 2/29 Bn. Immediately sent an officer and 50 men with stretchers and food and carried all our sick to their camp. Through an act of Providence, we did not lose a single patient. I owe great thanks to Col. Kappe, Col. Pond and Capt. Mills for their great kindness and prompt help, otherwise we would have been stranded. I must also mention the

---

40 In many respects the orderlies were the unsung heroes of "F" Force. One of those orderlies was Reginald Thomas Jarman. He left us an account of an average day for him and his fellow orderlies in Songkurai No.2 Camp: 'Up before daybreak to collect the "half ration" of food for those not working, i.e. the sick and dying; feed those who couldn't feed themselves; clean up all the mishaps of the night from dysentery patients who tried but couldn't make it to the latrines.

'The Japanese guard would then arrive to do a head count of all the sick while all the orderlies paraded outside. With this over, two orderlies would then go through both hospitals and remove all who had died during the night to an area outside. The daily average death rate was 4+. (I can remember one day when the death count was 10.)

great unselfish work, under the most trying conditions, that was done by the orderlies, particularly by L/Cpl Somerfield R. and Pte. Carlton of the A.A.M.C.[40]

On my arrival at Timonta I found the MO (Capt. Mills) sick and still working very hard. He was forced to go to bed and I carried out his duties. This unit was under great hardships, on half rations and there were about 400 sick including Cholera cases. After a week's stay here, I left with half 2/29 Btn. to Nikki, Capt. Mills remaining behind with patients and unfit men. This march was one of the worst I have experienced. I reported to Col. Harris on my arrival at Lower Nikki hospital and marched with Col. Harris and patients to Upper Nikki.

After a few days' work in Upper Nikki hospital, Cholera broke out again and I was detailed by Major Phillips to be i/c of Cholera Isolation Hospital, 3 furlongs away from the main hospital. In addition to our troops I was obliged to treat Burmese patients here. One incident here is worth mentioning. When under orders from Col. Dillon, I objected to admitting Burmese coolies to our Hospital, the Japanese threatened to hit me and gave me a long lecture about our "superiority complex", and about our being fed and paid by the Japanese Govt. and as such we have had to obey and work for them. The little success I have had in treating cholera was I think due to the following treatment. Large saline transfusions (about 4 pints on the first day, 2 or 3 pints on subsequent days depending on the condition of pulse, dehydration, vomiting, diarrhoea, etc.) M & B tablets, EnNO4 (weak solutions orally), cordise stimulants[41] when necessary, plenty of fluids, rest, nursing, etc.

'Each body was then carried on a makeshift stretcher to a guard post to be recorded, then to the burial ground away from the camp site. They would then dig the grave, remove any clothing before burial, complete the job, then return for the next body, and so on, until all the dead had been buried. This process could take most of the day as we only had one well-worn shovel to work with. Any clothing kept from those who died would be washed and, if not utilized as bandages, would be given to the those in the greatest need as, by this time, almost everybody's clothing had rotted off our backs from humidity, perspiration, mud and slush.' See the website Prisoners of War of the Japanese, www.pows-of-japan.net/articles/83.htm.

[41] This may refer to cordis which relates to the heart, so these might be heart stimulants.

At the end of the cholera epidemic, I worked a few days in the malaria ward at Nikki. On 1/8/43, I proceeded to Ronchi where I stayed for about 20 days i/c of staging section, Burma Hospital. I then went to Tanbaya where I was in charge of Dysentery Ward and did other small jobs such as M.I. Room and Isolation Ward at times. On final evacuation of Tanbaya Hospital, I came along with patients to Kunburi.

I owe thanks to all my superior officers particularly to Major Hunt and Cols. Huston, Harris, Dillon and Hutchison for the encouragement and help they gave me in my work and for their kindness to me.

CHAPTER 12

Report on Tropical Ulcers at Tanbaya

Lieut-Col J. Huston
S.M.O. "F" Force

Introductory

When the formation of a hospital in Burma for the treatment for all men of "F" Force who would still be unfit in two months' time was first mooted, it was obvious from our experience at Shimo Sonkurai, that tropical ulcers would form a considerable proportion of the cases to be dealt with. When the hospital was ultimately started in August, we had at Shimo Sonkurai almost a hundred tropical ulcers and their treatment was a great problem.

We had very little in the way of antiseptic and the routine treatment was frequent cleansing of the ulcers with hot water or saline, followed by a hypochlorite dressing made from bleaching powder. On one occasion we received a little idoform from the Japanese, and the results we obtained with it in a limited number of patients was very promising.

Included in the first batch of patients which arrived in Burma about August 12th, were about a dozen cases of tropical ulcer, of greater severity of any I had seen at Shimo Sonkurai. Ultimately of the 1900 patients who arrived, about 240 were suffering from tropical ulcers of varying degrees of severity, with or without complications.

A special section of the hospital was allotted to these patients consisting of two wards capable of holding 180 and 160 patients respectively.

Over the period of the existence of the hospital, approximately 420 cases of ulcer passed through our hands, of which about 185 developed in Burma.

The following clinical points were noted:-

1' Etiology[42].

The most striking feature in the etiology of these ulcers was that a considerable number started from very minute beginnings. A small scratch from a piece of bamboo seemed to be the commonest factor, usually in a patient who was debilitated from semi-starvation and exposure, and probably suffering also from clinical or subclinical malaria, or dysentery or beri-beri.

It was the rule rather than the exception for mild skin trauma to develop into frank ulcers.

I have seen one ulcer of the arm, which ultimately proved fatal, resulting from the abrasion caused by vaccination.

Scabies which became infected were the starting point of a number of ulcers, particularly on the hands and legs, and a striking feature was their multiplicity. Others started do move [?] particularly in severe cases of beri-beri and I have seen blobs arise on an oedematous[43] foot for no apparent reason whatever and within 36 hours these have extended into sloughing ulcers involving tendons and muscles, with an inevitably fatal result.

Many ulcers resulted from prolonged decubitus[44]. In patients with chronic dysentery and/or beri-beri, ulcers were very prone to develop on bony promontories, particularly in view of the fact that most patients were lying on bamboo slats. These ulcers followed the same course as those in other areas of the body. A contributary etiological factor, as pointed out, was the extreme debility due to recurrent malaria, dysentery, beri-beri and semi-starvation.

2. Site.

Ulcers were both single and multiple, the former being the more common. Multiple ulcers adjacent to each other tended to coalesce.

The common site for a single ulcer was the anterior aspect of the tibia. On other sites they tended to be multiple. The trunk was rarely affected, except in the case of pressure ulcers which involved the sacral and iliac regions[45]. The

---

[42] The cause, set of causes, or manner of causation of a disease.
[43] Swelling in the ankles, feet and legs, often caused by a build-up of fluid.

arms, apart from the hands were relatively immune. Multiple small ulcers on the hands, particularly in the region of the dorsal aspect of the m metacarpophalangeal and interphalangeal joints[46] were common, usually resulting from the infected lesions of scabies. Multiple ulcers on the foot were common; these commonly followed a type of pustular[47] eruption called tropical pemphigus.

In extremely debilitated patients, there were a few cases of multiple ulcers involving both legs, and showing very little reaction whatever. Most of these had a fatal termination.

The scalp was occasionally involved.

3. Pathology.
As previously stated, the ulcers, as a rule started from a small skin abrasion which became infected which led to localised death of tissue. The majority of ulcers spread with alarming rapidity, and a small infected abrasion became within 48 hours a sloughing ulcer, involving skin, subcutaneous tissue, fascia and muscle. In the latter stages bone became involved with superficial necrosis[48]. As a general rule there appeared to be very little associated tissue reaction, and necrosis spread rapidly. In a considerable number of cases there ultimately developed a line of demarcation, indicated by a zone of tissue reaction.

---

42 The cause, set of causes, or manner of causation of a disease.
43 Swelling in the ankles, feet and legs, often caused by a build-up of fluid.
44 Prolonged pressure on the skin.
45 The area between the sacrum and the pelvic bones. The Divisional Intelligence Officer, 18th Division, saw ulcers that had developed in this region of the body when he was at Tanbaya: 'One man's thighs and scrotum completely rotted away. Indescribable stench, ulcers were scraped away with spoons every day, or cleaned with leeches, accompanied by cries of men in their agony ... How they lasted as long as they did, Christ alone knows. Just a mass of moaning, stinking, decaying, gangrenous flesh.' Sir Harold Atcherley, *Prisoner of Japan, A Personal War Diary, Singapore, Siam and Burma, 1941-1945* (Memories Publishing, Cirencester, 2012), p.135.
46 The points where the thumb and the fingers hinge on the bones of the hand.
47 Reddish, scaly, pus-filled bumps.
48 Death of cells.

In other patients, particularly those in a very debilitated state, there was no attempt at limitation, and those patients usually died very rapidly from toxaemia[49]. In others the ulcers became limited in extent but remained in a sloughing condition with a putrid odour, and in these cases also death from toxaemia followed.

When the anterior aspect of the tibia became exposed, the periosteum[50] became rapidly necrotic and the surface of the bone developed a worm-eaten appearance. Sequestration[51] of a superficial flake of bone frequently occurred. In the more severe cases, pus tended to track around the entire circumference of the bone, and I have seen cases in which practically the whole of the daphysis[52] became a huge sequestrum surrounded by pus, and completely separated from all its muscular attachments.

In favourable cases, the ulcers ceased to spread and the necrotic [illegible] and muscular tissue separated leaving a granulating[53] surface which continued to discharge freely. If bone had been exposed in the floor of the ulcer this slowly separated, and during this process granulation tissue grew in from the edges. Separation or removal of the sequestrum must always occur before such an ulcer can develop a floor completely covered with granulation tissue. Once granulation had occurred epithelialization[54] under the methods of treatment available, was extremely slow, and it was quite common to see a clear granulating ulcer of diameter less than half-a-crown to take nearly three months to epithelialize.

Abscesses and pus pockets frequently formed in association with ulcers. These abscesses always required incision. Such abscess formation was common with ulcers of a severe degree on the anterior aspects of the tibia where pus could be found tracking downwards and backwards,

---

[49] Blood poisoning.
[50] Tissue covering the bones.
[51] Removal.
[52] The shaft or central part of a long bone.
[53] Granulating tissue is new connective tissue and microscopic blood vessels that form on the surfaces of a wound during the healing process.
[54] The repairing of the wound.

pointing on either side of the Tando Achillis[55]. Burrowing of pus up, and down beneath the skin on the anterior aspect of the tibia was also observed on a number of occasions.

Outstanding in the history of these ulcers was the rapidity and extent of their spread if the patient developed malaria or dysentery.

On numerous occasions I have seen patients with a clean gradulating and slowly healing ulcer, develop malaria; within 48 hours all the processes of healing had stopped, and the ulcer had rapidly increased in depth and area. The patients' general condition also deteriorated not infrequently death followed.

Despite all precautions many ulcers became flyblown and infection with maggots nearly always produced rapid spread of the ulcer. This was due to the absence of a surrounding wall of the fibroblastic[56] reaction to circumscribe the phagocytic activity[57] of the maggots. The maggots burrowed deeply into the tissues and their complete eradication was extremely difficult.

In some cases there was no sign of any leuceblastic reaction whatsoever, and the ulcer took on a dry, greyish black appearance with associated severe toxaemia[58]. Such ulcers were usually multiple and often fatal.

4. Complications.

The majority of patients with ulcers suffered also from malaria from beri-beri, from amoebic or bacillary dysentery, or from a combination of these diseases. The ulcer may have preceded or followed the systematic disease. These diseases played an important part in modifying the course of the ulcers.

(a). Beri-beri.

Beri-beri, usually of the odemateous[59] type was the most frequent accompanying disease. Ulcers usually complicated

---

[55] More commonly known as the Achilles tendon.
[56] A biological cell critical in the healing process.
[57] Phagocytic cells protect the body by ingesting harmful foreign particles.
[58] Blood poisoning by toxins from a local bacterial infection.
[59] This is a 'wet' form of the disease.

ber-beri rather than the reverse. In such cases, the ulcers were extremely indolent. Occasionally, however, they spread with alarming rapidity, as the waterlogged tissues offered very little resistance to the spread of infection. Death from toxaemia was frequent.

One type of ulcer was especially associated with beri-beri. A subcutaneous blob appeared on the dorsum of the foot. This blob filled up with a sere-sanguineous fluid[60], and very rapidly increased in size. Within 36 to 48 hours, the mermis [? dermis] beneath the blob had soured away, and a deep punched-cut ulcer had developed extending well into the subcutaneous tissue. There was always a surrounding cellulitis[61] of greater or less degree, and the patient rapidly became extremely toxic and died.

(b). Malaria.

An attack of malaria in patients suffering from an ulcer was often enough to cause its increase in size. The ulcer may have been healing satisfactorily for some weeks; an attack of malaria would, within 48 hours, undo all the improvement made in the preceding month and would cause a rapid spread of the ulcer into healthy tissue. Death often followed.

(c). Dysentery.

Dysentery was a particularly dangerous complication in a patient debilitated by ulcers. No specific therapy was available for either bacillary or amoebic dysentery. Very few patients who suffered from a combination of dysentery and ulcers survived.

(d). Secondary Haemorrhage.

This occurred in only four instances. The vessel involved in each case was the posterior tibial artery behind the medial malleolus[62]. The onset of the bleeding was always sudden and unexpected, and bleeding was profuse. The haemorrhage could always be controlled by direct pressure, but one patient lost so much blood before the haemorrhage was served (it occurred at night) that he died on the following day.

---

[60] This means that it contains both blood and the liquid part of blood.
[61] Bacterial skin infection in which the affected skin appears swollen and red and is typically painful and warm to the touch.
[62] One of the arteries supplying blood to the leg between the knee and foot.

5. <u>Clinical features</u>.

(1) <u>Pain</u>

Pain was a universal symptom. It was severe and aching, it was felt in the area of the ulcer and it was worse at night, preventing sleep. It was frequently referred to that part of the limb immediately below the lesion.

(2) <u>Oedema</u>

In medium and large size ulcers of the leg there was always oedema of the foot and ankle, due to venous and lymphatic obstruction. In three ulcer patients I have seen massive oedema of the foot and leg due to thrombosis of the deep femoral veins.

(3) Foeter[63]

The foetid nature of the discharge particularly in rapidly spreading ulcers was very characteristic; this added greatly to the general discomfort of the patient.

(4) <u>Nutrition</u>

The diet provided by the Japanese contained an adequacy of carbohydrates, but was grossly deficient in protein, fat, vitamins A, B1, B2 and C. The protein lack in ulcer cases was accentuated by the continued protein loss in purulent discharge[64]. This, associated with the lack of vitamin B was important in the lowering of tissue resistance and the rapid progress of most ulcers.

Nutrition was also grossly interfered with by intercurrent diseases such as dysentery and malaria, in which loss of appetite was a common symptom. This was particularly difficult to overcome in view of the monotony of the ration.

(5) <u>Treatment</u>

The treatment of tropical ulcers at Tanbaya was fraught with difficulty ... [due to a shortage of drugs which were] totally inadequate for the large number of ulcers in the camp (in all over 400). Moreover, idoform, cod liver oil or eusol, the drugs of election for the treatment of this condition, were completely lacking.

An extremely small supply of bandages, cotton wool, and gauze was available and various substitutes, chiefly

---

[63] Possibly meaning fetor, referring to offensive smell.

[64] A discharge of pus.

mosquito nets and leaves, were used to give protection against atmosphere and against flies.

Dressings obviously had to be used over and over again and here another difficulty arose, as the water supply was at all times inadequate.

The routine local treatment was to bathe the ulcer with hot boiling water and then to apply the dressing soaked in hypochlorite solution which was made from W.S.P. This treatment was carried out twice daily in acute purulent stages. A thrice-daily dressing would have been desirable but could not be carried out because of the water shortage. As the ulcer became cleaner and gradulation tissue appeared, saline was substituted for the W.S.P. solution. These simple measures carried out diligently did produce results provided that the ulcers were not in a very advanced stage. In these cases no local treatment was able to stay the rapid and usually fatal spread of gangrene.

The minute amount of sulphanilamide available was used on several cases of multiple ulcers on the hands. The results were more gratifying and I am sure that had anything approaching an adequate supply had been made available by the Japanese, the deplorable death rate in these series of ulcers would have been greatly diminished.

Dietary Treatment

300 mg of vitamin C were administered daily for 6 days in 6 severe cases. These patients received during the same period four capsules daily each containing an unknown quantity of vitamin A.

None of these patients showed any improvement at all and all subsequently died.

Prior to the 16th October, the camp dietary was outstandingly deficient in vitamin B. On this date rice polishings were first supplied. Within a few days it became possible to administer at least 3 oz daily throughout the camp. This dosage was continued until 30th January when the camp broke up. It was noted that no new severe ulcers developed after the early part of November, and that from this day there was a general trend towards improvement in the majority of the patients still surviving.

Although by November most of the patients with severe ulcers had died, a fact which renders comparative statistics valueless, nevertheless it is felt that this favourable trend was sufficiently outstanding to require explanation.

It is tentatively suggested that this is best provided by the great increase in the intake of vitamin B.

Surgical Treatment

Apart from palliative treatment mentioned above, the following surgical procedures came under consideration:-

(1) Curettage[65]

Curettage under general anaesthesia was attempted in two types of patient. Removal of hypertrophic granulation tissues gave satisfactory results. Removal of dead or dying tissue by curettage only accelerated the spread of infection into healthy surrounding tissue. The general devitalization of tissue was such that no adequate inflammatory barrier existed at the outer limit of the necrosed tissue[66].

(2) Excision[67]

In view of the uniformly unfavourable results of curettage of necrotic tissue, complete excision of ulcers was obviously impracticable, and was not attempted.

Where the nutritional state of the patient permits of adequate natural resistance to infection, excision is obviously a very valuable procedure in the treatment of tropical ulcer. Unfortunately, the resistance of our patients at Tanbaya had been reduced to a minimum by long months of hardship and privation.

(3) Amputation

Comparatively small ulcers spread very rapidly. Severe toxaemia developed with equal speed. In view of these facts it soon became obvious that amputation held out the only hope for the survival of a large number of patients.

The following considerations were important in deciding whether to amputate.

(a) Any patient with an ulcer more than 3 inches in diameter was considered a possible candidate for amputation. Such patients were watched extremely carefully and if palliative treatment showed no signs of

---

[65] The removal of tissue by scraping or scooping.
[66] Dead tissue.
[67] Excision is to cut out.

checking the spread of the ulcer, amputation was performed.[68]

(b) The tibia, apparently wormeaten, was frequently exposed in the depths of an ulcer of the leg. Amputation was always performed when such an ulcer was further complicated by the spread of suppuration lateral and posterior to the bone.

(c) An amputation was performed in the earlier cases of acute ulcer, occurring in association with severe oedematous beri-beri. Amputation however did nothing to avert the inevitably fatal outcome in these cases, and was therefore soon abandoned.

(d) The presence of ulcers on both legs introduced a further complication. At first I did not regard a small ulcer as necessarily contra-indicating[69] amputation of the other leg. Experience however showed that in these patients who developed severe ulceration on one leg, the ulcer on the other leg would inevitably deteriorate also. As soon as this became obvious bilateral ulceration became a definite contra-indication to amputation.

[68] Corporal John Charles 'Jack' Troedel of 2/4 Australian Army Field Workshop was one of those who had his leg amputated due to a single large ulcer, and one of the very few who survived to live a full life. He was told by Colonel Huston, in rather formal Harley Street fashion: 'You will have to have your leg off'. The amputation was high on his thigh. Lieutenant Colonel (Retired) Peter Winstanley OAM, RFD, JP, interviewed Jack in 2008: 'The operation was carried out on a bamboo operating table, with old fuel drums used for boiling water. The saw was borrowed from the work parties.

'The chloroform lasted a short time and Jack said that he experienced great pain. Notwithstanding the above, the operation was a success and there was no infection of the wound. Jack paid tribute to the care he received from the Medical Orderlies who with constant attention kept the healing wound clean. He had bamboo crutches made and existed in this camp until the Railway was finished and he, and others, were moved down to the Kanchanaburi area, probably in November 1943.' *Prisoners of War of the Japanese*, www.pows-of-japan.net/articles/ 96.html.

[69] A factor that serves as a reason to withhold a certain medical treatment due to the harm that it would cause the patient.

Site of amputation was as follows:-

(a) Surgical neck of the humerus	1 case
(b) Mid thigh	25 cases
(c) Upper third of leg	14 cases

Amputation was performed as low as possible but in a regrettable large number of cases, the "site of location" was itself included in the area of the ulceration.

Sepsis in the stump was extremely common. Tissue nutrition was so impaired that sloughing of flaps frequently occurred. The sloughing also involved vessel walls, leading to secondary haemorrhage. This was anticipated and watched for with great care. As soon as haemorrhage occurred a tourniquet was applied, the clot removed and the dressing changed. Twenty minutes later the tourniquet was removed, when it was always found that haemorrhage had ceased. In every case further haemorrhage followed at varying intervals.

Secondary haemorrhage occurred from the stump in five patients. In one case a re-amputation was necessary, while in another the haemorrhage was followed by severe sepsis in the stump which caused death from toxaemia. In two patients who bled from a mid thigh stump, the common femoral artery was tied just below Poupart's ligament[70]. In each of these patients the wound broke down and was followed by severe uncontrollable haemorrhage which ultimately proved fatal. One patient who bled three times from a mid thigh stump ultimately recovered.

Sequelae[71]
Among the after effects of ulcers, two require special mention.
(1). Joint Contractures.[72]
When any ulcer involved the skin over the flexor aspect

---

[70] Between the pelvis and the lower limb.
[71] The consequence of a previous disease or injury.
[72] A contracture occurs when your muscles, tendons, joints, or other tissues tighten or shorten.

of a joint[73] e.g. an ulcer in the popliteal fossa[74], the subsequent cicatrization might produce a flexor contracture of the joint.[75] This was observed on two occasions ...

(2). Sequestrum Formation.

Six patients, whose ulcers exposed extensive areas of tibia, survived their toxaemia, but were left with sequestra which at a later date required removal. Each of these ulcer subsequently healed completely.

Statistics

Accurate keeping of medical records at Tanbaya was impossible. It was rendered so by the lack of paper, by the extreme shortage of technical assistance, and above all, especially in the early days, by the necessity of devoting every minute of daylight to medical treatment.

Such figures as are now presented must be regarded as approximate only, they do, however, give a reasonably clear picture of what happened to ulcer patients at Tanbaya:

(i). Incidence

410 patients were treated in the ulcer wards at Tanbaya. In 235 of these the ulcer was present on arrival at the camp. In 185 cases, the ulcer or ulcers actually developed at Tanbaya.

(ii). Mortality

Of the ulcer patients, 250 (60%) and 170 (40%) recovered. The mortality was much higher in those patients whose ulcers were present upon arrival. Of the 235 patients in this category, 193 (83%) died and forty (17%) recovered.

Of the 185 patients whose ulcers developed after arrival, 55 (30%) died and 130 (70%) recovered.

In approximately one-third of the fatal cases the ulcer was uncomplicated. In the remainder, one or more of the three following diseases accelerated or actually determined the fatal issue. These diseases were, in order of importance, dysentery, beri-beri and malaria.

[73] The muscle that flexes a joint.
[74] The kneepit.
[75] In other words, the leg would be pulled upwards from the knee.

(iii) Amputation

Amputation was performed in 40 patients. No patient died during the operation. Only one patient died within 24 hours after operation. Four more patients died during the next six days. Thereafter, however, the death rate steadily rose. Intercurrent disease appeared to be particularly lethal to those patients. Sepsis in the stump was a further contributory factor. Three months after the last operation, only four patients on whom amputation had been performed were still arrive.[76]

Tropical ulcer at Tanbaya was a tragic affair, Manson writes that "Sloughing phagedena[77] is apt to attack the half starved, malaria stricken pioneers in jungle lands, overdriven slave gangs, and soldiers campaigning in the tropics"[78]. Every word of this description is literally applicable to the suffers from tropical ulcer among the men of "F" Force. Grossly undernourished – deprived of adequate protein and adequate vitamin – forced to labour outrageously long hours in mud and filth – constantly exposed to trauma and infection – unable to receive adequate rest – deprived of adequate drugs and dressings, it is little wonder ulceration and gangrene spread like wildfire in these poor victims of cruelty and oppression.

Means of treatment were inadequate. Water was short, food was short, drugs were short. It is possible that parts of this shortage were unavoidable. It is hard, however, to believe that the rice polishings and sulphur, which were supplied in October and November respectively, could not have been made available two or three months earlier. Had this been done, at least 100 lives would have been saved amongst ulcer patients alone.

In gloomy business two things stood out in clear relief. The first was the amazing cheerfulness and fortitude of the patients

---

[76] Harold Atcherley wrote of one such man who had 'his arms and shoulders bared, with the bone clearly visible. Complete amputation of arm and shoulder joint was carried out but what hope was there of the poor wretch living through it?' The man was dead within the hour. Atcherley, op. cit.

[77] The rapid spreading destructive ulceration of soft tissue.

[78] This refers to *Manson's Tropical Diseases*. First published in 1898, it has been continually updated since and is still considered the 'bible on tropical medicine'.

in the ulcer wards. They were pathetically grateful for what was done for them

And they cooperated fully in every aspect of their treatment.

The second redeeming feature was the steadfast devotion to duty of so many of the workers in the ulcer wards. Where so much good work is done it is difficult to single out individuals without doing apparent injustice to their fellows. The work of the following, however, was of outstanding merit:

Lieut. L. Turner [unclear] who acted as my assistant for several months and who took infinite trouble with the patients under his care.

Capt. E.J. Emery, RAMC, to whose skill in anaesthesia was due to the fact that no amputation patient, and many of these patients were appalling anaesthetic risks, died during an operation.

Capt. G.W. Gwynne, 2/4 Mc. Gn. Btn., who acted as Wardmaster in charge of ulcer wards and who was untiring in his efforts to maintain the feeding, washing, entertainment and morale of the patients under his care.

A/S Gordon Nichol, 2/3 M.A.C. who was in charge of nursing and was largely responsible for the relatively high standard of nursing under very difficult conditions.

Sig. N. Anderton, 8 Div. Sigs., L/c. F. Deans, 2/10 Fld Amb., Cpl. A.W. Rawlings, 8 Div. Prov Coy., Pte. L. Stone, 13 AGH., Pte. D. Whaley, 10 AGH., who were the best of an excellent collection of nursing orderlies.

QMS J.W. Franks, RASC, and Cpl. J. Scully, 8 Div. Sigs., who were responsible for the supply of wood and water and food for the ulcer wards, and who worked long hours, day after day without complaint maintaining the essential services of the ward.

Without the work of these men, the melancholy death roll, long as it is, would undoubtedly have been much longer, and I take this opportunity of recording my grateful appreciation of their work.

I would also like to express my thanks to Major B.A. Hunt, AAMC, C.O. Tanbaya Hospital, for the invaluable assistance he gave me in the preparation of this paper.[79]

Kanburi
A. Cahill, Cap.
AAMC
March 1944

79 'Captain F.J. Cahill, A.A.M.C., in reporting a series of 420 men suffering from tropical ulcers in Tanbaya camp hospital, described the almost incredibly unfavourable circumstances under which amputation became necessary for the rapid spreading of these ulcers. The tibia was often exposed and widespread sepsis was very common. Amputation was done on 40 men, at first as low a site as seemed advisable being chosen, but the site of election too often ran through an ulcerated area, and sloughing of flaps was frequent, often with secondary haemorrhage. Cahill found the association of oedematous beriberi with acute ulcer was very often fatal, and in this condition amputation was abandoned. The level of amputation was at mid-thigh in twenty-five cases and the upper third of the thigh in fourteen. Though these men survived immediate operation, only four patients were still alive three months after the last operation. Under more favourable conditions the hazard of spreading sepsis and chronic osteomyelitis in the lower limb could be reduced by an earlier and bolder policy of amputation at a reasonably high level before ulceration spread in the limb ... The pain was considerable, and sometimes intolerable, of a constant burning type, preventing sleep. Muscular spasm was an important associated feature, leading not infrequently to contractures perpetuating flexion of the knee or dropped foot.' Allan S. Walker, *Clinical Problems of War: Australia in the War of 1939-1945* (Australian War Memorial, 1962), pp.599-600.

CHAPTER 13

The Wardmaster System

The Wardmaster system came into operation in Thailand and Burma through forces of circumstance. The conditions which prompted its inception were unusual and difficult in the extreme. It will therefore be necessary to deal with these conditions in considerable detail in order to demonstrate fully the difficulties of hospital control which resulted in the inauguration of this system.

I am writing this as a combatant officer with no previous knowledge of hospitals or medical services; however, I have seen such services operating at Shimo Sonkural [sic], No.5 Camp, Kendo, Tanbaya (Burma) and Kanchensbri [sic]. At Shimo Sonkural my experience was as a patient, at No.5 Camp and Kundo, an O.C. of a party of sick personnel en route to Tanbaya, and at Tanbaya and Kenchemberi [sic] as a gaurdmaster [wardmaster?]. I am thus writing on a subject of which I have had first hand experience.

Generally speaking descriptions of conditions appertaining will apply to both Thailand and Burma, whereas particular instances will have occurred at Tanbaya which was a hospital only. All other hospitals with the exception of that at Kanchanabri were working camp hospitals.

"Hospitals" To the average person the word 'Hospital' conjures up the picture of a substantial building, adequately illuminated with iron bedsteads and white sheets staffed by sisters in spotless uniforms and clean and cheerful orderlies anxious not satisfy the requests and to attend to the comfort of their patients. The word also presupposes reasonably pleasant surroundings.

Imagine instead Thailand in the wet weather. If one has no experience of a wet season in the tropics let him picture himself living for weeks on end in a bath tub and shower running full strength and instead of granolithic floor a mud one. If this impression can be registered it is easy to realise the initial major problems with which hospitals administrations confronted – roofing and drainage.

When the troops arrived at their respective destination having marched under appalling conditions distances varying from 180 to 200 miles without adequate footwear, rest or food, they were met with the site of skeleton huts.

These huts were constructed of bamboo in their entirety with a passageway approximately 6 feet wide down the centre and contained 30 bays ten feet in width and 12 feet in depth at each side of the passage. Outside entrances appeared at intervals of ten bays each. The huts were constructed in the main on the side of hills consequently the bays were high on one side necessitating the use of ladders for ingress and egress while the other side was correspondingly low. The stagings were made of split bamboo, nets were provided but not in sufficient quantity to make more than 30% of the troops to any degree comfortable.

The passageways were obstructed at irregular intervals by roots of bamboo outcrops, roots and stumps of large trees which had been hastily felled during construction and water courses running through. At night it was only possible with the greatest difficulty to move from one end to the other. To add intention of the I.J.A. to cover the roofs with attap nut this did not become available for some weeks and then was laid by our own troops. Some tents and tent flys were provided after a few days but in the majority of cases they were perished and the protection they afforded was in inverse ratio to their nuisance value.

At Tanbaya the huts were constructed on a slightly different pattern. Each hut contained one length of 25 bays of similar dimensions with a passage on one side only. On the opposite side of the passage was an attap wall with doorways every four bays. The huts were roofed with attap which was in the majority of the huts the roofing afforded practically no protection. The flooring of the bays was also in very bad condition, large gaps appeared in nearly every bay rendering it almost impossible for patients to make themselves comfortable. Some mats and some bags were provided but again insufficient to go around. It was in these circumstances that hospitals were established.

The first troops arrived at Shimo Sonkurei [sic] on 15th May and on that day the hospital opened at the extreme northern end of the camp and at first occupied a portion of one hut only. On 30th May the hospital admissions had increased to 400 and on the following day increased to 600 when all ambulant dysentery patients were admitted.

Cholera broke out on 17th May necessitating the construction of an isolation hospital just north of a stream which bounded the camp. Almost from the commencement there were insufficient A.A.M.C. orderlies to cope with the increasing number of patients. Volunteers were called for with immediate response from members of combat units. Consequently at Shimo Sunkuri [sic] nursing was performed by A.A.M.C. orderlies and Volunteers working side by side.

At Shimo Sunkuri there were 4 Medical Officers who were working practically 24 hours a day on medical duties alone and had very little time to give the ward administration. As a result of this Major B. A. Hunt the Camp S.M.O. obtained the services of combat officers to manage wards, thus inaugurating the Wardmaster system which has so successfully operated there [and at] Kemi Sonkurai, Tanbaya and at Kanchanabri.

Wardmasters

It was quite clear that from the commencement of my association with hospitals that the secret of successful management was careful and intelligent organisation. How essential this was at Shimo Sonkuri can be judged by the fact that containers for the issue of food were so scarce that only two wards could be fed at a time. This is just an instance to show how rigorously a timed programme for meals had to be followed. In the wards the wardmaster was in the position of a Company Commander and Nursing sister. He has to watch carefully and organise unerringly his domestic duties paying particular to sterilisation of mess area provision of boiling water for drinking and cleanliness of quarters. Strange as it may seem it took weeks to educate troops to sterilise their mess gear as a precaution against cholera, and to drink boiled water only. With the aid of a ward C.S.M. and clerk – both ward inmates – the maintenance of fires, the obtaining of wood and the carrying, boiling and issuing of water was organised. At the time of writing this I almost wonder why such ordinary and apparently simple things should be mentioned but at the time they presented real difficulties owing to the shortage of manpower. The wardmaster who failed at any time to have such services running smoothly soon saw the failure reflected in the mental and physical condition of his patients.

Messing

With a ward largely consisting of bed patients, messing presented a difficulty which required careful attention. Firstly, all mess gear had to be collected, sterilized, and returned to the rightful owners. This necessitated in itself a considerable quantity of boiling water which was kept at the boil during the process of sterilization. Mess was then served with the maximum of speed under the supervision of an N.C.O., preferably an experienced man. Speed was essential so that containers could be returned for other wards. When the meal was concluded any swill was collected, mess gear washed up and returned to patients. With a ward of 180 finishing meals to everyone's satisfaction was a big job. It was probably the most essential of many in a wardmasters' day because so much depended on the consumption of all available food. To live, patients had to eat but if left to themselves a very large proportion would not look at food much much less eat it. They complained that food nauseated them, they could not eat rice anyway and all sort of other excuses, many of them quite understandable in view of their physical condition, but they had to be compelled to eat. The wardmaster soon got to know the finicky eaters and then spent each mealtime in persuading, cajoling, begging or bullying those articulate patients. On occasions I have had to resort to forced feeding and have had to hold men's noses to make them open their mouths. It was often necessary to make Nursing Orderlies feed people who refused to do so themselves but eat they must and eat they did. I believe that a considerable number of men on this force died of starvation alone. I am equally certain that the wardmaster system saved many lives in this way alone. You will probably say "What about Nursing Staff it was this anyway their job"? I will deal with that aspect later when discussing staffs. It was very noticeable at Tanbaya that the most difficult patients to feed came from camps such as Sonkurai No.5 Camp NIEKE, where wardmasters were not in operation. A great many of these troops were lamentably debilitated through self-starvation and resented [being] forced to eat. To my mind the strongest argument in favour of the system was a comparison of the physical condition of patients from Shimo Sonkuri with those from other camps.

Certain patients were in receipt of special diets and it was always necessary to check on the special orders to see that the patient received his extra food. It was not uncommon for a patient to say he did not feel like food and to endeavour to give away the very food which would probably save his life.

Treatment

Although the wardmaster had no medical training he was vested with absolute authority in his ward and everyone in that ward was responsible to him, including the medical N.C.O. in charge of medical staff. In the average ward treatments were many and varied. Admittedly patients with similar diseases were inmates of the same ward but even so their treatment differed. It was primarily the duty of the medical N.C.O. to keep his treatment records up to date each day after the M.O.'s round and to administer in due course any treatment required. The wardmaster had to continually satisfy himself that the correct treatment as laid down was being carried out. It was surprising the number of times that patients were overlooked or neglected particularly in busy wards. They would not have received adequate treatment in the absence of the wardmaster.

Hygiene

Absolute cleanliness of wards was one of the few safeguards against the spread of disease – particularly dysentery which could have resulted very easily into a more appalling death rate than actually happened. The greatest difficulty was experienced at Tanbaya in the initial stages in training patients in ordinary domestic cleanliness and preventing them from defecating and urinating just wherever and whenever they felt inclined. Bed patients were often too lazy to call for a bedpan or at any rate to call early enough and would defecate through the slats of the bay. Others – sometimes light duty personnel – would again through laziness – defecate in the passage way or through the slats without any thought of their health or that of anyone else. At Tanbaya this filthy and dangerous practice was so bad at first that picquets with bamboo canes were mounted on latrines and in wards during the hours of darkness in an endeavour to compel troops to use the latrines and not the adjacent surroundings. The most extraordinary aspect of this serious state of affairs was the disinclination or downright refusal of other patients to name the culprits who must have been known to some of them.

Some of the language used by me explaining to the ward what I thought of these people and what would happen to them if they were apprehended was neither printable nor credible, nor did it have much effect. However I caught a light duty man in the act of urinating between the slats of the bay one morning and promptly knocked him down. The condition of the ward improved overnight and eventually the average patient became hygiene minded. The lack of the wardmaster's influence was clearly reflected in the personnel from camps other than Shimo Sonkurai. Indiscriminate defecation and urination as well as general lack of ward discipline were characteristic of their behaviour.

Personal cleanliness also came within the purview of the wardmaster. The medical staff attended to the washing of the bed patients but walking patients had in many instances had to be driven to wash themselves and their clothing.

At Shimo Sonkurai 4 M.O.s were available and as many as 1456 patients while at Tanbaya 10 (of which no more than 5 were ever available for duty) attended to 1750. That it was impossible for M.O.s to take part in Ward Administration is self-evident.

2. The object of the system depended upon the wardmaster being vested with absolute authority and he must receive full support from his S.M.O. As it was unpopular with Medical Staff generally who resented non-medical interference.

3. It is the only system which ensures the patient receiving the best possible treatment.

4. It is the only possible means of enforcing Ward discipline immediately and effectively.

Morale

Apart from looking after and attending to the physical requirements of the patients the wardmaster's primary object was the maintenance of morale. The most effective way of doing this was by personally visiting every man at least once a day, listening to his troubles and discussing with him any subject as far removed from his complaint; also keeping him advised of any camp gossip. Food and the iniquities of the kitchen staff were a constant source of conversation. The patience of Job was required. The same stories were told day after day and the same answers given. Another visit was advisable after dark because I consider a cheerful word at that time of day when things always appear worse, very helpful.

Entertainment at night was also the wardmaster's responsibility – lectures and talks generally – and was found to be the greatest help in the bolstering up of morale. It must be remembered that there was no illumination of any kind – except of course fires – and the hours between 2100 and 2230 were pretty miserable without something to distract the patient's thought from his ailments.

Canteens came under this heading. At Shimo Sonkurai and Tanbaya canteen supplies were neither regular nor adequate but were of tremendous importance to troops when they did arrive. Tobacco was in particular request, and the immediate distribution made a great difference. If for instance tobacco was held overnight when it could have been issued late in the evening, the spirits of the average ward showed a marked decline.

Staff

The handling of ward staff, particularly in a very sick ward, was the most difficult task a watdmaster had to perform. As previously stated, for the system to work properly he must have absolute control over the medical N.C.O. who is nominally in charge of the nursing side of the wad under the supervision of the ward medical officer. Otherwise, if his common sense suggests to him that patients are not being properly handled, he is powerless to act.

At Tanbaya the medical personnel were drawn from N.C.Os. and men of the R.A.M.C. and the A.A.M.C. who had previously worked at various camps from No.5 to NIEKE, excluding Kami Sonkurai from which no personnel sick or otherwise were sent to Tanbaya. I do not know how or by whom these medical personnel were detailed for Burma, but I do know from personal experience that they were not truly representative of their units. Many were particularly lacking in those attributes which are normally associated with Army Medical Units.

As regards R.A.M.C. personnel generally I found a lack of

adaptability which I can only attribute to their training. They were slow to improvise where improvisation meant existence. There were a number of particularly able and conscientious dressers among them but a greater proportion were lazy. If a member of the R.A.M.C. was good he was excellent – if not he was useless in a technical sense.

The A.A.M.C. personnel were more at home in the difficult and uncomfortable conditions in which they were compelled to work but they were often unreliable and on occasions their attitude to patients left a lot to be desired.

There were however some outstanding N.C.Os. from both Corps. Chronic illness was of course rife among medical personnel. One small medical unit lost 29 N.C.Os. and men by illness.

The volunteer orderlies, often N.C.Os. were by and large a long way ahead of the personnel of the medical units. They were enthusiastic in the extreme and individually took a personal interest in their patients. They never hesitated to perform the most unpleasant and dirty jobs, and very soon acquired the art of dressing. Procrastination so evident in medical personnel, was not one of their faults.

Deaths

The death rate during the cholera epidemic and later at Tanbaya was naturally high and every individual death required the immediate attention of the wardmaster to take possession of any kit. It was not possible to trust anyone – again with the exception of a few N.C.Os. – to take charge of a dead man's kit which if not immediately taken over by the wardmaster rarely contained anything of value. At night it was not possible to do this but often men died during the night without being discovered until dawn. Consequently the wardmaster's first duty at reveille was to collect what was left of the gear of men then discovered. The neighbours of the dead were often less trustworthy than the orderlies. If the sick man was in possession of a watch, the wardmaster usually endeavoured to obtain possession of this by some subterfuge or other. Rarely was a watch discovered in the possession of a dead man.

Paper

The duties of a wardmaster were not any easier by the complete lack of paper. He became accustomed to writing on bamboo in

Thailand but Burma suitable bamboo was unavailable and it was necessary to use long narrow strips. Cemete rolling leeping [correct record keeping?] was consequently a work of art. One's patience was tried to its limits when a sudden deluge of rain swamped the administration bay making all bamboo records unreadable.

General System
Once a day all the Wardmasters attended a conference called by the S.M.O. hut which one subject of peeting [keeping?] the general running of the hospital was considered. This resulted in a Wardmaster being kept right up to date in all hospital affairs, likewise the administration was fully aware of what was going on in the wards.

Conclusions
The system is an excellent one anywhere and is absolutely essential in hospitals were M.O.s. owing to pressure of work cannot possibly control the internal organisation of wards. Understand the normal establishment for a 600 bed hospital provided for at least 15 M.O.s.

A Wardmaster is on duty 24 hours a day. He must be even-tempered but willing and able to hit hard if necessary.

I am satisfied that no one can eulogise sufficiently the work of the medical officers who staffed the hospitals at Shimo Sonkurai, Tanbaya, and Konchanabri, particularly the two former where conditions were at their worst. Never have I seen such untiring efforts made to save life and relieve pain at all hours of the day and night.

Only first class organisation and daily attention to detail prevented Tanbaya from becoming a place of death and misery.

(Sgd) George W. Gwynne
Captain
2/4 M.G. Bn. A.I.F.

CHAPTER 14

Extract from the Report of Capt. Wilson R.A.M.C. Nutrition Expert with "F" Force

<u>Nutrition.</u>

<u>Rations.</u> Ready cooked food was supplied during the five day train journey from Singapore, and the three weeks or so on the march. The meals consisted of boiled rice and watery vegetable stews containing a few pieces of cucumber, pumpkin or onion – only suffice to stave off the pangs of hunger for a few hours. The usual issue was two meals a day, plus some cold and occasionally pieces of dried fish as a haversack ration for the midnight halt. People in possession of Thai currency could buy extra food from wayside hawkers during the first week of the march, but even with this addition few men were able to maintain weight and strength during this period of exertion. At the fixed camps the I.J.A. supplied uncooked rations. Theoretically, the ration was the same as at Changi, but in practise the amount handed over each day varied according to the stocks in hand, the state of communications with the outside world and the mood of the Japanese Quartermaster. Another cause of variation was the idea held by some officials, and at times openly expressed by them, that sickness, even though not feigned in order to avoid work, was a gross breach of discipline and an act of sabotage against the Japanese War Effort. Instructions were actually issued officially from the I.J.A. HQ fixing a scale of 600 gms rice daily for those working for the I.J.A. on the road and railway projects; 400 gms daily for those on camp duties; and only 200 gms daily for those classified as unfit or sick. As sick and convalescents always exceeded the workers, sometimes by three

or four to one, this order meant a marked a reduction in the total amount of food issued to a camp. Although some adjustment and improvement of the sick men's rations was usually possible in our own cook-house, the manual workers dare not be penalised to much for the benefit of the sick. Items such as potatoes and boxed meat provided another cause of variation. The Japanese Q.M. would issue a certain number of bags or boxes of these commodities regardless of their state of fitness for human consumption and this total number would be shown on his records. The preserved meat, a course fibered meat, probably buffalo meat without bone, was partially salted or pickled and arrived packed in boxes. It usually swarmed with blow fly maggots and was usually in such an advanced state of decomposition that, as a grey-green fluid it dropped through the seams of the boxes. Only one box might be salvaged of meat worth cooking from four or five issued. Sacks of potatoes suffered greatly from wet during transit and storage, and many were only fit for the refuge pit. (We may add that our standard of what was fit for consumption was a local one far below anything held before leaving Changi). The rice provided was a highly milled, medium grade Burma rice; both it and the dried beans were heavily infested with weevils. Cattle which had been driven on hoof all the way from Burma provided the fresh meat; they were just as exhausted by their walk as the prisoners; they often died on the way and there was usually great anxiety to get our butchers to work before too many succumbed on arrival at the camps.

Supplements to the ration. It was impossible to supplement the rations at all adequately by local purchases, Nieke village was the only trading centre in the neighbourhood of the camps, and the one storekeeper with whom trading was permitted had a meagre selection of foodstuffs at high prices. Palm sugar cost 40 ticals (Thai dollars) per 15 oz tin. The men received pay at the rate of ¼ tical (25 cents) when working. The sick received no pay. The camp hospitals had first claim on valuable foods such as green grams which came in later. Coconut oil cost 35 ticals per 4 gallons, canned herrings 3 ticals per 15 oz tin. At no time were the amounts available sufficient to make any appreciable difference to the food value of the camp rations as a whole, until after the return to Kanburi at the end of November, where food was more plentiful and supplementary items cheaper. A supplement which may have made some difference to food in general was when a specimen of green leaves was shown to Maj. J.A. Reid by a Burmese at Nieke. Later a large patch of these plants was found nearby and sufficient was collected daily to add to the stew for the whole camp. It was a leguminous plant, later identified as a species of Cassia (family-Leguminosae), popularly known as wild-peanut. Near Sonkrai camp, a large area of ground was covered with a species of wild gourd akin to snake-gourd (family-Cucurbitaceae) the leaves of which made a palatable stew when cooked. The use of this was suggested to the officers of the camp by Maj. Reid. At Sami-Sonkrai the leaves of a certain climbing plant were similarly used. This was not identified with certainty but was thought to belong to the family Sterculiaceae. The leaves were large and hairy but fairly soft when boiled and produced a syrupy soup. Parties of convalescents were organised to pick these various plants daily, special quantities were given to those suffering from Beri beri and other deficiency conditions. The men had great faith in the value of their green stews.

Collection of data. Ration figures were collected from a number of camps on the spot, others were obtained later on from the "Q" staff of camps who had sufficient paper to keep records. One Q.M. replied to our request for information by stating that he had been in the habit of keeping his records on the shoulder blade of an ox which he had not brought back to Changi with him ...

Remarks on the diet. (a) Rations for June and early July were particularly poor. This was the time when some camps, notably those in Konkoita and Nieke area were almost cut off from communication with the outside world. No adequate reserve stocks were laid in before the rains came, and as it was uncertain how long it would be before more supplies could get through rations were cut drastically. At Nieke in the middle of June the whole camp was receiving an issue of white rice 270 gms, dried lima beans 24 gms, fresh meat 50 mgs including bone, per head per day. This works out at an energy value of 1200 calories, less than that required for basal metabolism. At about the same time the Konkoita camps for 8 ton 10 days were on a diet of 300 gms white rice daily, and a little salt, varied occasionally by the omission of the salt. On this diet men were compelled to do heavy manual work on road and railway

133

cuttings. (b) The later months showed an improvement in energy value except where there was a discrimination against the sick men, but only once did this food value reach a reasonable figure for the work being done. (c) Approx. 80 % of the total energy value was supplied by carbohydrate, and about 90 % of this carbohydrate was derived from highly-milled rice. (d) Protein was usually small in amount and little of it was animal origin. (e) The amount of fat was inordinately low at all camps. (f) There was a complete absence of green leaf vegetables and fruit, except later on return to Kanburi, consequently very low figures for vitamins A and C. (g) The Thiamin (Vitamin B1) values were well below the estimated normal requirements except at Tanbaya Hospital, Burma, from the last week in Oct. onwards when rice polishings were supplied in reasonable quantities. ...

Given only these details one could have predicted with certainty that a severe outbreak of beri beri must develop sooner or later. When to them we add periods of semi-starvation, the widespread occurrence of cholera, dysentery, diarrhoea and malaria, tragic results were inevitable.

CHAPTER 15

Sickness and Death Rates

Lack of Medical Records makes it impossible to compute accurately either the amount of sickness caused by the different diseases or the total amount of sickness from all diseases. The best that can be done is to make rough estimates based on information supplied by our own observations and by observations of other M.Os.

(a) Incidence of diseases. Cholera attacked about 1300 persons with an immediate mortality pf about 50% but the ultimate mortality may have been 80-90%. Few of the cholera convalescents made a complete recovery and many eventually succumbed to other diseases. Malaria attacked about 80% and there were a few cases of blackwater fever. Dysentery and diarrhoea were widespread throughout, and almost everyone developed a state of incipient beri beri. Bugs, lice and scabies affected practically everyone. These pests were responsible for much loss of sleep, and infected scratches were frequently the starting points of septic sores and ulcers.

Lung disease like bronchitis and pneumonia were surprisingly rare considering the living and working conditions.

(b) Total sickness. Certain records still exist showing daily number sick and number at work. Here are a few examples:-

Camp	Date	Camp population	Number sick	Number demanded for work
Shimo-Sonkurai	19th July	1850	1350	353
Kami-Sokurai	16th Aug	1670	1075	450
Takanun	Mid July	564	464	160
Sonkurai	25th July	1300	1050	280

Remembering that the prisoners themselves supplied all the labour for the cookhouse (including water carrying and wood cutting and collection in the surrounding jungles) and for camp maintenance and also all medical staff required to deal with such large numbers of sick, one can readily perceive from these figures that the I.J.A. demands for workers were indeed excessive. But the records do not show the true position in other respects. Had the medical standards for the unfit for work been anything like normal, the proportion of sick to workers would have been very much higher than recorded above.

A progressive deterioration in physical condition occurred as the months went by. This deterioration was noticed at the time, but it became strikingly obvious when one was able to compare the returned men of "F" Force with the men who had returned to Changi. Some idea of it is given by the results of an inspection made by I.J.A. medical officers in February 1944. 1420 Australian troops (excluding those in hospital) were examined two months after returning to Changi, and only 125 were classified as fit for heavy duty.

One can conclude that only an insignificant fraction of the "F" Force survivors can have remained free from disease; the overwhelming majority suffered from several diseases either in succession or in conjunction.

(c) <u>Death and death rates.</u> Of the 6998 men who left Singapore in the second half of April 1943, 3087 died during the 12 months May 1943-April 1944, giving a crude death rate of 441 per mille per annum[80]. Analysis and discussion of individual causes of death must be prefaced by a reminder of the prevalence of diarrhoea, beri-beri, malari and ulcers. Failure to mention any one of the diseases in the actual death report may mean that it was not an immediate cause of death, but certainly does not exclude the possibility of it contributing thereto. This fact has influenced the remarks that follow ...

The only deaths not based on medical officers' reports are some of those occurring in transit camps and in about 20 escapees who are assumed to have died in the jungle. About 30 death

---

[80] Per mille means parts per thousand.

reports gave three or more causes ... Movements of populations make it useless to attempt comparison of the health of different camps by months. Thus the sudden drop in deaths at Sonkurai from 275 in August to 12 in September, was due far more to the removal of all the sick men to Tanbaya and their replacement by fit men from Shimo-Sonkurai and Nieke than any miraculous improvement of conditions at the camp itself. We will deal then mainly with the time sequence of deaths in the force as a whole. Grouping of the deaths into periods of four months each, to correspond with the distinct phases of the Force's existence, helps to bring out the main points.

Death rate per mille per annum

Population at beginning	Cholera	Dysentery & Diarrhoea	Beri-beri	Malaria	Ulcers	Total
May-Aug 1943						
6998	269	176	38	27	10	595
Sept-Dec 1943						
5613	5	218	163	31	77	841
Jan-Apr 1944						
-	10	15	7	2	-	93

The first period, May, June, July, August, 1943 covers the march and the greater part of the monsoon; by the end of it the move to Tanabaya Hospital in Burma was practically completed.

Cholera was the greatest killer, causing half of the total deaths, with dysentery a close second, and all other diseases lagging well behind.

The second period, September, October, November, December, 1943, includes the last months of the monsoon, the finishing of the railroad and the return move to Kanburi and Singapore, 500 were at Kanburi and only 300 still in Burma. Cholera had become negligible as a direct cause of death, and dysentery, beri-beri and ulcers were all powerful. The total death rate had increased by 246 and averaged 841 per mille per annum over this four month period.

The third period, January, February, March, April, 1944, was the period of recuperation. All I.J.A. work had ceased, and living conditions, food and drug supplies were better for everyone. The death rate fell rapidly and averaged 93 per mille per annum over the period, although this was still very high in comparison with the Singapore rate of 13 per mille for the first twelve months of imprisonment ...

The crude death rate from all causes per mille per annum for each month was:-

1943

May	June	July	Aug	Sept	Oct	Nov	Dec
314	748	451	1048	1082	928	1006	778

1944

Jan	Feb	Mar	April
226	79	37	37

Reference to the table will show a rough time sequence of diseases with cholera as the prime cause of death in May and June; dysentery deaths increasing rapidly in July with a sharp peak in August; ulcer deaths at a maximum in September; and deaths from beri-beri alone at their highest in November, but those from beri-beri combined with other diseases remaining at a high level from August to December.

The very high rates for August and September must to some extent be attributable to the movement of the sick to theTanbaya Hospital camp in Burma. About 1900 men participated in this move, which started at the beginning of August and was completed by the second week in September. The journey was a trying one even for the more or less fit men of the hospital staff, its effect on the sick can be judged by the fact that, out of a total of 748 deaths occurring at Tanbaya during the six months of its occupation, 310 deaths took place during September. There was a much smaller step up in the death rate at the time of the return move to Kanburi in November.

Our impression however, was that the men who died during a move or shortly afterwards would almost certainly have died later on i.e. that the moves acted mainly as accelerators of the fatal ending. The records for Kami-Sonkurai, the one camp north of Nieke which did not send patients to Burma, tend to confirm this impression. This camp had originally consisted of 396 Australians, and up to the end of July they had lost 23 men, 14 of them from cholera. It was filled up to a strength of 1685 in the first week of August with batches of men from Nieke, Shimo-Sonkurai and Changaraya. Many of these men were unfit and would have been sent to Tanbaya Hospital had it not been that the number to go there had been fixed by the I.J.A. sometime beforehand and could not be increased. At Kami-Sonkurai it will be noted that the food was sufficient in quantity but just as unbalanced dietetically as elsewhere; while working conditions were among the worse experienced. The only changes in population were the losses from deaths and the arrival of a small party of 54 men from Changaraya in September. From the first of August until the 28th of November, when the camp was finally vacated, there occurred 490 deaths. The transformation of deaths per month into death rates per mille per annum exaggerates the figures considerably when dealing with figures in general. The death rates from all causes were: August 481, September 787, October 1150, November 1399, with a steady increase from month to month in the death rate from dysentery, beri-beri and ulcers.

One can only wonder what the December death rate might have been; it is certainly not surprising that everyone in the camp was convinced that their one hope lay in a speedy removal to the more cultivated areas near Kanburi, and that morale fell to a very low level when this removal was repeatedly deferred.

We think it quite probable that, had it not been for the mass move to Burma, the deaths for the Force as a whole would have followed a similar course to those at Kami-Sonkurai. We can express our opinion of the total deaths by saying that about 73% could well be grouped together under the composite heading of Dysentery, Ber-beri, Ulcers and Malaria (with cholera as an additional contributary cause in about one-fifth of these); with 21% being put down as directly due to cholera, and 6% being caused by small-pox, diphtheria, pneumonia, and "other diseases".

REPORTS TO IMPROVE CONDITIONS

To become prisoners of war is a considerable error of judgement. It will be realised that we were not our own masters. Every effort was made by the "F" Force Commander and his staff from the outset, and by the officers of each marching party and working camp, to help to get big and little things put right. A heavy strain was put upon them and upon the interpreters. Stereotyped methods such as letters produced little or no result and verbal and very diplomatic means were tried, varying from "a firm stand" to trading one's cigarette case or fountain pen, or giving English lessons to Korean guards – all with the same end in view and with regrettably little result ...

The S.M.Os. visits to other camps to attempt to coordinate or improve medical work were almost impossible to achieve and, when permission was granted, they were so brief as to be valueless. During the whole period I saw Camps 1 and 4 once, Tanbaya Hospital twice, Camp 3 four times, Camp 5 never. The S.M.O. worked at Nieke, Sonkurai and Kanchanabri (Kanburi) for varying periods.

ACKNOWLEDGEMENTS

In this sombre report it is pleasant to record the immense help and support received from the Force Commander (Lieut-Colonel G.W. Harris, O.B.E., R.A.) who used every resource to improve our lot. To Lieut-Colonel F.J. Dillon, M.C., R.A.M.C, who commanded Nieke and later No.2 Camp and who managed financial aid for our Camps and the Hospitals at Kanburi and Tanbaya. To his diplomacy, ingenuity and energy, the members of this Force are under a heavy debt.

I am indebted to Lieut-Colonel C.T. Hutchison, R.A., for much good advice and for his work as an Administrative Commandant, Tanbaya Hospital. The whole Force owes much to the efforts of the Interpreters, Major C. Wild, Oxf. & Bucks L. I., Captain G.G. Waller, F.M.S.V.F.[81], Lieut. Fletcher, Gordons; large demands were made upon their courage and ability. Many Combatant officers worked as Wardmasters under the exceptional conditions prevailing in Thailand and were of the utmost use, special mention should be made of Lieut. R. Eaton, A.I.F., Lieut. A. Ellerman, A.I.F., Lieut. Geikie, A.I.F., Capt. Gibson, A.I.F., Major Auld, R.O.A.C., Major M.D. Price, R. Sigs., Capt. J. Ainger, R. Sigs., for their invaluable services. Capt. T. Wilson, R.A.M.C., who was the expert in nutrition with "F" Force has been good enough to collect from many sources the figures for rations issued by the I.J.A. and to make an analysis of the food value therein. On return to Changi he also re-checked these figures and the figures

---

[81] Federated Malay States Volunteer Forces.

for deaths by diseases. This has been work of great complexity and magnitude and every credit is due to him for the results obtained ...

Not least, the Medical Officers of this dismal expedition gave their best to their patients and loyally supported me. I am indeed grateful to them for their sustained and unfortunately often unavailing efforts against appalling odds.

SUMMARY

The main factors which contributed to the appalling sickness and death rates in "F" Force have been mentioned in this report. The apportionment of blame for the conditions described is a matter for consideration by higher authority. These factors may be briefly recapitulated:-

1) Wrong information was given at the onset to the effect that the party would have light work amid pleasant surroundings and that food would be better than at Changi. This led to the inclusion in the force of a large number of delicate men suffering from the effects of previous disease and dietary deficiency.

2) Almost complete lack of transport and general organisation to get the force to its working camps in Thailand. This led to the forced march under shocking conditions, to the loss of practically all our own medical supplies, and to the breaking down of the strength of even the fittest elements in the parties as they had to overtax themselves with carriage of stores and sick comrades.

3) Failure to provide provisioned staging camps on the way.

4) Siting of camps in malarious and insanitary areas often in the close proximity to disease infected coolies.

5) Not stopping movement on the first information that cholera had broken out.

6) Lack of provision of adequate provisions and accommodation (during monsoon weather) on arrival at working area. Bad siting of camps. No time or personnel allowed to get the camps in order when the parties arrived.

7) Excessive demands for labour and excessive hours under cruel conditions resulting in a heavy sick rate and inadequate camp maintenance staffs.

8) The pernicious system of reducing the ration scale for the sick far below basal metabolic requirements.
9) Failure to call a halt to the above conditions even when the results were blatantly apparent to the most ignorant and stupid of our guardians.
10) Lack of provision of special transport or accommodation for the sick. (Ambulance cars were used for transporting rations and the sick were carried by their less sick comrades).

SUMMARY ON RETURN TO CHANGI
British

Departed April 1943		3336
Died in Burma and Thailand	2012	
and earlier parties on return		
to Changi up to 27-4-44	17	2029
Escapes (fate unknown)	5	
Missing	1	
Unconfirmed death report	1	7
Alive		1300
		3336

A.I.F

Departed April 1943	3662
Died in Burma and Thailand	
and earlier parties on return	
to Changi up to 27-4-44	1058
Alive	2604
	3662

J. Huston
Lieut-Colonel, R.A.M.C.,
S.M.O. "F" Force

CHAPTER 16

Report on Tanbaya Hospital Subsequent to Departure of Main Body 24 Nov 43

The I.J.A. ordered the occupation of huts 4, 5, 6, 7 and 8 and the move of patients was carried out before the main body left. No.8 Hut remained the H.Q. Hut.

The administrative problems were the same as before – shortage of labour (in the initial stages), lack of tools and shortage of water being the main ones. With the smaller numbers to cook for a more varied form of meals was possible. Canteen supplies became more readily obtainable and eggs at a reasonable price became almost plentiful.

About 16 December it was realised that the water supply would present a serious problem in the near future and water for the cookhouse had to be obtained from the well (Well C) besides the stream, a lift and force pump being provided. A month later washing points had to be established at the well. Towards the end of January the well on the west side (Well "B") went dry and the well on the east (Well "B") showed signs of doing so and it was therefore necessary to impose restrictions on washing for a couple of days or so.

The rations had to be collected from ANAQUIN by a yak cart, which was manhandled. This required a minimum of six men and was an every other day fatigue, which was initially a strain on the manpower situation. At first the rations were good but at the end of December the rice was reduced to a ration of 600 grs per day, seldom though were more than 550 grs received; some extra vegetables were issued. After about three weeks the rice ration was increased a little. On the whole, however, the ration was adequate, though of course not properly balanced. The issue of rice polishings continued all the time. Special Xmas Day fare was put on by the cooks and a free issue of cheroots, eggs and bananas was made to the patients. Great credit id due to Lieut. Dean and his cookhouse staff for their herculean efforts, which were appreciated to the full.

CHAPTER 17

Extract from Health of "F" Force May to November, 1943

The staple article of diet was rice, supplemented by small and varying quantities of dried "Chinese radish" beans, whitebait, dried meat, oil, and in some camps (e.g. No.2 during June and July) some lean local beef. During 4 months at No.2 Camp one bag of Rice Polishings was supplied. Rice Polishings were also supplied to Tanbaya Hospital, Burma, after repeated requests from 15 October 1943 until it closing down – with very beneficial results in the health of the patients and staff there. The amount of rice issued for the men working was slightly deficient in total calories, that for Camp staff more so, that for the sick was totally inadequate for the maintenance of body weight, and the recovery of health. Efforts were made in all camps to use local produce e.g. wild pumpkin leaves, to build up deficiencies. There is a report from Capt. T. Wilson, R.A.M.C. Dietician with "F" Force [see below] which gives an accurate picture of this diet, its intended distribution and effects.

No.2 Camp
31.7.43

Diet.

Major Dobson R.A.S.C. has supplied figures for the rations actually received for the 16 day period 6-21 July 1943, of different amounts to separate groups, such as working parties, camp duty men and the sick, but the main difference is in the amount of rice supplied to each group. Assuming that items such as onions, beans, potatoes, whitebait, dried meat and oil were supplied and divided equally I estimate that these supply only 340 Calories per man per day.

2.   The remainder of the energy requirements have to be made up from the rice issue. Rice provides approximately 360 Calories per 100 grms. (dry weight). Sick men receive roughly 300 gms of rice per day so that their diet only gives about 1420 Calories. This is below the amount needed basal metabolism and maintenance of the body weight even in health, and quite inadequate to help a patient through an attack of disease or to enable him to recuperate afterwards. In other words once a man goes sick he either dies of disease or he is gradually starved to death. I consider the present very high death rate, in the absence of acute epidemic disease, must be largely the result of this very poor diet.

3.   The energy values for the camp duty men, assuming 600 gms. of rice is 2500 calories, and for working parties, assuming 700 gms. rice and 100 gms. dried fish, is 3,000 calories. These figures are better though still well below normal requirements for the type of work done, but the diet of all groups is seriously lacking in vitamins, particularly those of the B Complex; Beri-beri is already prevalent and increasing. The diet is also lacking in fat and protein.

4.   I consider it essential that the ration for sick and convalescents should be increased to at least 400 gms. rice per day and that an essential, Rice polishings, more towgay, peanuts, potatoes, green leaf vegetables and fats should be provided for everyone to make good the existing deficiencies. There is sufficient wild pumpkin leaf growing in the isolation camp area, with leaf green vegetables for quite a long time. The leaves have been pointed out to several people including officers."

The poor diet, especially defective in Vitamins A & B was, in my opinion, the most important factor in producing the enormous sick and death rates which prevailed in "F" Force during the whole period. The ration of the sick was supplemented by deductions from that of the fitter personnel, while local purchases from Camp Funds, of tinned milk, fish, sugar, the only articles procurable, were used to make the diet of the very sick a little more nourishing and attractive. This could only be done in a very small way and only in some camps. No sick man could lose a single day's feeding without the direst consequences. With the neuses of Malaria or the flux of dysentery upon them, eating was difficult, and sometimes impossible. Thus many prisoners died.

4. Working Conditions.

The day after arrival, despite exhaustions, unroofed huts in the torrential rains, the presence of cholera in all parties, the maximum numbers of men demanded by the Japanese Army Engineers for work on road and railway making. This continued every day. In general the work was heavy – clearing jungle, building bridges, digging cuttings and embankments and road-making. The working hours were long and arduous. Men arose at 7 a.m. had breakfast and were marched out at 8 a.m. (dawn) they returned from work 12 to 19 hours later. They worked 7 days a week. Many men did not see their camp in the day light for weeks on end. Insufficient men were left in camp to improve conditions there. Latrines, washing places, food serving points where containers could be sterilized, awaited construction or improvement everywhere. The daily sick rate mounted rapidly. Here are the figures for No.3 Camp (at that time probably the fittest and best fed camp) for the first 9 days after their arrival on the evening of the 25th May 1943.

26th May. Original strength 7 officers, 386 O.R. (all A.I.F.). Cleaning camp which was very foul as it was occupied by Cholera and dysentery infected coolies.

		Working	Sick	Camp Duties
May	27th	330	50	13
	28th	285	90	18
	29th	282	93	18
	30th	271	103 (1 death)	18
	31st	267	107	18
June	1st	260	113 (1 death)	18
	2nd	215	160	18
	3rd	215	160	18
	4th	182	193	18

That the Engineers were quickly destroying their source of labour was explained to our I.J.A. Headquarters by the Force commander. Even Lt. Col. Banno understood this, but the state of affairs continued.

The condition of the sick was demonstrated to the local Engineers. They would rush out of the sick huts rather than endure the sight of the results of their inhuman treatment.

Numbers were demanded and if they were not supplied they were taken out of the hospital huts in camps, despite the utmost protests of our officers and Doctors. The 8 a.m. parade was generally known as the "Murder parade" and not without foundation.

By the end of June 5,000 men north of Neieke, 700 were at work daily and at least half of this 700 were unfit and useless for heavy work. Apart from the Red Cross men and the small camp staff, the remainder were lying ill in Camp hospitals. Working conditions continued in this way until the railway was completed at the end of October.

Our own administration and camp staffs made repeated pleas and suggestions to ameliorate working conditions with slight or little success. The Engineers appeared to have complete control of working conditions and were insensible to and of our requests. The I.J.A. Administrative Staff on the other hand, appeared in certain camps to be concerned about the condition of their prisoners. Camps at Niele, Shimo Sonkurai, (from early August) managed to improve sanitation and accommodation by getting a proportion of working men off outside work for short periods.

At Tanbaya Hospital (August 1943-January 1944) men were only required to work on maintaining their own camps.

5. Accommodation

Accommodation was always totally inadequate. Prisoners, whether in hospital or fit, lay closely packed, touching each other on platforms made of split bamboo. In many huts there were two decks of platforms so that men had to climb ladders to get to bed. These added to the difficulties of reaching the latrines in the dark. Scabies was universal owing to the crowding. Louse infestation was widespread. At No.2 Camp these conditions were so bad that epidemic typhus seemed likely to occur. Fortunately the transfer of large numbers of sick to Tanbaya in August removed this threat. The huts were made of bamboo, roofed with attap. (At Timonta and Tarkanun only (Camp No.4) men were accommodated in tents. Huts were partially or completely roofless for the first week or two. The roofs leaked and gullies of storm water ran through them during rainstorms.

Bugs were universal. They added to lack of sleep and sceptic skin conditions. Accommodation to segregate cholera patients from others was not provided at Camp 5 until mid-June though the epidemic started in mid-May. The same happened at Tarkanun. At the hospital at Kanburi (Dec 43-April 44) where general conditions had improved enormously accommodation was still tight. Huts 132 ft x 21 ft held 120 patients.

6. Water.

At all camps water was available from adjoining streams or the river, except at Tanbaya where there were 2 wells (which dried) and a river 800 yards away. At Kanburi II there were 2 small wells and a water cart service from the river 1 mile away. At no camp or hospital was there a piped supply.

Drinking water had to be boiled before use, mess tins and eating utensils had to be sterilized for each meal. Shortage of containers for water storage and sterilization was a most difficult problem (except at Kanburi where containers brought from Changi were available). 44 gallon drums were used (extensively) where they could be procured. In some cases e.g. Camp 5, although there were plenty of drums, we were not allowed to use them. Our own water sterilising powder and tablets were conserved for use during moves.

Ablution. Men bathed in the river when opportunity occurred. Bathing parades were allowed at both camps – the difficulty was that the working parties did not get back to camp until dark – when bathing was prohibited. At Camp 3 the only bathing place available was a small creek which ran through the middle of the camp. It drained the seepage of the area and was most foul.

7. Cooking.

This was done in saucer-like metal bowls (Kuelas)[82] holding 12 gallons, heated over open trench fires or built up on mud platforms. Cooking was done in the open with light bamboo and attap superstructure. Working conditions were difficult in the rains.

8. Latrines.

At halts on the march and at camps on arrival latrines were

---

[82] Possibly he means kawalis.

open trenches of varying depths – 2 ft to 4 ft as a rule. These were foul and teeming with fly lava. Dysentery was rife. On pointing this out to I.J.A. I was told that flies made no difference, all men had been anal swabbed at Changi, and there were no dysentery carriers!! At most camps the latrines were on higher ground owing to high subsoil water. Rainwater washed down the effluent into the living huts and fouled areas of the camps. Efforts were made to improve matters by making deep trench latrines (12 ft to 14 ft) with solid wooden coves and lids making the structure flyproof. Where this was done for sufficient numbers (as in Camp No.1) it was successful. The difficulties in obtaining tools and labour were enormous. More often the trenches were left semi-open with bamboo straddle slats. All latrines were of the squatting type. Separate places were kept for dysentery patients. Bamboo bedpans and later improvised commodes, made from oil tins, were used for the lying sick. Apart from a scanty supply of lime there were no crude antiseptics except a few bottles of our own stock of cresol which were used diluted in bamboo drop bottles for disinfection of hands. Latrine paper was not supplied except later in Burma. Fouling of ground by demoralised men suffering from diarrhoea and dysentery was common. Corduroy tracks to latrines were made gradually to aid men in their journeys through the mud which was difficult to negotiate in the darkness. Strong disciplinary action had usually to be taken to prevent fouling of the ground. Sanitary squads at all camps worked hard and some showed amazing ingenuity in overcoming difficulties.

9. Medical Stores issued by the I.J.A.

Until the return of "F" Force to Kanburi the amount of drugs and dressings issued was minute. Upcountry small issues of drugs were made (as far as I am aware) on three occasions. For months camp hospitals had no drugs to treat dysentery or diarrhoea except charcoal made locally. Torn up shirt sleeves, mosquito netting and banana leaves were used to cover the thousands of ulcers. It was difficult to preserve sufficient wool or gauze to cover the stumps of freshly amputated limbs. Considered carefully it is probable that 70 % of the Force was (and still is) infected with Amoebic Dysentery. Yet the only issue of specific drug was 100 ⅓ grains Emetine Ampules to the Tanabaya Hospital where there were 1500 men in hospital, hundreds of them in need of this particular drug. (The amount received was sufficient for 3 patients judged by normal British standards). Two other camps received smaller quantities and the remainder none. I implored Col. Banno to inform the International Red Cross of our urgent needs of drugs and invalid foods, if the I.J.A. could not supply them. He said I was a "theorist".

On the return of the Force to Kanburi, the supply of drugs was much better and the I.J.A. Commandant (Lieut. Wakabyashi) did everything he could to help us.

Quinine and Anti-Cholera vaccine (given every 3 months) were supplied more liberally. Quinine tablets ($3\frac{1}{2}$ gr) were however much short of our requirements. Suppressive quinine could rarely be used as it was required for treatment purposes of Malaria which eventually affected 50% of the Force. Even then it too frequently fell short of normal treatment requirements. At Kanburi it was possible to provide adequate treatment and adequate suppressive dosage during the greater part of the period with the resulting improvement in the malarial sick rate (50% reduced to 10%). Sulphur was urgently needed for the specific treatment of scabies which affected the whole force. A few grammes only were ever supplied. Our own Administration purchased small quantities through the Canteen supplier at fantastically high prices from September onwards. The supply of this drug was sufficient at Kanburi. Constant demands were made for concentrated Vitamin B extracts or Rice polishings to treat and prevent Beri-beri. From September onwards a supply of Ebios (Yeast) tablets was issued to Camp 3, and Rice polishings was issued to Tanbaya only. At Kanburi it was purchased out of Camp funds. Small quantities of Vitamin B1 ampules for injection were issued by the I.J.A. These were most useful in the acute cardiac emergencies of Beri-beri.

It is hard to conceive why Rice Polishings, which would have saved many cases of Beri-beri, should be difficult to obtain in Burma, Thailand or Malaya, countries with many rice mills. The only answer given was at Kanburi – "They are difficult to obtain because we use them to feed our Cavalry horses."

10. Conditions during movement of prisoners.

Presumably to reinforce labour at various points, or to make room for coolies, frequent movement took place. Conditions then were generally nightmarish. Only a few examples need be quotes (not necessarily the worst).

Camp 4 (400 strength) moved from Taimonta on 21/6/43 carrying by hand their tents, cooking gear, kits and sick, about 50 kms, arriving near Tarkanun. The road was a muddy morass entailing an enormous expenditure of energy; it also entailed walking men over a skeleton bridge 50 ft above a river torrent and across a precipitous cliff face. When this party eventually marched back to Nieke at the beginning of November their numbers were reduced to 100 fit men.

At the end of July orders were received to move all sick and fit men from Nieke to No.2 and No.3 Camps apart from those earmarked to go to Tanbaya Hospital. No transport was to be provided. Force Administration eventually prevailed upon Col. Banno to leave the very ill lying men (about 120). The remaining hospital sick had to march 12 Kms. To Camp 2. We were allowed frequent halts as the men were pathetically weak and ill and the road extremely broken and muddy.

The move of men unlikely to recover under 2 months to Tanbaya Burma commenced at the end of July and continued piece-meal for the following 6 weeks. Transport provided was open lorries on roads and the usual metal rice trucks on rail. At all camps involved there was always complete uncertainty of the time and numbers to move; the I.J.A. guards were always excitable at these times. The sick would be laid out on the sides of the road for hours on I.J.A. orders awaiting lorries; they were frequently taken back to their huts in the evening owing to them not arriving. There was never bedding or straw on the metal floors of the lorries or railway trucks. We had not been able to bring more than half a dozen service stretchers from Bampong (where 200 were left) so bamboo stretchers made with matting or rice sacks were used to carry the lying. The I.J.A were kind enough to provide a quantity of rice sacks in lieu of blankets or bedding. The sick on this move were passed through one or more staging camps at Camp 5, Kandu, Ronchi, on their journey (Nieke-Tanbaya was 83 Kms). The trouble was that no extra accommodation was provided. Camp 5 had shockingly inadequate facilities. One of our Medical Officers with a small medical party was at each of the above camps but arrangements were bad. Only part of the railway in Burma was completed at the time. Guards jabbed ulcerated buttocks and stoned them to "speedo" the unfortunate out again. A party of ulcer patients had to walk 4

Kms from Ronchi to the railway. Their ulcers poured blood over their ankles as they stumbled along. Accomodation in railtrucks varied, the worst case reported was 54 men plus pannier and containers (these trucks measure 19 ft 3 in x 7 ft 3in).

There were some 50 deaths on the move to Tanbaya and hosts of men died soon after arrival there. This table of deaths speaks for itself:-

CAMP	British		Australian	
	Died	Arrived	Died	Arrived
Nieke	71	160	35	143
No.1	-	-	81	342
No.2	408[83]	751	109	380
No.5	70	133	-	-
	549	1044	225	865

Last death 30 January 1944

The move from the Burma-Thailand border to Kamburi was carried out by rail. At the end of November all fit and sick were moved to Kanburi except 316 of the very sick and small staff left at Tanbaya. The latter party moved down at the end of January 1944, their move was well arranged and they were not too overcrowded in the usual metal trucks. There were two deaths on the journey.

The main body at the end of November was not so fortunate. All heavy sick from Nieke, Nos. 2 & 3 Camps – some of them moribund, were ordered to move. Trains were loaded in a hurry – sometimes at night. The guards were sometimes excited. Accommodation – average 30-40 per truck – including very ill men. Our own I.J.A. Administration did try to get more transport and Lt. Wakabyashi and Dr Tanio were obviously distress by conditions, when the parties commenced this journey. 46 men died during the journey and 186 during the first three weeks at Kanburi.

11. Camp Hospitals.

The conditions described in the foregoing paragraphs applied to all Camp Hospitals. Patients were accommodated in tents and

---

[83] Includes six dead on arrival.

huts in the same way as the fit men. There were no special hospital facilities anywhere. The nursing staff consisted of RAMC, AAMC and volunteer orderlies. The sick rate among these was heavy (upcountry there was an average sick rate of 60%) and men had to work like the outside workers when ill, a high proportion died. There were many outstanding workers, who gave of their best without stint; others were of poorer quality, and suffered from lowered morale; medical officers and assistant surgeons were overworked and many were sick (about 60%). It was found that the Wardmaster system – the placing of Combat officers in charge of discipline and detailed administrative arrangements in each hut had great advantages and helped to make things work more smoothly and efficiently. The method was adopted at No.1, 2 and 3 Camps and Tanbaya and Kanburi Hospitals.

Advantages were:-
- (a) It relived the medical staff of much non-medical work e.g. wood, water, feeding, discipline, returns, disposal of effects.
- (b) ensured continuous supervision – which medical officers were unable to do.
- (c) shared the heavy responsibilities of the care of the sick with Medical officers and kept the whole camp informed of current difficulties and the progress of patients ...

This system was first adopted by Major B. Hunt at No.1 Camp and much praise is due to his energy and enthusiasm in training many officers in this work. Officer wardmasters needed to be strong characters, with the wisdom of Solomon and the patience of Job. Their adoption must not be taken to infer criticism of my medical colleagues nor of the other ranks' nursing. They worked endlessly and under as miserable conditions as anyone can imagine. Attending to incontinent and dying men in the darkness of long nights with only the light of a fire or bamboo flares to guide them, required stamina and endless patience. Maintaining the strength of men suffering from disease on the rations issued has been discussed under food. Little could be done to vary the preparation of rice etc. and patients had to be forced to eat to enable them to maintain their weight which once lost could not be regained on the ration. Cooking facilities and the rations did not permit much variety. Rice pep and tea for breakfast, rice and thin stew for dinner, rice and rissole or vegetable hash and tea for supper was the usual fare. Lest it be thought that the subject of food has been laboured this was the I.J.A. ration at Kanburi Hospital (we were fortunate enough to be able to supplement it there with peanuts, eggs, fish and rice polishings bought with officers' subscriptions and Canteen profits).

12. Main diseases.

The predisposing factors – prevailing illness, poor quality and quantity of food, hardship and exposure have been described.

The main diseases were of one general pattern. Most patients suffered from two, three or more conditions at the same time i.e. Malaria, dysentery, ulcers, beri-beri, in any combination.

Cholera epidemic. I.J.A. Medical authorities diagnosed Cholera among the Thai labourers in huts at Konkoita on 15.6.43. Prisoners from Train parties 1-6 had passed through this Camp and occupied its huts. Movement was ordered to continue by the I.J.A. 2 cases of Cholera appeared at No.1 Camp on 17.5.43 and further cases on the 18th, and following days, appeared at Shimo-Nieke on 15th May at No.2 Camp, on 21 May at No.3, 4 and 5 on 26th May. It should be noted that there were great numbers of Tamil, Thai and Burmese labourers in or close to all camps. In some the same huts had been used by them until our arrival (e.g. in Camp 3).

The disease presented no unusual features. The main wave of the epidemic was over by mid-June, but carriers and cases occurred in Camp 3 as late as August and September. The mortality rate varied from 66% to 45% (Nieke and Camp 1). There was a much heavier preponderance of cases and deaths among British Troops than among Australian. This seems to be due to the fact (a) the A.I.F. were a fitter body of men when we left Changi (b) they had been left intact in main units e.g. 26th, 29th and 30th Bns. whereas the British were composed of bits and pieces of many units who had supplied previous Forces from Singapore (c) there were a number of British and Volunteers who had been on Asiatic service for years before the war without a break (d) conditions at Camp 5, a wholly British Camp, were deplorable, accommodation, medical supplies and local I.J.A. Administration were worse than anywhere in our area (d)

Australian troops were better at adapting themselves to strange conditions e.g. many of our British troops after generations of living in towns were at a disadvantage in fending for themselves under these primitive and stark realities (f) the A.I.F. troops in general were more healthy and hygiene minded. They seem to have been taught and learnt the fact that the rules of hygiene are one of the most important essentials in soldiers' training and not merely "the doctors' fad" (g) the A.I.F. part of "F" Force had made considerable progress on the road march before the main force of the monsoon. Free fluids – tea, rice, water and nutrine, when available, were employed widely and with success. Potass-Permang, drinks and morphine were the mainstays. Sulphenamides were tried in a very few cases with no apparent result but the cases were too few anyway to determine its value.

Isolation measures were only very partially possible at No.5 and No.4 Camps. At the former no separate accommodation was provided until mid-June despite repeated representations and these highly infectious patients had to be nursed at one end of the hospital hut. There was much sadism in the earlier days of this camp which left 140 out of 240 cases of cholera out of an original camp strength of 690.

Anal swabbing in the search for carriers was done by the I.J.A. Carriers were placed in such isolation as could be provided. Carriers and recovered cases were declared non-infectious after three negative swabbings at weekly intervals. The Force was inoculated with Cholera vaccine at the onset. In several places the supply was short and this was not completed until mid-June. Men were subsequently inoculated at three monthly intervals.

Malaria. There had been relatively little Malaria at Singapore. Heavy infections occurred on the march. Nieke, Camp 1 and Tambaya were breeding areas ... and practically 100% of the population of these camps contracted the infection. As mentioned under Medical Supplies, the supply of quinine, while more liberal than any other drug, was inadequate for suppressive and therapeutic use. The supply of Atebrin was very small until arrival at Kanburi at the end of November, when it was possible to place men who had chronic relapsing malaria, on suppressive Atebrin, with marked benefit. Plasmoquin supply was unsatisfactory but when available was used with quinine in the treatment courses; the recommended course for M.T. and B.T. cases was Quinine sulp. grs. 30 (in 3 doses) with plasmoquin

.03 or .04 grams (in the doses) for 14 days. Often the amount of quinine available up-country allowed of only a 7 or 10 day course of 24 grains of quinine daily. The I.J.A. supplied Begnon ampules (soluble quinine) for parenteral use. It was found satisfactory. The incidence of M.T. and B.T. infections was almost equal. There were many mixed infections. As there was only one microscope available for the Force detailed observations were impossible. Many cases of prolonged resistance in oral quinine were substantiated in undoubted malaria cases in Burma and Thailand. Intra-muscular or Intra-venous quinine was given in these usually with success but all medical officers observed cases which relapsed on 7th to 10th or 12th day of malaria while on full doses of quinine. Plasmoquin added to the quinine throughout a course definitely lengthened the interval between relapses.

Most of the clinical variations of malignant malaria were seen. The most common and dangerous being cerebral. It yielded satisfactorily to parenteral quinine as a general rule but there were fatal outcomes.

The small supply of Atebrin at our disposal was used suppressively with success on personnel e.g. on Interpreters, Medical Officers, Cookhouse superintendents, etc., but in a proportion of these (taking two Atebrin tablets twice weekly regularly) overt M.T. or B.T. infections appeared. Suppressive Quinine was largely ineffective unless used in dose of 10 grains daily – given on parade. We could only afford this for a period at Kanburi, (January-February 1944).

Mosquito nets were supplied by the I.J.A.; they were eventually taken out of use as they effectively trapped mosquitoes entering through the bamboo slats on which we slept.

Where an attack of malaria supervened in another disease there was rapid deterioration and in the very emaciated it frequently heralded the end of the struggle.

Dysentery. Troops of this force suffered heavily from this disease prior to leaving Changi – more especially the British element. Conditions on trains, the march and the insanitary state of all camps in the early days produced an enormous amount of acute dysentery – with insufficient treatment and the incessant demand for labour, relapses were very common. Even among those who made a satisfactory recovery the heavy labour and prodigious hours almost inevitably brought a return of the condition.

The clinical features were frequent copious stools especially at night and in the morning hours, with tremendous urgency, severe abdominal colic and generally little tenesmus[84] (unless it was an acute attack). The stool contained undigested food and thin mucus or traces of blood and muco-pus. In time practically the whole force suffered from this disease. At the end of the period under review one cannot meet any officer or man who has not had it – most of them had it for many months.

There were few drugs to treat dysentery. The very limited amount of Sulphapyridine was successful in acute bacillary cases used in 0.9 gm. Doses for the first 24 hours. It was much less successful in the chronic conditions ...

It is probable that a high proportion of the chronic cases had a mixed bacillary and amoebic infection. Their histories often suggested it. From the use of Emetine, the clinical features, the results of a limited number of microscopic examinations of stools and sigmoidoscopic observations (by Major Hunt at Kaanburi) it appears certain that 70%-80% were infected with E. histolytica.

Incessant requests for specific drugs to the I.J.A. resulted in enough Emetine to treat 8 cases.

In a wasting disease such as this, with food of limited calorific value, it was essential to use all means to make patients eat every grain of rice procurable for them otherwise they consumed their body proteins which on the diet could not be replaced. Where attention to this principle was successfully enforced, results were decidedly less deplorable than where the orthodox doctrine of "initial starvation" to enable the bowel to rest, lingered in the minds of certain medical officers.

The incidence of Amoebic hepatitis and Liver abscess was very low as would be expected in overt dysentery.

Tropical Ulcers The prolonged march with blistered and sore feet, lack of footwear, wet muddy camps and roads, debility and lowered body resistance to local infection is the soil in which ulcers were sown. The condition rapidly became one of the "big four" diseases. We might add starvation or malnutrition to make a "big five", as it was the solid background of all serious diseases

---

[84] Cramping rectal pain.

in the force – a sort of Bank of England to the Commercial Banks.

Ulcers affected the parts of the body most exposed to injury, commonest sites were (a) the region of the ankle, the front of the leg and dorsum of the foot[85] especially over the base of the toes (all these from knocks and abrasions). (b) The buttocks, back and area over the crests of Ilium and great Trochanters[86] (due to pressure sores from sleeping on split bamboo platforms acute abscesses often preceded these). (c) The skin creases of the body – flexures of the elbow, knee, and groin (caused by abrasion, the result of scratching scabies areas).

These ulcers commenced as small abscesses and infected abrasions and spread superficially involving increasing areas of skin and deeply involving subcutaneous tissue, deep fascia tendon sheaths and muscle, and finally bone in the progressive cases.

In severe oedematous Beri-beri the origin of the ulcer was frequently a blob on the skin or of the dorsum of the foot. In consequence of ulcers, every break of the skin, however minute, was suspect and had to be meticulously treated until, and if, healing took place ...

As regards amputation results – and amputation was resorted to as the last means of saving a patient's life, of 53 amputations done in our camps in the Burma-Thailand area, there are only 5 survivors in April 1944. The vast majority lost their lives from other diseases – beri-beri, malaria, dysentery, subsequent to operation. Results of the few amputations done after reaching Kanburi gave much better results by reason of better nutrition ...

Beri-beri The state of nutrition prior to leaving Changi has been noted. Conditions which affected "F" Force subsequently have been described. A number of Beri-beri cases developed on the march ... The supply of beans in the I.J.A. ration appeared to prevent rapid development but this supply unfortunately fluctuated very considerably. The disease lacks behind the deficiency of this and so we found that there were 5 deaths ascribed to Ber-beri in June, 20 in July 87 in August, 156 in September. Lack of the necessary vitamins was all the more felt because the resting disease cholera and dysentery, and the hard

---

[85] The mid and fore part of the foot.
[86] Parts of the hip bone and femur respectively.

physical toil used the body reserve which could not be made good from the existing diet.

Neuritic[87] beri-beri was relatively rare but cases of wrist drop, foot drop, ensosthesis [?] of the lips etc. were seen. Oedematous beri-beri was the commonest variety seen, it affected the feet and the legs in the milder degrees, but by July camps had patients resembling water-beds, so swollen were they. Despite strenuous efforts to make good the diet deficiency in these by giving extra beans from the rations of the fit men any liver procurable, and Yeast Tablets (I.J.A. but very scare) most of them succumbed to Cardiac Beri-beri, Dysentery, Chest Conditions, Malaria and Ulcers. Tapping of ascites[88] and hydrothoraces[89] gave no more than temporary relief ...

Sudden passing of faeces during sleep or temporary mental aberration followed by epileptiform fits were seen occasionally. These fits were more often than not, fatal. They were afebrile[90] and previous routine examination of this central nervous system was usually negative. Cardiac abnormalities in association with Beri-beri were common and became more so as general health deteriorated ... Medical Officers noted the prevalence of conditions not usually attributed to this disease. The left side of the heart was affected more often than the right, there was bradycardia rather than trachycardia[91]. A forceable slapping cardiac impulse could be seen and felt ...

The subject of Beri-beri and cardiac disorders were much in the minds of medical officers. A history of Beri-beri was found in a very high percentage of our population as was that of recurrent malaria attacks with major degrees of secondary anarmia [anaemia?]. One hesitates to dogmatise on the aetiology[92] of these heart conditions – they were abnormal and were heated by as complete recumbency[93] as possible and extra [vitamin] B1.-containing diet where this was procurable.

---

[87] Continuous pain in a nerve.

[88] A build-up of fluid in the abdomen.

[89] An accumulation of fluid in the pleural cavity.

[90] Not feverish.

[91] Meaning a slower heart rate rather than a faster heart rate.

[92] The study of the causes.

[93] The state of resting or reclining.

CHAPTER 18

Selection of Correspondence and Reports Between "F" Force and I.J.A.

INSTRUCTIONS GIVEN TO PoW ON MY ASSUMING COMMAND

I have the pleasure to lead you on the charge of last stretch of Railway Construction Wardoom. In examination of various reports as well as to the result of my partial inspection of the present conditions, I am pleased to find you in general keeping discipline and working diligently.

At the same time I regret to find seriousness in health matters. It is evident there are various causes inevitable for this and but to my opinion due mainly to the fact of absence of firm belief as Japanese.

Health follows will and lease only when the enemy is annihilated.

Those who fail to reach objective in charge by lack of health or spirit is considered in the Japanese Army most shameful deed.

Devotion to death is good. Yet still we have the spirit of Devotion to the Imperial Cause, even to the 7th of life in reincarnation the Spirit which cannot become void by death.

You are in act of charge in colleagues of the I.J.A. You are expected to charge to the last stage of this work in good spirit by taking good care of your own health. Beside you are to remember that your welfare is guaranteed only by obedience to the order of the Imperial Japanese Army.

Imperial Japanese Army will not be unfair to those who are honest and obey them, but protect such.

You are to understand this fundamental Japanese spirit and

carry out the task given you with perfect ease of mind under protection to the Japanese Army.

Given in Kanchanabri, June 26th 1943, by Col. Sijuo (?) Nakamura, Comm. PoW Camps in Thailand

----

NOTICE!

1. The hour of daily work is stipulated as belows:-

(1) Get up   7.00
(2) Breakfast   7.30
(3) Morning Roll Call   8.20
(4) Set to work   8.30
(5) Consultation to Surgeon   10.00
(6) Tiffin   12.00
(7) Resume work of afternoon   14.00
(8) Evening Roll Call   18.30
(9) Supper   19.00
(10) Consultation to Surgeon   20.00
(11) Go to bed   21.00

2. The Captive who can go out of fence in the daytime are as belows:-
    I. Water-drawer, Firewood-carrier, Watchman around the camp, and persons in charge of the dead.
    II. The Captive who take bath after work. But the time limit is till 21 o'clock (9 pm.)
    All the Captive with the exception of the items mentioned above should ask for Permission of the Chief of this Prisoners' quarters.
    Everybody who went out of fence without permission is strictly punished.

3. The Captives who disobey or oppose to the orders of the Nippon Army are strictly punished or condemned to Capital Crime.

4. Measures to the Deserter:-
    I. The Captives who devised to run away and were captured are condemned to Capital Crime.
    II. The Chief of Section which produced the Deserter and

concerned officer are severely punished in joint.

III. When the Deserter cannot be found within two days from the day of desertion, the chief of section concerned will be punished to Capital Crime owing to their Responsibility to Soldier-men.

> 7th July 2603 (1943)
> Chief of the 5th Detachment of Malaya
> Prisoners' Quarters

————————————————————————

Headquarters Camp
Ninkh
12th July 1943

Sir,

Food

Further to my interviews with you on this subject, I now forward a report of my senior medical officer, which summarises the situation and shows its extreme seriousness.
I have the honour to be, Sir,
Yours faithfully,
Sgd/ F.W.H.
Lieut-Colonel,
Commander
Commander
PoW Camps
Imperial Japanese Army

Commander,
"F" Force

The present ration scale for this force is viewed with the utmost concern by the medical officers attached to this force. The present scale is entirely deficient in Vitamin B, fat, protein, calcium and if persisted in will result in the rapid deterioration of health of the, at present, moderately fit men, and the impossibility of recovery of the already sick.

My appreciation is that on the present scale the force will be entirely incapacitated in one month's time and that the death rate will be extremely heavy.

Most alarming is the very rapid increase in disease caused by the absence of Vitamin B in the diet – Beri-Beri, Pellagra[94], failing eyesight and in some cases blindness, Asthenia[95] and general weakness. The entire force is on the verge of Beri-Beri, and most men are already showing mild symptoms. These will increase at an alarming rate in the near future and many deaths and total invalidity will be the result.

The additions necessary to make the present ration a suitable one are as follows:-

(1)	Vitamin B –	Rice polishings	2 ozs per man per day
		Towgay[96]	3 ozs per man per day
		Beans	3 ozs per man per day
(2)	Fat (which is not only necessary as a food, but also conserves Vitamin B		
		– Cooking oil	1 oz per man per day
(3)	Protein –	Meat or fish	4 ozs per man per day
(4)	Calcium –	Whitebait	2 ozs per man per day

[94] Pellagra manifests itself in dementia, diarrhoea, and dermatitis.

[95] Lack of energy and strength.

[96] Bean sprouts.

[97] The story of these men is an horrendous one. Lieutenant J.B. Bradley RE was isolated in the cholera ward outside No.2 Camp Sonkruai where his job was to incinerate the corpses of cholera victims. This was a place the Japanese stayed well clear of, which allowed Bradley to wander around a little and he found a way through the jungle to the bank of a small river, the Huai Song Kalia. Along with Colonel Wilkinson RE, he planned to escape to tell the world what was happening to the prisoners of "F" Force. They aimed to travel down the Huai Song Kalia, through the mountainous jungles to reach the Ye River and from there to the Andaman Sea.

Joining the two men were captains W.H. Anker, RASC, J. Feathers, RASC, lieutenants Robinson, RASC, I.M. Moffat, RE, G.A. Machade, SSVF, T.P.D. Jones, Malay Regiment, Corporal Brown, SSVF, and Nur Mohammed, an Indian fisherman who had been taken prisoner by the Japanese.

They successfully escaped on 5 July 1943, and made their way along the river but found the dense jungle on the slopes of the mountains so thick that progress was pitifully slow. Their rations dwindled until, on 28 July, they ate the last of their rice. During the night Corporal Brown walked out into the jungle to

The above additions would constitute a diet on which steady improvement of health and working capacity of this force could be confidently predicted.

> (Signed) R.H. Stevens, Major
> S.N.O. A.I.F. "F" Force
> 12 July 1943

Headquarters Camp
Nieke
19th July 1943
Sir,

I have the honour to inform you that yesterday I was told by Lieut. YAMADA that some British officers had been arrested for escape, that they would probably be condemned to death and that I must hold myself in readiness to witness their execution.[97]

die, not wanting to be a burden upon the rest. Others developed injuries from hacking their way through the undergrowth and Lieutenant Moffat's legs had become covered in tropical ulcers. On 2 August, Captain Feathers died during the night and three days later Colonel Wilkinson died from heart failure. On 9 August Lieutenant Jones collapsed unconscious and had to be carried to a hut by a tributary of the Ye. In the hut Lieutenant Robinson died from septicaemia and dysentery, and the same night Jones begged them to carry on without him as he was virtually unable to move.

On 14 August, after six weeks, the last two of which were without food, the survivors reached the Ye and built a raft. This took three days, and on 17 August they set off down the Ye. They did not get far before the raft broke up in rapids. Three managed to reach the shore where they were found by Burmese hunters. They were taken to the native village and eventually arrested by the Japanese.

Thanks to the efforts of the British and Australian officers, particularly Cyril Wild, the Japanese were persuaded to drop the death sentences and the men went back to work on the railway. Paul H. Kratoska, *The Thailand-Burma Railway, 1942-1946: Documents, and Selected Writings* (Routledge, New York, 2006), pp.288-90. See also James Bradley's own account, *Towards the Setting Sun*, op.cit.

If this is so, then as senior British Officer and therefore the representative of the British Government on the spot, I wish to make a formal appeal to the Imperial Japanese Government (on behalf of the British Government) not to exact the death penalty.

While I have no information as to the reasons that impelled these officers to escape, the basis of this appeal is:-

(a) It is contrary to the Laws and Usage of War to exact the death penalty from prisoners of war who escape, nor is capital punishment imposed by other Great Powers.

(b) There is a feeling of despair among some officers at their continued inability to mitigate the severe and unprecedented hardships of the men of whom they have been put in command by the Imperial Japanese Army. These hardships have already caused in the space of three months the deaths of over 600 men and the sickness of 90% out of this force of 7,000 men. I have no doubt that this feeling of responsibility weighed heavily on the minds of these officers.

In the meantime I urge that immediate action be taken to postpone execution until such time as a reply to this appeal is received.

I have the honour to be, Sir,
Yours faithfully,

> Lieut.-Colonel, Commander
> Colonel Banno
> Commanding Malayan P. of W.
> Thailand

Dear Capt. Barnett,

From this morning I order you to the working number because the work is very very hurry. Therefore of course you must select and collect this number from the some sick party.
Today – soldier 130 men, the officer 8 men.

> (Sgd.) Capt. Maruyamma
> Received at Tarkunun, Thailand on 19th July 1943.

No.2 Camp
4 Aug 43

Sir,

Now that the HQ of this force is situated away from your own HQ, it would be of great assistance in ensuring the accuracy of the various reports submitted to you if you would allow the duplicate copies of the Force Nominal Rolls at present in your office to be retained by this HQ.

If this could be arranged, and No.3 Camp could be instructed to send all death notifications and other reports through this HQ, it will be possible in future to avoid mistakes in making reports to you.

The role of NIEKE personnel has been amended to date to show movements of all troops. As this HQ will not know when hospital patients are moved from NIEKE to the Burma Hospital, could Lieut. Wing please be instructed to keep a record of these movements so that the roll may be kept up-to-date.

> Sgd Dillon
> Lieut-Colonel
> Commander
> Mr. Saji
> Headquarters
> I.J.A. PoW Camps
> Nieke

To: Lt-Col Banno,
       Headquarters Camp,
       Nieke (through "F" Force Headquarters)

I wish to endorse the action of A.I.F. officers under my command who have deemed it necessary to submit a protest against the conditions to which the members of CHANGI "F" Force are being subjected. I forward herewith two further reports, one from Lt-Col POND, Commander No.4 Camp (in which I am quartered) and the other from Lieutenant LILLIE, 2/29 Bn, who is in charge of personnel at the staging camp of KONKOITA. These reports speak for themselves.

As commander of A.I.F. personnel and as the senior Regular Commanding Officer in MALAYA, I consider myself the representative of the Australian Government in this area and therefore respectfully submit that the following memorandum be passed to Lt-Col BANNO for transmission to the International Red Cross.

In my considered opinion, which is supported by medical opinion, the present physical condition of the Force is such that in a few weeks there will scarcely be a man fit to carry out work of any nature and in addition the death rate is certain to increase. The men are so debilitated by the conditions of the long and arduous march of 260 kilometres through a series of insanitary staging camps that the majority have little physical resistance to diseases such as cholera, dysentery, severe diarrhoea, diphtheria. etc. The food situation is serious. In 18 days, the men have had only rice and thin onion stew and occasionally beans and towgay. The quantity of the items is insufficient to maintain a reasonable standard of health. Two days ago the rice ration was reduced from 4 to 3 bags for 700 men.

For three weeks there has been insufficient cover to protect the men from the rain which has fallen every day – on one occasion 230 men were completely soaked and another 300 men were unable to keep dry. Many men are obliged to sleep on the ground under the huts. Many have no boots at all, while some have boots which have little or no service left and badly need replacing. The supply and repair of footwear has been a problem since capitulation. Clothing is also urgently required, many men being in rags, and several having little bedding. Considerable bedding had to be jettisoned by the men at BANPONG to enable them to undertake the march to this area.

There is now a grave shortage of essential drugs. Requisitions have been submitted repeatedly but little relief has been given for the reason that the I.J.A. state that they have no supplies. A requisition was submitted for extra food for the sick but I was informed that nothing could be done for even one sick man. Lately a small supply of tea and sugar has been made available for the dangerously sick cholera cases.

From the outset I have endeavoured to put my case to Lieutenant MURAYAMA. I made a request for an interview to discuss the questions of accommodation for the sick, the food situation, the evacuation of the sick, canteen supplies etc. I have since submitted a further request for consideration of the food situation. To both of these I have received no acknowledgement – on was asked to be despatched to Lt-Col BANNO if the local camp authorities could not act.

It was also pointed out that the digging of latrines to replace those already existing, which were conducive to the spread of disease, was delayed because all so-called fit men were required for road work. Whereas we were informed by the I.J.A. that they were moving "F" Force to an area where food was more plentiful, the reverse was the case.

On the grounds that the soldiers under my command, who fought honourably and well and who have been commended for their work and discipline, are not being treated in accordance with international agreements, I forward this request for investigation and necessary action by the International Red Cross.

I appreciate the problems of supply in an area with no railway and a bad road is immense, but the danger is great and the lives of many hundreds of men are at stake, particularly as the worse months of the monsoon are still to come. I am convinced that Lt-Col BANNO is doing what he can to improve conditions but to my mind relief can only be obtained by reference to the highest authority.

(Signed) C. H. Kappe Lt-Col
Commander A.I.F Troops, "F" Force

————————————————————————————

To: Lt-Col Banno
     I.J.A. Headquarters, Nieke

I respectfully desire to bring to your notice the conditions of Australian soldiers in this camp and to request that sympathetic consideration be given to improving conditions.

1. The party under my command, originally 700, now consists of 523 of whom 37 are at Tamarumpat [Tamerompat][98] and

---

[98] This was an Australian camp twenty-three kilometres from Konkoita.

the balance are here. The party at Tamarumpat consists of men too sick to move and their number is decreasing by death every few days. They are without a medical officer and cannot obtain permission for nearby English and Australian doctors to visit them.

2. At Takaeun[99] there are 112 fit men, 19 light sick and 356 heavy sick men. Of the latter 58 are isolated with cholera in this camp but the epidemic now appears to be under control. I would like to express appreciation of the efforts made by the Japanese medical authorities to assist in checking this epidemic – they have been most helpful.

3. We were recently permitted to send 70 men to a hospital down the river but there are at least another 185 men who should be evacuated to hospital as they will be unable to work for at least two months

4. At the present I am required to send 200 men to work every day and also to have to provide 20 cooks and 24 nursing orderlies. As a result about 120 heavy sick men have to go to work on the railway even though suffering from Beri Beri, Malaria and Dysentery. The work party leaves camp about 08.15 hours and returns normally about 21.30 hours or later. The work is heavy, particularly in the almost constant rain and as a result sickness is increasing. I anticipate that if men with heavy malaria and dysentery are to continue to go to work many of them will die.

5. Of the men in this camp about 150 have no boots at all and over 150 have boots which are worn out beyond repair. The number of bootless men increases by about 30 per week. To provide boots for working men I took the boots of the men evacuated down the river to hospital. I have made several applications for an issue of boots but without success. Most of the men without boots now have large septic sores on their feet through having to work in continual wet and often on rocky ground and they endure great hardships. We also have 117 men without a shirt and 54 men without a pair of shorts, while 256 men have only one shirt and 317 have only one pair of shorts, 134 men have no towel and 181 have no ground sheets. Thanks to the issue by the I.J.A. all men now have a blanket.

---

[99] This was situated twenty-two kilometres from Tamerompat.

6. Food has improved somewhat during the past three weeks but there is a serious lack of meat and fish. We have had meat on only five occasions in the last five weeks and that at the rate of at the rate of 40, 55, 70, 80 and 40 grammes per man only. There has been no fish even for the working men in the past week – vegetables only. In English camps in this vicinity meat is issued daily at the rate of 200 grammes per man as well as vegetables and fish. We also need tea and sugar.

7. I have received orders that sick men in this camp are only to receive two meals a day and this order has been obeyed. I feel sure that as a result many of the sick men will not regain their health and strength and will not be able to work again. Some will no doubt die as a result.

8. Accommodation has improved a little with the building of three double-decker stages and with the evacuation of 60 [70] men to hospital but nevertheless most men become wet at night in bed when it rains as it does every night. In consequence the deaths of a number of men have really been caused by exposure.

9. I request that if this Force is required to move again some transport be provided for its baggage, tents, cooking utensil and rice, all of which have been required to be man-handled in the past. In my opinion if this is not done, there will not be 100 men in the Force capable of doing any work after another move. Furthermore most of the sick men need transport though some would be able to march if they carried no baggage.

In conclusion, Sir, I trust that something may soon be done to improve the conditions of my men as I am very concerned at the number of deaths and the amount of sickness that have occurred.

> I have the honour etc.
> (Signed) S.A.F. Pond, Lt-Col,
> Commander A.I.F Troops[100]

---

[100] This is reproduced from Lieutenant Colonel C.H. Kappe's report in the National Archives of Australia, reference NAA A6238, 23.

Headquarters
"F" Force
8th August 1943

Dear Colonel Banno,

I regret to have to forward this report as I know and appreciate all that you and your administration have tried to do on our behalf. However, the present situation is so scandalous and its consequences in loss of life is proving so widespread that it is bound to be made the subject of an official enquiry by the British Government after the war with serious and lasting diplomatic repercussions between our two countries.

I feel, therefore, in the interests of all concerned that there should be no delay in forwarding this statement through His Excellency General ARIMOURA to the highest quarters.

> Yours faithfully,
> Lieut-Colonel ,
> Commander
> "F" Force

————————————————————————

Headquarters
"F" Force
Colonel Banno,
Imperial Japanese Army,
Commanding,
Malaya Prisoners of War in Thailand
8th August 1943

Sir,

I have the honour to submit a report from my Senior Medical Officer on the medical situation at this camp. This report fills me with the gravest concern as 25% of the original strength of the camp are already dead and the remainder are dying at a rate of 2,800 a year, which is an appalling state of affairs.

Col. Huston in his report points out the possible remedies, and I should be grateful if immediate steps could be taken to implement them. To my mind our most urgent and pressing needs are (i) no unfit men to be forced to go on working parties and working men to be allowed one day off in seven to wash themselves and their clothes.

(ii) The cessation of ill-treatment by the I.J.A. engineers. Cases are occurring every day of severe beatings of prisoners of war. Men have been knocked unconscious and left to lie in the mud.

(iv) Improvement of rations particularly for the sick and the provision of the foods enumerated in Col. Huston's report, rice polishings, cooking fats, sugar and flour being the most urgent.

(v) The provision of medical stores, antiseptics and disinfectants.

Present conditions are so disgraceful that they are steadily and rapidly destroying the men of this force and will undoubtedly grossly undermine the health of any survivors. None of the other belligerents in this war are treating their prisoners in this manner, and it was to save prisoners of war suffering such treatment that the Great Powers became party to the Geneva Convention, numerous clauses of which are now being flagrantly disregarded here. It is my belief that if the Imperial Japanese Government in Tokyo were made aware of the present situation and if the Japanese representatives of the International Red Cross Society could see the disgraceful conditions in which our sick are perishing in the so-called hospital in this camp, immediate steps would be taken to come to our rescue.

The establishment of the hospital in Burma for 1,250 patients is much appreciated but it only touches the fringe of the problem as there are over 1,400 sick in this camp alone, of whom only 350 will be sent to Burma.

I therefore request that this letter be forwarded as soon as possible to His Excellency General Arimura for transmission to the Imperial Japanese Government.

Sgd
Lieut-Colonel,
Commander
"F" Force

Colonel Banno
Commanding Malayan PoW

MEDICAL REPORT BY LT-COL J. HUSTON, SENIOR MEDICAL OFFICER

Lt-Col S.W. Harris, OBE, RA
Commanding "F" Force, Thailand.

The high death rate and medical situation generally in this camp is causing me the gravest anxiety, and unless stringent and immediate steps are taken to remedy existing conditions the death rate, which is now at the rate of 100 % per annun, will continue in an increasing ratio.

The following report on this situation is submitted for your information and possible action:-

1. AVAILABILITY. On 6 Aug 43 (excluding officers)

	Fit	Light Duties	In Hosp	Red Cross Non-Combatants		Total
On road	214	83	-	-		297
In camp	70	35	1463	86		1654
Total	284	118	1463	86		1951

2. DEATHS (out of an original total of 1,600)

Cholera	209	Starvation and Dysentery	119
Beri-Beri	28	Malaria	17.
Diphtheria	14	Tropical ulcers	7
Misc Causes	5		
Making a total of	399		

3. CAUSES OF ILL HEALTH AND HIGH DEATH RATE

   (a) Defective diet during the past 2½ months, the present ration for sick men contains 1400 calories only, which is not sufficient to maintain life much less to enable desperately sick men to recuperate.

   (b) The prolonged march here of a force in which there were 30% unfit men. Excessively long working hours and ill treatment of men on road and rail working parties.

(c) Sick men being forced to work on outside working parties. After working long hours some of these men have been found dead in their huts.

(d) A lack of medical supplies and hospital equipment.

(e) Inadequate rations and non-payment of unfit men.

4. SUGGESTED REMEDIES

(a) Immediate improvement in camp conditions, sanitation, cooking facilities and hygiene generally. (This is now being done under the orders of Lieut. WAKADYASHI and we are very grateful for this dispensation).

(b) Only fit men be allowed to work on the roads and railway. At present sick men are forced to work – men suffering from malnutrition, beri-beri, sore feet and malaria. If it is true that the daily working party is to be increased from 300 to 700, then I anticipate that the number of sick men will steadily increase and that there will be a rapid rise in the death rate.

(c) Supply of a good mixed diet containing rice polishings, fresh vegetables and cooking fats to produce 3,500 calories daily for all men whether sick or fit. As I have already stated the present ration for sick men contains only 1,400 calories, which is not sufficient to support life, with a consequence that unfit men are dying in large numbers and the number will undoubtedly increase unless the rations are improved.

(d) Supply of medical equipment which was brought from CHANGI with this force. This has been dumped at BAMPONG, KANU (HQ of "H" Force) and TARKANAN. We are also in urgent need for dressings, cotton wool, gauze, Emetine, Vitamin B tablets, Magnesium Sulphate tablets, Bismuth and Opium for diarrhoea, Idoform and Sulphur for treating ulcers and skin disease.

(e) Invalid foods are urgently needed, fish, oil, eggs, sugar and flour.

(f) Antiseptics are also urgently needed for disinfecting hands and preventing the spread of disease. (Creosol, Lysol, Xylenol).

(g) A supply of tools, utensils, basins, buckets, and scrubbing brushes are also needed for keeping the sick and their quarters clean.

(h) Finally in particular I must warn you that at present
     without disinfectants and with inadequate food the
     whole camp is defenceless against another outbreak of
     cholera.

Sgd/
Lieut-Colonel, R.A.M.C.
S.M.O., "F" Force
8 Aug 43.

Colonel Banno
Commanding Malayan Prisoners of War,
Thailand
No.2 PoW Camp
Sonkrai
18th August 1943

Sir,

Knowing your good will and sincerity, and since you are
entrusted by His Excellency General ARIMURA with the
responsibility of this force of 7,000 prisoners of war (now
unhappily reduced by death to less than 6,000), I must make
this further personal appeal on behalf of these men, of whom I
am the senior British officer.

As anticipated in my letter of 8 Aug 43 the situation is steadily
worsening, as the sickness and death rate is accelerating day by
day. Since my arrival in this camp about two weeks ago, 120
men have died (12 during the last 24 hours) and this is not due
to an epidemic but to diseases mainly caused by overwork, ill-
treatment, and malnutrition.

Lieut. WAKABAYASHI has always done his utmost to help us
and with his kind assistance we have been able to improve
greatly the sanitation, hygiene and cooking facilities in this
camp. In spite, however, of these and other measures our 1,400
sick grow weaker and more men fall ill every day; until now have
only 150 fit men to send out to work, with 250 others who
should be excused duty on account of illness to make up the
daily working parties of 400. The causes of this disastrous
situation are:-

(i) Lack of suitable food apart from rice (see Colonel Huston's report of 8 Aug 43) which weakens all men and causes actual starvation among the sick.

(ii) Excessively long hours and ill treatment at work.

(iii) Lack of drugs and suitable nourishment for those in hospital.

I must therefore implore you to take suitable measures immediately to prevent this situation developing into an overwhelming tragedy. I should also welcome the chance of an early interview with you.

Yours faithfully,

Lieut-Colonel,
Commander
"F" Force

————————————————————————

Colonel Banno
Commanding Malayan Prisoners of War,
Thailand
No.2 Camp
Sonkrai
30 Aug 1943

1. Lieut. Wakabyashi advised me to write to you with the following difficulties about pay:-

(a) When are the other ranks going to be paid for the period of the march up, especially the various camp cooks, who were promised heavy duty rates?
Amount required – approx $15,000.

(b) When are the other ranks going to be paid for the working period 10 May to 20 June? Camps 1, 2, 3, 5 and 5 were all at work by 23 May. Camp 4 (Konkoita) started work on 10 May and the others in between.
Amount involved – approx $16,000.

(c) When are the officers and Red Cross personnel going to be paid?
Amount involved – approx. $14,000.

2. From the above it will be seen that the force has been owed $45,000 for more than one month.

3. We expect that all these matters would be put right in this month's pay, but it did not happen.

4. In addition to the above, officers and Red Cross personnel are now due for pay for August (approx. $14,000), which brings the total amount owing to $59,000.

5. Our total capital is about $10,000 and so we cannot support this big debt owing to us.

6. In spite of Changi promises we cannot get Malay money changed. Can nothing be done about this? I have here $2,000 and Col. Kappe and Col. Hutchinson have similar amounts or more.

7. We will be glad to help in any way we can to clean up this mess.

8. Lastly, there is the matter of the Red Cross W.OsI ... What can be done to have this mistake put right?

I hope to see you up here one day.

> Yours sincerely
> ???
> Mr. Saji,
> PoW Headquarters,
> Nieke

————————————————————————

Subject: Immediate Medical Requirements:
No.2 Camp
To: Commander "F" Force
2 September 1943

Sir,

It is requested that the following needs of the of the force be brought to the notice of the I.J.A. as soon as possible:-

1. <u>Medical Officers</u> – to be moved as soon as they can be spared

Capt. A. Barber RAMC from NIEKE to No.2 CAMP
Capt. Lloyd Cahill AAMC from No.1 to No.2

Capt. J. Taylor AAMC from No.1 to No.3
Major D.G. Gillies RAMA from No.5 to No.3
Capt. Mannion Australian Dental Officer from TAMARAN PAT to Burma Hospital.
Capt. J. Frew AAMC and Capt. R. Brown RAMC – These two officers to not belong to "F" Force but owing to the heavy sick rate their services are required as the Thailand administration has depleted the number of medical officers of "F" Force (Major Rogers AAMA at KAMBURI, Major Brand AAMC at TAMARAN PAT). Capt. Frew is required at the Burma Hospital and Capt. Brown at New Light Sick Camp.

2. Medical Equipment – It is requested that Dental Equipment (one grey box marked "F.D.O. Capt. Dix, Dental Stores" thought to be at TAMARAN PAT be sent to New Light Sick Camp. ...

——————————————————————

COPY OF LETTER SUBMITTED TO I.J.A.

To:- IJA Officer Commanding Tanbaya Hospital Camp
From:- Major B.A. Hunt, Commanding Tanbaya Hospital
Date:- 20 Sep 43

Sir,
I regret to have to inform you that the health of the men in this camp, instead of improving, is steadily getting worse. This is in spite of all efforts on your side and on ours to make things better. The number of men well enough to carry on the essential services of the camp – nursing, cooking, woodcutting, hygiene – is becoming daily smaller and very few are well enough to be discharged from hospital to take their place. Seventeen of the working staff were admitted to hospital this morning. It is much to be feared that unless a marked improvement takes place at an early date the whole camp service may break down.
    The diseases which are causing the present appalling death rates and the large number of admissions to hospital are:-

I. Beri-beri. Although we know that you are doing your utmost to increase the vegetable supply, the green vegetables and potatoes which are being supplied contain very little vitamin B, so that beri-beri is steadily

179

increasing. Many patients, already sick from other diseases, are suddenly developing acute cardiac beri-beri and dying from it. Many of the camp hard workers – cooks, woodcutters and such – who naturally require a larger supply of vitamin B and are not receiving it – are becoming attacked by beri-beri each day. The beri-beri patients already in hospital – between 500 and 600 – are getting no better, and in many cases are actually becoming worse despite complete rest.

II.   Dysentery. NO medical treatment or drugs are available for this disease. In the absence of such treatment there seems little hope of saving more than a very small number of the 450 (approx) patients now suffering from dysentery.

III. Malaria. The malaria in this region is particularly virulent and responds very slowly to quinine. It is hoped that the recent increase in the supply of quinine may affect some improvement in this respect, but this is not to be expected for several weeks to come and in the meantime the relapse rate is very high.

IV. Ulcers. In many patients these are rapidly spreading in the devitalised skin of the patients, whose vitamin lack is so great that they can offer no resistance to the infection. Blood poisoning from ulcers occurs and ulcer patients are dying at the rate of 2 or 3 daily.

V.   Typhus and typhus-like fever. A persistent fever lasting for 2 two or three weeks resembling typhus (tsutsugamushi[101]) in many respects but not quite typical of that disease is occurring in increasing numbers. It is extremely weakening and shows no response whatever to quinine.

Medical Officers
1. Australian
Major Hunt: still weak after cardiac beri-beri and malaria.
Capt. Cahill: well.

---

[101] Mite-borne infectious disease caused by a microorganism, which results in a fever, headache, a rash, swollen glands and a dark, crusted ulcer at the site of the bite.

2. Britain

Major Phillips: very ill for the past 12 days with typhus. Not improving – condition serious and still in bed.

Capt. Silman: ill for the past 9 days with typhus – not improving and in bed.

Capt. Lowe: ill for the past 5 weeks with typhus – now improving but very weak and unable to work.

Capt. Pantridge: suffering from cardiac beri-beri – working only half-time.

Lieut. Turner: suffering from dysentery and working half-time (both these officers would, if the need for doctors were not so urgent be kept in bed, as would also Major Hanbury).

Major Hanbury: suffering from cardiac beri-beri – working half-time.

Capt. Emery: well

W.O Wolfe: Ill with malaria.

Thus only two of the ten medical officers are at present capable of a full day's work.

Future Prospects

(i) If the present circumstances continue I anticipate at least 400 deaths in the next 6 weeks and possibly more.

(ii) If for any reason it were suddenly decided to move the camp population and considerable distance by train (for example, a five or six days' journey) at least 300 lives would be lost on the trip even under favourable circumstances of weather, food and the like.

Suggestions

The only suggestion for improvement I can offer – and I realise that most of these are beyond your immediate control – are set out below. [Then followed a list of medicines and their purpose]

I have the honour to submit the above report regarding the present state of the health of the camp for your information in the hope that you will be able to help us to save the lives of many of the pitiable invalids now in hospital.

(Sgd) Bruce Hunt
Major A.A.M.C.

<u>Copy of letter from Major Hunt which was handed to I.J.A. Colonel (Medical) on 25 Sep 43</u>

<u>Tanbaya Hospital Camp</u>

Total Patients in Camp – 1632

<u>Admin Staff</u>	Perm Admin Staff	4 Offrs	51 O.Rs.
	Sick – working		7
	Working Patients		52
		<u>4</u> Offrs	<u>86</u> O.Rs.

<u>Med Staff</u>	Perm Med Staff	10 Offrs	109 O.Rs.
	Sick – working	4	60
	Working Patients	6	49
			81
		<u>6</u> Offrs	<u>130</u> O.Rs.

<u>Chief Diseases</u>

Malaria –	537	Very virulent and resistant to quinine. High relapse rate.
Beri-Beri –	492	Increasing daily especially in working staff. More than half these cases contracted in this camp. Much heart involvement – many recent deaths.
Dysentery –	521	All cases getting steadily worse in the complete absence of drugs and dressings.
Ulcers –	317	Most getting worse in absence of Vits. A, B and C, drugs and dressings.

<u>General Health</u>

The health of the camp as a whole is getting worse, not better, every day. The increase in Beri-Beri being the chief cause under present circumstances and in the absence of immediate supply of very large quantities of vitamin containing foods, drugs and dressings. I anticipate not less than 500 deaths in 6 weeks. To this must be added over 280 deaths which have occurred in the past 6 weeks. The patients are extremely debilitated and all come from "F" Force, a body of 7,000 which left SINGAPORE in April and has already had about 2,000 deaths.

In 20 years of medical practice and after extensive experiences of two wars, I have never seen men in a more pitiable condition of health than the men in this camp. The real tragedy lies in the fact that much of the disease is really curable if proper vitamin containing foodstuffs such as beans and towgay and proper drugs are made available in sufficient quantity, and I earnestly impress upon whatever authority this may reach, that through no fault of their own, men are dying in hundreds and will continue to die until help comes.

> (Sgd) Bruce Hunt,
> Major A.A.M.C.
> Commanding Tanbaya Hospital

——————————————————————

Colonel Banno
Commanding Malayan Prisoners of War,
Thailand
No.2 PoW Camp
Sonkrai
9th September 1943

Sir,

1. Now that road conditions are improving I should be grateful if you could arrange for certain individuals to be brought up to the forward area. Details are as follows:-
   Chaplain Rev. A. Jackson now at TAMARAN PAT[102] to be sent to Burma Hospital.
   Chaplain Rev. E. Cordingley now at KANCHANABRI to be sent to Burma Hospital.
   Interpreter Capt. Waller now at KANCHANABRI to be sent to KAMI-SONKRAI.
   Dentist Capt. Mannion now at TAMARAN PAT to be sent to KAMI-SONKRAI.
2. I have in a previous letter already asked for two doctors Major Rogers from KANCHA and Capt. Brand from TAMARAN PAT, to be sent forward or, alternatively, to be exchanged for Capts. Brown and Frew now at SHIMO-SONKRAI and NIEKE in charge of Tamil labour groups. My request in that letter for

---

[102] Tamaran Pat is fifteen kilometres south of Konkoita.

Capt. Mannion to be sent to the Burma Hospital is now cancelled, as another dentist, Capt. Dix, has been sent to the hospital.

3. All except the interpreter are Red Cross non-combatants.
Yours faithfully,

Lt-Col, Commander "F" Force

————————————————————————————

No.2 Camp
SONKRAI
To:-   Lieutenant TANIO
       Medical Officer
       19 Oct., 43.
       HQ, Malaya PoW Camps,
       NIEKE,

Sir,

I have just visited the PoW Hospital at No.1 Camp, KAMI-SONKRAI, where the Medical Officers are deeply concerned by the lack of dressings for the many ulcers and for the amputations which have been caused through these. I am sorry to say that they now have to make dressings by cutting off the arms and legs of men's shirts and trousers and by cutting up officers' private mosquito nets.

Please do your best for us by providing dressings or any material from which to make them, as this is now absolutely essential for both No.1 Camp and the Burma Hospital.

J. Huston
Lieut-Colonel, RAMC
S.M.O., "F" Force

————————————————————————————

To: Headquarters
       Kanchanabri Camp
       Malaya Prisoners of War Administration
       29 Nov. 1943
       Malaya

Health of "F" Force

The attached report on the medical situation of "F" Force is submitted for your information. The departure of the party of 1,000 prisoners of war who are due to leave for Singapore in the near future will leave the following position here:-

2,000 ill in hospital
1,500 fit for light camp duties only

These 3,500 men are broken in health and suffering from malnutrition and vitamin deficiencies. To remedy this, it is essential that they receive extra food such as milk, eggs, sugar, flour and cooking oil.

At a meeting between the I.J.A. representative (Captain Hachisuka and Mr Fujibayashi) and the British Red Cross representatives at Changi on 13 April 1943 it was agreed that when things settled down, if the force urgently required money it could apply for a grant from the International Red Cross through the I.J.A. administration, which would be the same as at Changi.

Money is urgently required by "F" Force for the purchase of special food and drugs for the 3,500 PoW remaining here. This amount is estimated at $350,000 for a period of three months. At present hospital patients and sick men are not paid by the I.J.A. and during the past seven months the sick of the force have been financed by voluntary contributions from the officers who contribute 3/8ths of their limited pay they receive in cash for this purpose. I do feel that the provision of extra food and medical requirements for the force should not be the responsibility of the officers, and in any case their contributions (although, of course, these will continue) are now totally inadequate to meet this urgent situation.

It would be greatly appreciated if the I.J.A. would allow the International Red Cross Society to:-

1. Supply the necessary drugs and dressings for this force which the local I.J.A. administration is unable to provide.
2. Furnish the force with a sum of money ($350,00) to purchase extra food and necessities for the sick.

The clothing of this force is in a deplorable condition, a big proportion of the men are without boots and are literally in rags.

It would be appreciated if an issue of clothing could be made at the earliest opportunity.

Although the 1,000 Prisoners of War that have been selected to go to Singapore from this force in the near future are the fittest available, nevertheless, 200 are unfit and of the remaining 800 over 90% have suffered during the past seven months from malaria and dysentery and they are bound to have frequent relapses. It is respectfully requested therefore that whatever work is allotted to this detachment should not be of too arduous a nature.

Signed S.W. Harris
Lieut. Colonel, R.A.
Commander, "F" Force

––––––––––––––––––––––––––––––

Copy of letter submitted by Major B.A. Hunt AAMC to O.C. Tanbaya Hospital Camp, dated 14 October 43

Sir,

I wish to draw your attention to certain facts and figures concerning disease and sickness amongst the body of 7,000 Ps.O.W, British and Australian which left SINGAPORE at the end of April, 1943. In particular I shall detail certain facts and figures concerning the men of that force who are now patients in this camp. I should be grateful if you would, after reading this document, forward it to the General responsible for the administration and care of PsoW

(1) When the original order for the despatch of this force was issued, no indication that long marching would be required was given (the contrary was implied). As a result, many old men otherwise unsuitable for marching were sent. These men naturally broke down very early on the march and many of them have been in hospital ever since, or have died of other diseases contracted in Thailand.

(2) The force has been in Thailand and Burma for just over 5 months. During that period over 2,000 men have lost their lives from disease – approx. 30%.

(3) The chief causes of death have been:-

(i) CHOLERA. This arose from the troops being herded

186

together in camps in close proximity to Tami and Thai coolies amongst whom cholera was widespread. The essential article in the treatment of cholera is intravenous saline – none was provided

(ii) DYSENTERY chiefly AMOEBIC. It is a matter of common medical knowledge throughout the world that Thailand is the most heavily amoebic-infested country in the world. Yet no effort was made to protect the troops at the Staging Camps, where the sanitary arrangements were filthy, and where many hundreds of men became infected. It is again universally recognised that the only treatment of any value in amoebic dysentery are emetine, yatren, and ovarsol[103]. Despite numerous requests none of these drugs have been supplied, and as a result hundreds of innocent men have died unnecessarily.

(iii) BERI-BERI. The causes of beri-beri are very well known, especially to Japanese scientists, who have done much valuable work in the treatment of this disease. Yet, on many occasions, and especially in this camp, for no apparent reason a diet has been supplied which was certain to produce, which we informed the I.J.A. would produce, and which has in actual fact produced, many hundreds of cases of beri-beri and caused many deaths. Why this camp should have received a small and inadequate bean ration for over two months, while the hospital camp at 55 km has throughout this period been getting all the beans it needed, passes our comprehension. In this connection we are most grateful to you for increasing our bean ration to 2½ bags daily, and hope that it may soon be possible to increase this ration still further to 4 bags. A small supply of B.1. tablets and ampules was given in July – only adequate for a few cases – no official supply since.

(iv) MALARIA. It is well known that Thailand is very highly malarial, yet troops were not supplied with nets until most of them were infected, and quinine supplies were never adequate to give long enough courses of treatment to check relapses.

---

[103] The editor has been unable to identify the drug ovarsol.

(v) <u>TROPICAL ULCERS</u>. The very gross deficiency in vitamins A and C in our diet has so lowered the resistance of the skin to even the most trifling infection that huge ulcers have developed in hundreds of cases, causing loss of legs or loss of life. The only satisfactory local treatments are idoform and sulphonomide – very small supplies of these drugs were made available in July, enough to last only for two to three days – none before or since.

(4) In addition to the above fatal diseases, scabies has spread rapidly throughout the force, and especially through this camp. The only possible treatment for scabies is sulphur, a common and cheap product, yet all our appeals for sulphur have produced no results and over 1,100 men in this camp are now infected with scabies. Infected scabies often goes on to the formation of ulcers.

TAMBAYA HOSPITAL CAMP

This camp was established at the beginning of August to accommodate between 1,500 and 2,000 of the sick of "F" Force. We were informed before the camp was formed that the food here would certainly be better than it was in the working camps and that medical supplies would possibly be available. In actual fact the food has not been better than in the working camps and in the particular item of beans has been much worse, so that instead of improving from beri-beri, they have actually become worse and in many cases died. Moreover, several hundred new cases of beri-beri have developed particularly amongst the working men of the camp, more than half of whom are now in hospital. Apart from what trifling quantities we had left from our own British and Australian supplies at Changi no medical stores whatever have come into this camp despite very frequent representations on this matter by every possible channel.

PRESENT MEDICAL SITUATION
The diseases are Malaria 275, Dysentery 426, Beri-Beri 630, Ulcers 265, Scabies about 1,150. In general the health of the camp is <u>not</u> improving, but rather is getting steadily worse – chiefly on account of the poor diet. Fewer and fewer really fit men are available to perform camp work and are not well enough to come out of hospital to take the place of the fit men as they fall

ill. As an example – of the total of 142 RAMC and AAMC personnel in this camp (including barbers and hygiene men as well as nurses) 63 are actually working at the moment, the remainder being sick in hospital.

FUTURE MOVE

We have been informed that a move of part or the whole of this Hospital Camp is likely at an early date, and we have been asked to give certain figures. As Hospital Commander the prospect of this move fills me with horror. During the past two days I have completely surveyed all the wards in the hospital. I find the health of the patients so bad that in my considered opinion not less than 320 men will probably lose their lives during or shortly after a move of any duration (say 3 to 4 days). Above and beyond these, about 400 men will require to be carried by stretcher.

If it is decided to leave many or most of these very sick men behind, the staff of fit men to look after them will be just as numerous as is required at present because there will not be the supply of semi-fit patients who are able to help their fellow sufferers by doing light jobs in the wards.

Since there will be no men available whatever for carrying the stretchers on to and off the trains, if these men are to be moved, the only possible solution which I can see, will be to bring some fit men down from the working camps to help with the move.

So far as the future is concerned, the only possible means of getting any of these desperately sick men sufficiently well to enable them to travel in safety will be to improve camp rations, especially as regards beans and meat, very considerably and to make available at a very early date full and adequate supplies of the necessary drugs.

SUMMARY

If we had been taken prisoner by a barbarous race unaccustomed to the usage of warfare between civilisations, complete lack of medical precautions and the failure to provide the sick the drugs they so urgently need, would be understandable. But we find it very difficult to understand why such treatment be meted out to its prisoners to a great and powerful nation like Japan, whose doctors and scientists are amongst the best in the world and whose proud boast is of chivalry to the vanquished. Is it too much to hope that even at this late date these poor, helpless suffering prisoners may receive the consideration, the food and the medical supplies which they so badly need and which I know – because I have personally inspected many PoW camps – are always supplied by Great Britain and Australia to the PsoW who are in their care?

(Signed) Bruce Hunt
Major AAMC
Comd. Tanbaya Hospital.

–––––––––––––––––––––––––––––

To: Officer in Charge
     Shino Sonkrai Camp

The medical situation in this camp is extremely grave and is becoming worse every hour. At the present moment cholera is raging – there have been 37 deaths and there are over 90 patients in hospital – new cases are occurring at the rate of 35 or more daily.

Dysentery is still a serious problem and many men are so debilitated from prolonged dysentery and diarrhoea that it will be many weeks before they are fit for any form of work; meantime their resistance to cholera or any other disease is seriously impaired.

Malaria is rapidly increasing, and we anticipate that within a week or two there will be hundreds of sufferers.

Taking the situation as a whole, it is our anticipation that within one month there will NOT be 250 men in this camp to do a day's work.

The reasons for this situation are that the men in this camp have been subjected to treatment which is wrong for any civilised nation to inflict on its prisoners of war.

In detail:-
1. The men before leaving CHANGI were weakened by dysentery and deficiency diseases (beri-beri and pellagra) and were in no condition to withstand infectious diseases.
2. An assurance was given by the I.J.A. at CHANGI to the commander A.I.F. at CHANGI that food would be better here than at CHANGI and that troops would not have to march from the train to their destination. Neither of these

promises have been kept. Replying on the second promise many men totally unfit to march were included in the force – very many of these are now in hospitals – some here died.

3. The hygiene of the camps on the road was appalling and hundreds of men were successively affected by dysentery, by malaria and finally by cholera, the present tragedy is the result.

4. The conditions on marching were extremely arduous and in some cases unwarrantedly cruel. Sick men were driven out on to the road night after night, in some cases with high fever of active dysentery. As a result men arrived here completely exhausted.

5. After arrival men were put in an unhygienic, badly situated camp, roofless and with very bad latrine accommodation; all conditions ideal for the spread of disease were present and disease has, in consequence, rapidly spread – your own report that 58 positive reports for cholera were found in about 500 apparently healthy men showed how rapidly and widely the spread took place.

6. No adequate rest was given to men, nor was any assistance given to requests for help. On the contrary, men were sent out to work and kept out of camp 12 to 13 hours a day in the pouring rain – conditions typical NOT of the honourable treatment of prisoners of war, but of slave labour.

At the present moment (approximately):-
37 men are dead of cholera
95 men are in hospital with cholera
250 men are in hospital with other diseases
140 men are excused all duty on account of sickness, and many of these would be in hospital if there was enough room, or drugs, or nurses. 150 men are so weakened by illness that they are only fit for light duties. 120 men are being used (or have been used) to the care of the sick and of these 30 have already become so sick to have been already admitted to hospital.

Thus about 800 men out of 2000 have become invalid or have become required to nurse the sick within 14 days of arrival in this camp – and the number is likely to increase rapidly.

In view of the above facts, we recommend:-

191

1. That this document be forwarded to the International Red Cross in Bangkok and Rangoon.
2. That all work shall cease, NOT for three days but indefinitely until the present cholera epidemic has been fully got under control. In these circumstances we draw your attention to the promise given on the 27th May 1943 that all work would cease for three days. This promise was broken the day after it was given.

The reasons for asking for all work to cease are:-
   a)   To enable all necessary construction work around the camp on latrines, roofing and drainage to be done.
   b)   To enable hundreds of debilitated men to rest and recover their health
   c)   To permit enough men to be allotted to nursing work to give adequate treatment to the hundreds of sick and rest the present overworked and exhausted nursing staff.
   d)   The supplies of adequate drugs, disinfectants, soap, lights and other medical supplies.
   e)   The supply of blankets for the sick.
   f)   The supply of invalid foods and soups, and tea and sugar for the sick.
   g)   The improvement of the camp diet by extra vitamin-containing food e.g. rice polishings, towgay, meat, oil and fats.
   h)   The supply of suppressive atebrin for the whole camp – the present small quinine dosageis quite inadequate and without effect.
   i)   The supply of water containers especially 44-gallon drums to enable water to be used on a large scale, and also smaller containers for water boiling, to make sterilisation possible.
   j)   The supply of a large number of tents (waterproof) for the cholera area which is extending daily. At least 30 large tents are required apart from what is now in the camp.
   k)   The supply of oil for dealing with mosquito-breeding places in the camp – a visit from Captain WILSON, Malarial expert, at HQ Camp is urgently necessary to locate these.

l) The supply of protective clothing – white coats for nurses handling cholera.

m) As soon as the health of the camp has been improved, which may NOT be for several months, the evacuation of the area by troops and their subsequent treatment in a manner befitting the honourable JAPANESE nation whose reputation must suffer gravely if the present conditions continue.

We demand that this document is laid before Lt. Col. BANNO and the senior Japanese Medical Officer for the area and also before Lt. Col. HARRIS at the earliest possible moment – preferably tonight.

Signed: W. McJohnston, Major
Comd. AIF Troops,
Shimo Sombrei Camp

Bruce Hunt, S.M.O., Major,
S.M.O. Camp, A.A.M.O.

Tracey, Major
Commander No.1 Bn

R.H. Anderson, Major
Commander No.2 Bn

CHAPTER 19

POSTSCRIPT
War Crimes Trials, Tokyo and Singapore, September and October 1946

On 29 November 1945, just thirteen weeks after the end of the war, an article was published in the *West Australian* newspaper by Major Bruce Hunt, which revealed to the world the conditions endured by the men of "F" Force. It also gave him an opportunity to express himself more openly than when he was a prisoner. He spoke first about the march from Bampong: 'Men toiled through the pitch blackness, sometimes knee deep in water, sometimes staggering off bridges in the darkness: sprains and bruises were common, broken arms and legs occurred and stragglers were set upon and looted by marauding Thais. Of the large and growing number of sick many fell by the wayside, and they and their kit had to be carried by their comrades.'

Hunt also wrote of the work the men were compelled to perform and the state of the camps: 'The work demanded of all men, without consideration of their physical condition, was heavy navvy labour on the rushed construction of the 30 mile stretch of the railway through the hilly and flooded jungle immediately south of the Three Pagodas Pass on the Burma-Thailand border. This work was arduous in the extreme, men having to carry logs far beyond their capacity and pile-drive up to their waists in water. The hours were generally from first light to dark; but frequently men were kept out as late as 2 am the following morning. Men working in quarries without boots had their feet badly cut and these cuts developed into tropical ulcers ... The hospital, so called, in every camp was nothing but a dilapidated hut with leaky roof, no walls or lighting and with split bamboo flooring on which men were crammed, their bodies touching on another. In these grossly overcrowded conditions even such mosquito nets as the Japanese provided could not be used, with the result that over 90 per cent of the force were speedily infected with malaria.' Also, Bruce Hunt described the brutal treatment handed out by the Japanese: 'There were daily beatings of officers and men at work, some of them even being beaten into unconsciousness. These beatings were not for disciplinary purposes but were intended to urge sick and enfeebled men to physical efforts quite beyond their remaining strength, or to punish officers for intervening on their behalf.'

Hunt concluded: 'The Japanese are a race apart from us: they do not see things the way we do, they do not think the same way, their instinctive reactions in given circumstances are different, their attitude towards life, towards honour and towards keeping one's word are different …

'If you are dealing with a Jap the only argument he can understand is one where you can "put it across" him, preferably with a Tommy gun. He understands "force majeure" and so the only way to meet him is to have that "force majeure" yourself.'

It was evident that people would have to answer for these crimes and fortunately the reports and correspondence written by the officers of "F" Force had been preserved – indeed, one of the reasons for the preservation of these documents was that of bringing to the attention of the world the treatment the prisoners endured at the hands of the I.J.A. and to hold those responsible to account. This bore fruit when seven of the Japanese involved with "F" Force were brought before the United Nations War Crimes Commission – and a key figure in the investigation of the crimes committed by the Japanese was another member of "F" Force, Major Cyril Wild.

As someone who spoke Japanese and who had lived and worked in Japan before the war, as well as having witnessed war crimes first-hand, Wild was perfectly equipped for the task he was set as a member of E Group of the War Crimes Investigations in Malaya and Singapore. He continued with this work until he was able to finally return to the UK in December 1945. But the British authorities wanted him to continue his work, to which he agreed on the proviso that he was raised in rank to that of full colonel to give him equal status with many of his U.S. counterparts.

He returned to Singapore on 16 February 1946, this time accompanied by his wife Celia, as War Crimes Liaison Officer, Malaya and Singapore.

Colonel Wild worked assiduously in this role, seeking out and apprehending more than 170 suspected war criminals.[104] But the

---

[104] More details are recorded in Bradley's *Cyril Wild, The Tall Man Who Never Slept.*

crimes that Wild wanted investigated more than any other were those he and his comrades had endured on the Burma Railway. This he was able to do when the International Military Tribunal for the Far East resumed its proceedings in the War Ministry Building at Ichigaya, Tokyo, on Friday, 13 September 1946.[105]

Prompted by questions from British lawyer Sir Arthur Comyns Carr, Wild related many of the stories recorded in the medical officers' reports and correspondence. Among the many incidents he spoke about was the incident in August 1943 when the Japanese threatened to expel the PoWs from Sonkurai camp because so many of them were sick and couldn't work and replace them with native labour. Colonel Banno's administration had endorsed this action which would see 700 sick men being cast into the jungle to die.

Under questioning, Wild spoke of another incident which took place at the end of May 1943: 'We heard ... that about twelve of our men were still at Konkuita camp. Konkuita was the cholera camp ... about thirty miles south of us. We therefore got permission from the Japanese to send Assistant-Surgeon Wolfe, an Anglo-Indian, to Konkuita. He found eight of the twelve men in a small tent. Four of them were suffering from cholera. They had had no food or attention from the Japanese for several days and were lying in their own filth. Wolfe paid three visits to the Japanese medical major ... whose hut was in that camp. He asked for medical supplies from quite a well-stocked dispensary there. All he was given was some disinfectant to wash his own hands with. He made a strong appeal to this Japanese medical major, saying that the men would die without medical attention. The Japanese major said, "It can't be helped; if they die, they die".'[106]

While not acknowledging anything to do with this particular incident, the defence said that: 'Since the proposed site of the railway line was virgin jungle, shelter, food provisions and medical supplies were far from adequate ... During the rainy season of 1943 transportation was frequently interrupted and both Japanese soldiers and prisoners of war were obliged to put up with much hardship.' The defence also claimed that: 'The Japanese Army Medical Corps tried in vain to stem the violent outburst of malaria and sickness of digestive organs.'

This was later repeated in a similar vein: 'Though the Japanese Army did its best in taking the best possible measure conceivable at that time

---

[105] The full transcripts of the trials can be found at imtfe.law.virginia. edu/collections/sutton/8/45/trial-transcript-september-13-1946#expanded
[106] Bradley, pp.149-50.

in order to improve the treatment of the prisoners of war cooperating with the Japanese troops, laying stress on billeting, rations and health, many prisoners of war fell victim of the work at last much to our regret.

'We should like to declare the Japanese troops participated in the joys and sorrows of the prisoners of war and native labourers in the construction work.'

Of course, if there had not been a mass of documents written and preserved by the medical officers, it would have been difficult to corroborate in detail Cyril Wild's allegations. Colonel Wild continued to give evidence until 19 September, though the trials did not conclude until 10 April 1948.

Wild's next assignment was in Singapore for the trial of those Japanese soldiers held directly responsible for the atrocities inflicted upon "F" Force. This was the trial Cyril Wild had been waiting for. Arthur Lane, a drummer and bugler with the Manchester Regiment, told *Post Magazine* that prisoners in the camps were asked to pass on to Wild information concerning the ill-treatment of British and Australian personnel. 'I was a bugler,' said Lane, 'and, as such, I had to attend many funerals in prison camps along the route of the railway. I was able to supply Major Wild with the names of any men who had not died of natural causes. Those who had been killed. Wild hid his information in a vestment case that belonged to a padre [Duckworth] and which Wild carefully buried close to the camps.'[107]

Wild was unable to find a seat on any direct flight between Tokyo and Singapore, but he managed to get a flight to Hong Kong, though he was stranded there until 25 September, at last finding space on a flight to Singapore. The RAF Dakota took off from Kai Tak airport at 09.39 hours. Just moments later it crashed to the ground, killing all fourteen passengers and crew in circumstances which have never been explained. Cyril Wild was killed on the very day that what was referred to as the 'Banno Trial' was due to begin.

SINGAPORE TRIALS

Of the Australian investigations into war crimes and the subsequent trials, twenty-one were in connection with the ill-treatment of PoWs on the Burma-Thailand Railway. Of these, eighteen were held in Singapore and three in Hong Kong. The accused were for the most part N.C.Os. and guards in close contact with the PoWs and the typical crimes were

---

[107] See also fepow-community.org.uk/monthly_Revue/html/colonel_wild.htm.

assaults and forcing the sick to work. In only five of the twenty-one trials were officers charged.[108] The trials relating to "F" Force, were held in Singapore on 25-28, 30 September and 1, 3-4, 7-12, 14-17, 22-23 October 1946.

Seven men were put on trial: Lieutenant Colonel Banno Hirateru, Captain (Medical) Tanio Susumu, Captain Muruyama Hajime, Captain Fukuda Tsuneo, Civilian Toyoyama Kisei, Lieutenant Abe Hiroshi and Civilian Ishimoto Eishin.

All seven faced the charge of 'Committing a War Crime in that they in Siam, between April 1st 1943 and December 31st 1943, in violation of the laws and usages of war, when engaged in the administration of a group of British and Australian Prisoners of War known as "F" Force, employed in the construction of the Burma-Siam railway, were together concerned in the inhumane treatment of the said Prisoners of War, resulting in the deaths of many, and in the physical suffering of many others of the said Prisoners of War.'[109]

In addition, Banno Hirateru, Tanio Susumu, Muruyama Hajime, and Fukuda Tsuneo, faced a second charge of 'Committing a War Crime in that they in Siam, between April 1st 1943 and December 31st 1943, in violation of the laws and usages of war, while engaged in the administration of a group of British and Australian Prisoners of War known as "F" Force, employed in the construction of the Burma-Siam Railway, were concerned in the internment of the said Prisoners of War in conditions which were unhealthy and unhygienic.'[110]

After a summary of the decision to send the 7,000 men (that comprised "F" Force) to work on the railway, and of the severity of the journey, the following was related to the court:

"F" Force remained under the general administration of Major General Arimura's HQ at Singapore the local Japanese Commander was Lieutenant-Colonel Banno. The Camps were commanded individually by Junior Japanese officers or N.C.Os. of the Malaya PoW Administration.

Cholera broke out soon after arrival in early May. This outbreak was due to the fact that during the course of the march all the marching parties had camped at Konquita for

[108] D.C.S. Sissons, *The Australian War Crimes Trials and Investigations (1942-51)*, p.36.
[109] ICC Legal Tools Database, document reference 2f0912.
[110] ibid.

a period of one or more days within a few yards of huts filled with hundreds of cholera-stricken coolies. A protest was made to Lieutenant Colonel Banno without effect and the result was that by the end of May, cholera was epidemic in all of the 5 labour camps.

The evidence will show that conditions in the camps was of the utmost severity. The work demanded of all men without consideration of their physical wellbeing was severe manual labour on the construction of a 50 kilometre stretch of the Burma-Siam railway immediately south of the 3 Pagoda Pass. The hours of work were generally from first light until dark, but frequently men were kept out as late as 0200 hrs the following morning. Capt. ABE was responsible for forcing sick men to work and forcing all working Prisoners of War to perform tasks beyond their strength, driving them by the use of brutal methods. There were daily beatings of Officers and men at work, not for disciplinary purposes but intended only to force sick men and enfeebled men to physical efforts beyond their strength or to punish Officers for intervening on their behalf. TOYOYAMA (No.6 accused) was noted for his continual beatings of officers and men, often using a steel shaft of a golf club as a weapon. Capt. FUKUDA (No.4 accused) who was Commandant at Lower Songkurai and Upper Songkurai and was, as such, responsible for much ill-treatment of Prisoners of War, revealed his attitude by 2 remarks made at official interviews:

'International Law and Geneva Convention does not apply if they conflict with the interests of the Japanese Army.'

'You have in the past spoken somewhat boastfully of the Geneva Convention and humanity, you must remember that you are our Prisoners of War, that you are in our power and that under the present circumstances these things do not apply.'

Capt. TANIO, as Medical Officer in charge of "F" Force was responsible for the shortage of medical supplies, medical staff and for the faulty hospital accommodation and all other matters pertaining to the health of the Prisoners of War by neglect of which many deaths were caused.

Protests as to these conditions were made to Lt. Col. BANNO

and to Major-General Arimura's H.Q., but no answer was ever received.

The following are tables and statistics showing the consequences of these conditions.

Deaths by Month

<u>1943</u>

May	183
June	425
July	249
August	537
September	506
October	395
November	396
December	280

<u>1944</u>

January	76
February	26
March	12
April	12 [111]

In November 1943, the Force was moved back, first to Kanburi and later to Singapore. The conditions endured on the return journey were as severe as those suffered in transit from Singapore to Siam.

Nine men had provided the court with affidavits, with the intention that Cyril Wild would have given verbal confirmation of the accuracy of Lieutenant Colonel Hutchison's "History". Those presenting affidavits were Major Johnson, Major Hyde, Major Hunt, Captain Havells, Captain Mills, Chaplain Polain, Sergeant Berry and Private Robert Ward.

All the accused denied the charges that were levelled against them, and claimed that they did all they could, given the circumstantial factors beyond their control.

[111] Death by disease was also itemised after this list.

According to a report compiled by Stephanie Beckman, at the U.C. Berkeley War Crimes Studies Center it was demonstrated that there was a great deal of evidence, even in the prosecution case, which showed that the main causes of the high mortality of "F" Forces were factors beyond the scope of responsibility of these accused, for example:

a) "F" Force started off from Changi with 30 per cent of its number unfit and suffering from beriberi, dysentery, and other diseases, and the majority unfit for work on account of malnutrition.

b) Throughout the evidence stress was placed on the fact that one of the most important factors leading to the high mortality of "F" Force was the fatigue resulting from the march from Bampong to the camp sites, and the cholera that was picked up en route and subsequently became an epidemic. None of the 4 accused were responsible for that march, or the staging arrangements en route.

c) None of these accused was responsible for the shortage of medicines, which might have prevented many deaths. Most of the deaths were due to diseases.

d) There was ample evidence to show that the climate and terrain were important factors which impeded the provision of adequate supplies.[112]

The defence also argued that the conditions of the camps were 'quite reasonable'. There were, no doubt cultural, economic and social disparities between the Japanese and the British and Australians which might have led to different perceptions of what might or might not be considered 'reasonable' and the Japanese would not have wished to visit the unhealthy hospital wards – especially the cholera wards – too often. The Japanese perception of the camps must be seen through their eyes and not of those who had to live there.

The defendants also sought to shift the blame, declaring that the whole 7,000 men of "F" Force were submitted to blood examinations before being sent into Thailand, and that vaccination against small-pox, inoculation against dysentery, plague, cholera and enteric bacteria, were given in two doses at weekly intervals under area management, but that "F" Force took malaria and dysentery with them from

---

[112] Stephanie Beckman, U.C. Berkeley War Crimes Studies Center, Singapore Cases: No.235/1034 Banno Case.

Singapore.[113] According to Colonel Huston's "History", it may be recalled, the cholera inoculations had not been completed by the time the Force had to leave Changi.

The defendants pointed out that the British and Australians took their medical supplies with them when they left Changi. This was true, of course, but no transport was provided to help move the supplies from the railhead at Bampong, which is where they remained.

The cholera outbreak, the defence claimed, occurred due to 'unforeseen circumstances'. The defence argued that it was in fact the Imperial Japanese Army medical men who first alerted the "F" Force doctors of the presence of cholera on 15 May, after half the Force had passed through Konkoita, the epicentre of the disease. Though this is not how it is recorded in the "History".

Some of what was written in the correspondence that was preserved worked in favour of the defendants. It may be recalled that Colonel Harris wrote to Colonel Banno towards the end of June 1943 stating that he appreciated 'the fact that Colonel Banno and his administration are doing everything they can on our behalf' and on 18 August he praising Banno for his 'good will and sincerity' and that 'Lieut. Wakabayashi has always done his utmost to help us and with his kind assistance we have been able to improve greatly the sanitation, hygiene and cooking facilities.'

It was certainly the case, as the defence stressed, that the circumstances the Malayan PoW Administration found itself in were extremely challenging. Banno had only a staff of 150 for 7,000 PoWs, with just eight lorries, and one ambulance. For all other transport, huts, food and medical supplies, they were dependent on the Railway Administration.

Banno argued that he had done as much as he could to improve the conditions faced by the PoWs. He stopped sick officers from being compelled to work (though this was a somewhat spurious argument as the Hague Convention forbade the forced working of officers). He did, in fairness, intercede when the re-captured escapees faced the death penalty and saved their lives.

Some of the defendant's claims were clearly unfounded. Banno declared that 'plenty' of good food was issued to the PoWs. The medical officers' reports and the correspondence with Banno emphasized on every occasion that the prisoners' inability to resist disease was to a large degree due to the poor diet.

---

[113] ibid.

Muruyama Hajime pled that he was never on the railway and had an alibi to prove that. It was a case, he claimed, of mistaken identity.

Tsuneo said that there was no proven case of individual cruelty or neglect, while Kisei, and Eishin declared that that any ill-treatment that they carried out was for disciplinary measures and nothing else, which they said was 'necessary'.

It was also claimed that those sick men who were sent to work were always selected by the prisoners' doctors and never any of the accused.

THE KAPPE REPORT

In support of the Australian War Crimes Commission was the report written by the commander of the A.I.F. contingent of "F" Force, Lieutenant Colonel Charles Henry Kappe, in May 1944 at Changi prison. With regards to some of the accused, of Captain Fukuda, Kappe wrote: 'He [Fukuda] said that if he ordered that 1000 men would go to work, they would go, despite any protests which we would make – the Japanese Engineers were prepared to die, and the prisoners also must be prepared to sacrifice their lives for the railway.

'He went on to threaten that not only would the camp commander and his staff be punished, but all men in the camp would be made to suffer for the disobedience of his orders.

'Their own particular punishment was to consist of being made to stand in a fire … he pointed out that the construction of the railway had to go on without delay, as it was required for operational purposes, and had to be finished within a certain time at all costs, irrespective of the loss of lives of British and Australian prisoners … He said that it was of no use our quoting the articles of the Geneva Convention … If necessary, he concluded, the men would be required to work three to four days on end without rest.'[114]

Toyoyama Kisei was called Fukuda's 'notorious assistant', by Kappe, referring to a number of brutal events, including one on 16 August: 'A stormy incident occurred when the guards entered the hospital and attempted to intimidate the sick by striking the flooring close to the men's bodies. The Camp Commander ordered the men not to budge, and he protested on humanitarian grounds. Toyama [sic] then appeared and threatened all forms of punishment, and stated that unless 50 men were out of the hospital within five minutes the whole

[114] "F" Force Report by Lieutenant Colonel C H Kappe, op. cit.

camp would be placed on half rations and that the guards would forcibly eject men picked at random.'

With regards to Lieutenant Abe, Kappe recorded: 'Their [the PoWs] work task had been the construction of a large bridge over the river adjacent to the camp. So severe were the demands on them by the engineer officer-in-charge, Lieut. Abe, that men unfit to walk had to be carried on their comrades' backs to parade and thence to work on the bridge, where they were forced to haul heavy logs and beams from a sitting position.

'Men had been, and continued to be, beaten (until the completion of the bridge on August 20) with wire whips and bamboo sticks, and unfit men were punched and kicked, not for disciplinary reasons, but to drive them to make efforts beyond their strength. Lieut. Abe made no attempt whatsoever to stop this brutal treatment by his men.'

Complaints about Captain Muruyama feature heavily in Kappe's report, mostly regarding his captain's failure to respond to Kappe's frequent appeals for improvements in the prisoners' conditions. Kappe also wrote that during an outbreak of dysentery at Kami-Sonkurai camp all work ceased and the camp was quarantined: 'In addition to these troubles the ration position became more serious than ever – rice dropped to 7.5 ozs. per man per day. This meant two meals only per day of plain rice, the supply of onions having been exhausted.

'Apparently Lieut. Murayama considered that as no work was being performed the issue of a minimum ration to prevent starvation was justified.'

Kappe later added: 'Murayama, in order to bring up the working figures to the required strength, would drive even the sickest man out of camp.

'It is literally true that only men who were close to death were allowed to remain in camp. It is equally true that deaths of many men were caused, or at least accelerated, by this callous drive.'

Kappe also wrote: 'From information furnished by Korean guards it is certain that Murayama was not distributing rations issued to him for the prisoners of war.'

At the conclusion of the trial, identification of all the accused was well established, and thanks to the 'mass' of documents provided there was ample evidence to support the findings of the court. Colonel Banno, Captain Tanio Susumu, Captain Muruyama Hajime, and Captain Fukuda Tsuneo, were found guilty of both charges, resulting in a sentence of three years' imprisonment for Banno and five years for Captain Tanio Susumu. Captains Muruyama Hajime and Fukuda

Tsuneo were sentenced to death by hanging, as were Toyoyama Kisei, and Lieutenant Abe Hiroshi.

However, the evidence before the court did not sufficiently establish that the third, fourth, fifth or sixth accused actually caused the death of any PoW, or participated in such brutality as would justify the imposition of the death penalty.

The conclusion was, therefore, that all the sentences would stand, but that the death sentences would be commuted. This resulted in life imprisonment for Tsuneo and Kisei, and fifteen years each for Hajime and Abe Hiroshi. Ishimoto Eishin was given the lightest sentence of all, just eighteen months.

Index of Persons

A

Ainger, Captain J., 138,

Agnew, Major, 41

Anderson, Major R.H., 193

Anderton, Signaller N., 120

Anker, Captain W.H., 164

Arimura, Major-General Tsunemichi, 26, 173, 176, 198, 200

Auld, Major, 140

B

Banno *see* Hirateru, Lieutenant Colonel Banno

Barber, Captain A., 16, 178

Brand, Captain, 183

Brand, Major, 179

Barnett, Captain Ben, 24, 166

Berry, Sergeant, 200

Boyle, James, 5

Bradley, Corporal Bernard, 65

Bradley, Lieutenant J.B., 28, 65, 164, 165

Bradley, Sergeant Ian, 65

Brown, Corporal, 164

Brown, Captain R., 179, 183

C

Cahill, Captain A, 120

Cahill, Captain F.J., 91, 121

Cahill, Captain Lloyd, 178

Carlton, Private, 105

Carr, Sir Arthur Comyns, 196

Cordingley, Chaplain Rev. E., 183

D

Dawkins, Joe, 65

Dean, Lieutenant, 144

Deans, Lance Corporal F., 120

Dillon, Lieutenant Colonel F.J., 6, 18, 30, 36, 67, 71, 103, 104, 105, 106, 140, 167

Dix, Captain, 179, 184

Dobson, Major, 145

Duckworth, Padre J.N., 64, 65, 197

E

Eaton, Lieutenant R., 140

Eishin, Ishimoto, 198, 203, 205

Ellis, Corporal 'Taffy', 65

Ellerman, Lieutenant A., 140

Emery, Captain E.J.,78, 91, 120, 181

F

Feathers, Captain J., 164

Fletcher, Lieutenant R.G., 44, 79, 140

Furze, Lieutenant, 79

Franks, Quarter Master Sergeant J.W., 120

Frew, Captain J., 179, 183
Fujibayashi, Mr, 185

G

Gairdner, Major, 44, 80
Geikie, Lieutenant, 140
Gibson, Captain, 140
Gillies, Major D.G., 179
Godman, Lieutenant Arthur, 67
Gwynne, Captain George W., 120, 130

H

Hachisuka, Captain, 185
Hanbury, Major, 181
Hasegawa, Captain Saburo, xi
Hajime, Captain Muruyama, 198, 203, 204, 205
Hardie, Robert, 41
Harris, Lieutenant Colonel S.W., ix, 2, 6, 9, 10, 12, 16, 26, 30, 31, 33, 34, 36, 39, 40, 42, 53, 54, 77, 79, 93, 103, 104, 105, 106, 140, 174, 186, 193, 202
Havells, Captain, 200
Hedley, James, 65
Hendry, Dr Peter, x
Hirateru, Lieutenant Colonel Banno, xi, 12, 13, 15, 16, 21, 22, 26, 28, 29, 30, 31, 37, 39, 40, 41, 48, 54, 55, 71, 71, 91, 104, 147, 151, 152, 166, 167, 168, 169, 172, 174, 176, 177, 183, 193, 196, 197, 198, 199, 202, 204
Hingston, Lieutenant Colonel A.T., 63
Hiroshi, Lieutenant Abe, xii, 57, 198, 199, 205

Holding, Private W., 67
Hutchinson, Lieutenant Colonel G.T., 32, 8292, 96, 178
Hunt, Major Bruce Atlee, 5, 11, 15, 17, 32, 45-7, 82, 91, 96, 102, 106, 120, 124, 154, 158, 179, 180, 181, 182, 183, 186, 190, 193, 194, 195, 200
Huston, Lieutenant Colonel J., xiii, 6, 12, 15, 16, 37, 106, 107, 116, 142, 172, 173, 174, 177, 184, 202
Hyde, Major, 200

I

Iraiwa, Lieutenant, 91

J

Jackson, Chaplain Reverend A., 183
Jackson, Corporal Peter, 65
Jarman, Reginald Thomas, 104
Jones, Lieutenant T.P.D., 164, 165
Johnson, Major, 200

K

Kanada, Second Lieutenant, 44
Kappe, Lieutenant Colonel Charles Henry, x, 2, 12, 33, 43, 104, 169, 178, 203-5
Kisei, Toyoyama, 193, 203, 205
Koriyasu, I.J.A. civilian interpreter, 5

L

Laird, Adjutant Richard, 8, 57
Lane, Drummer Arthur, 107
Lowe, Captain, 181

M

Machade, Lieutenant G.A., 164
Mannion, Captain, 179, 183, 184
Maruyamma, Captain, 166
McInerney, Tom, 11, 22
McJohnston, Major W., 193
Mills, Captain Roy M, 43, 104, 105, 200
Miyasaki, Captain, 2
Moffat, Lieutenant I.M., 164, 165

N

Nichol, Private Gordon, 120
Nur Mohammed, 164

O

Onishi, Lieutenant, 29, 30

P

Pantridge, Captain, 181
Percival, Lieutenant General Arthur Ernest, vii
Phillips, Major W.J.E., 40, 105, 181
Polain, Chaplain George, 200
Pond, Lieutenant Colonel S.A.F., 12, 43, 73, 104, 167, 171
Pope, Lieutenant Colonel, 63
Price, Major M.D., 91, 140

R

Raw, Lieutenant, 44
Rawlings, Corporal A.W., 120
Reid, Major J.A., 133
Robinson, Lieutenant J.F., 164, 165
Roges, Major, 183
Ross-Dean, Reverend, 11

S

Saji, Mr, 30, 167, 178
Scully, Corporal J., 120
Sijuo, Colonel, 162
Singleton, Sergeant Jimmy, 65
Somerfield, Lance Corporal R., 105
Silman, Captain Harry, 78, 103, 181
Stevens, Major, R.H., 15, 16, 165
Stone, Private. L., 120
Susumu, Captain Doctor Tanio, 198, 204

T

Tanaka, Captain, 2
Tanio, Lieutenant Dr., 21, 153, 184, 198, 199, 204
Taylor, Captain J.L., 14, 15, 179
Tracey, Major, C., 193
Troedel, Corporal John Charles, 116
Tsuneo, Captain Fukuda, 5, 198, 203, 205
Turner, Captain, 79
Turner, Lieutenant L., 120, 181
Twigg, Private Reg, 4

W

Waller, Captain G.G., 140
Walker, Allan S., 121, 183
Ward, Private Robert, 200
Wakabyashi, Lieutenant, 29, 30, 33, 34, 151, 153, 177
Warren, Lieutenant Colonel, 41
Whaley, Private. D., 120
Wild, Colonel Cyril Hew Dalrymple, 2, 6, 11, 34, 36,

41, 46, 65, 74, 119, 140, 165, 195, 196, 197, 200

Winstanley, Lieutenant Colonel Peter, 116

Wilson, Captain T., xiii, 131-4, 145, 192

Wolfe, Assistant-Surgeon P., 17, 42-3, 72-3, 103-6, 196

Wolfe, Warrant Officer, 181

Y

Yamada, Lieutenant, 165